GOING PLACES

GOING PLACES

THE
HIGH-SCHOOL STUDENT'S
GUIDE TO
STUDY, TRAVEL,
AND
ADVENTURE ABROAD

1993–1994 EDITION

Council on International
Educational Exchange

St. Martin's Press   New York

IMPORTANT NOTE

All information listed in this book, including prices, exchange rates, and program fees, is subject to change. To the best of its ability CIEE verified the accuracy of information at the time *Going Places: The High-School Student's Guide to Study, Travel, and Adventure Abroad* went to press. The most up-to-date bargain fares and travel information may be obtained from the latest issue of CIEE's *Student Travels* magazine or from any Council Travel office.

GOING PLACES. Copyright © 1993 by the Council on International Educational Exchange. All rights reserved. Printed in the United States of America. No part of this book may be used or reproduced in any manner whatsoever without written permission except in the case of brief quotations embodied in critical articles or reviews. For information, address St. Martin's Press, 175 Fifth Avenue, New York, N.Y. 10010.

Library of Congress Cataloging-in-Publication Data
Council on International Educational Exchange.
 Going places : the High School student's guide to study, travel,
and adventure abroad, 1993–1994 edition / Council on International
Educational Exchange.
   p. cm.
 Includes index.
 ISBN 0-312-08799-3
 1. Foreign study—Handbooks, manuals, etc. 2. Voyages and
travels—Handbooks, manuals, etc. 3. American students—Foreign
countries—Handbooks, manuals, etc. 4. High school students—United
States—Handbooks, manuals, etc. I. Title.
LB2376.C68 1993
370.19′62—dc20
                92-40077
                CIP

First Edition: February 1993
10 9 8 7 6 5 4 3 2 1

CONTENTS

ACKNOWLEDGMENTS

*M*any people deserve credit for helping put together the 1993–1994 edition of *Going Places: The High-School Student's Guide to Study, Travel, and Adventure Abroad.* First and foremost is Max Terry, who gathered and updated the information, organized the program listings, and edited the text. Credit must also be given to Lazaro Hernandez, who oversaw this project.

Thanks also to Angene Wilson at the University of Kentucky for her contribution of Chapter Five on the subject of reentry into one's own culture after an experience abroad. In addition, special recognition goes to Marjorie Cohen, the original author of the book, who created much of the style, format, and text that still appear in this edition. Finally, I want to thank all of the organizations who cooperated with CIEE and provided the information included in this book.

Del Franz
Director, Information and Student Services
Council on International Educational Exchange

GOING PLACES

About CIEE

*T*he Council on International Educational Exchange (CIEE) is a nonprofit educational organization with offices in the United States, Europe, and Asia. In nearly fifty years of service to the educational community, CIEE and its travel subsidiaries, Council Travel and Council Charter, have emerged as three of the foremost organizations concerned with international education and student travel.

CIEE was founded in 1947 to help reestablish student exchange after World War II. In its early days, CIEE chartered ocean liners for transatlantic student sailings, arranged group air travel, and organized orientation programs to prepare students and teachers for educational experiences abroad. Over the years CIEE's mandate has broadened dramatically as the interests of its member institutions have spread beyond Europe to Africa, Asia, and Latin America. Today, CIEE's responsibilities include developing and administering study, work, and voluntary service programs throughout the world; publishing books, academic papers, and informational material on international educational exchange; and facilitating inexpensive international travel for students, teachers, and other budget travelers.

Study Abroad

Among CIEE's most widely recognized educational services are the academic programs that it administers for college and university students in Argentina, Australia, Brazil, Chile, China, Costa Rica, Czechoslovakia, the Dominican Republic, France, Germany, Hungary, Indonesia, Japan, the Netherlands, Poland, Russia, Spain, Thailand, and Vietnam. These programs are administered by CIEE's University Programs Department on behalf of sponsoring colleges and universities that participate in policy and curriculum formation, ensure academic credibility and quality, and serve the particular academic field for which the program has been developed. Programs are available on the undergraduate and graduate levels and are open to all qualified students.

Secondary School Programs

CIEE's Secondary Education Programs Department administers School Partners Abroad, a school-to-school partnership program that matches junior and senior high schools in the United States with counterpart schools in Costa Rica, France, Germany, Japan, Russia, and Spain. The program provides resources for the enhancement of foreign language and social studies curricula, as well as short-term reciprocal exchange opportunities for groups of students and teachers. Each exchange provides participants with the opportunity to live with local families and attend regular classes in the partner school. For more information, see page 125.

Adult / Professional Programs

CIEE's Professional and Continuing Education Programs Department designs and administers a wide variety of short-term seminars, study tours, and in-service training programs for groups of international professionals, including secondary-school teachers and administrators, university faculty, business managers, and other "adult learners." Among these programs is the International Faculty Development Seminar series, for faculty and administrators at two- and four-year institutions of higher education. These overseas seminars and professional interchange opportunities are designed to assist institutions with internationalizing home-campus curricula. At the K-12 level, CIEE arranges short-term "teaching visit" opportunities in overseas schools for U.S. teachers, with reciprocal opportunities in the United States for educators from abroad.

Work Abroad

CIEE's Work Abroad Department operates a series of reciprocal work exchange programs which enable college and university students to work in each others' countries, primarily during summer vacation periods. Through these programs students are able to obtain temporary employment in Australia, Britain, Canada, Costa Rica, France, Germany, Ireland, Jamaica, New Zealand, Spain, and the United States. The Work Abroad programs allow students to cut through the red tape that usually accompanies the process of getting permission to work in another country. Along with the necessary employment authorization, Work Abroad participants receive general information on the country, tips on employment, and helpful hints on housing and travel. In each country the program is offered in cooperation with a national student organization or CIEE office that provides an orientation on the country's culture and society, advises on seeking jobs and accommodations, and serves as a sponsor during the participant's stay.

International Voluntary Service

CIEE's Voluntary Service Department operates an international work-camp program for young people interested in short-term voluntary service worldwide. Volunteers are placed with organizations conducting projects in Algeria, Belgium, Canada, Czechoslovakia, Denmark, France, Germany, Ghana, Hungary, Lithuania, Morocco, the Netherlands, Poland, Slovenia, Spain, Russia, Tunisia, Turkey, Ukraine, the United Kingdom, and the United States. Projects include restoring historical sites; working with children or the elderly; constructing low-income housing; and taking part in nature conservation efforts. Workcamps bring young people from many different countries together to work in local communities. For more information, see page 228.

Student Services

CIEE's Information and Student Services Department answers more than a quarter million inquiries on work, study, and travel abroad each year. In addition to its capacity as an information clearinghouse, it also administers the International Student Identity Card, the International Youth Card, and the International Teacher Identity Card in the United States. Nearly 200,000 International Student Identity Cards are issued each year by CIEE's New York headquarters, its 38 Council Travel offices, and more than 450 issuing offices at colleges and universities around the country. Cardholders receive travel-related discounts, basic accident / medical insurance coverage while traveling abroad, and access to a 24-hour toll-free emergency hotline. The International Youth Card, for those under 26, and the International Teacher Identity Card, for full-time faculty, both provide benefits similar to those of the student card. For more information, see page 61.

PUBLICATIONS

In addition to *Going Places,* CIEE's Information and Student Services Department produces the following books for travelers:

- *Work, Study, Travel Abroad: The Whole World Handbook,* published biennially by St. Martin's Press. Divided by geographic region and country, this book contains essential information on work and study opportunities worldwide. It also shows the traveler how to experience another country as an insider.
- *Where to Stay U.S.A.,* published biennially by Prentice Hall Press. This guide is a state-by-state listing of more than 1,700 places to spend the night for under $30, with special city sections and general travel advice for anyone touring the United States.
- *Volunteer! The Comprehensive Guide to Voluntary Service in the U.S. and Abroad,* published biennially in cooperation with the Council of Religious Volunteer Agencies. For anyone who wants to volunteer, this book describes more than 200 organizations that sponsor long- and short-term voluntary service opportunities for all age groups, both in the United States and abroad. Also included are a section on the basics of volunteering and essays written by former volunteers.

CIEE also publishes a wide range of informational materials that are available free of charge. Among these are

- *Student Travels,* a new 48-page travel magazine for students, replacing CIEE's *Student Travel Catalog.* This magazine includes in-depth articles and travel tips, all from a student's perspective. Special sections contain information on the International Student Identity Card, the Work Abroad program, international workcamps, study-abroad programs, and updates on Council Travel's student airfares and services.
- *Basic Facts on Study Abroad,* a booklet compiled in cooperation with the Institute of International Education and NAFSA: Association of International Educators. This booklet provides general information for students interested in an educational experience abroad.
- *A Guide to Educational Programs in the Third World,* which provides brief descriptions of over 200 programs offered by CIEE-member institutions in developing countries. Included are study, work, and voluntary service programs.

- *Update,* CIEE's monthly newsletter. *Update* keeps campus advisers and other professional educators informed about the latest developments in the fields of international educational exchange and travel.

SCHOLARSHIPS AND FELLOWSHIPS

CIEE provides financial assistance for U.S. students and professionals to participate in educational programs abroad. The following funds are available:

- *International Student Identity Card Fund.* This fund provides travel grants to enable full-time high-school or undergraduate students attending CIEE-member institutions or participating in a program sponsored by a CIEE-member institution, to participate in study, work, voluntary service, internship, or homestay programs in the developing nations of the world. For more information, see page 62.
- *Education Abroad Scholarship Fund for Minority Students.* This recently established fund supports members of minority groups who want to participate in any of CIEE's educational programs, including study, work, voluntary service, internship, and professional opportunities. Funds are available for high-school, undergraduate, and graduate students, as well as professionals, who are United States citizens or permanent residents of the United States.

TRAVEL SERVICES

Council Travel, a subsidiary of CIEE, operates a network of 38 retail travel offices across the country that provide travel assistance to students, teachers, and other budget travelers. (See pages 8–12 for office locations.) Council Travel's services and products include

- low-cost flights between the United States and Europe, Asia, the South Pacific, Africa, the Middle East, Latin America, and the Caribbean on scheduled and charter carriers (many special fares are available only to students or young people)
- rail passes, including Eurail, BritRail, and French Rail passes

- International Student Identity Card, International Teacher Identity Card, and International Youth Card, which entitle eligible bearers to discounts and services as they travel in the United States and abroad (for more information, see page 61)
- car-rental plans in Europe
- language courses in seventeen European cities and Japan
- travel insurance, guidebooks, and travel gear
- the New York Student Center, a low-cost accommodations and travel advisory service for visitors to New York City

Travel Services for Groups

Council Travel offices provide schools and other educational institutions with a complete range of travel services designed to simplify travel planning for groups. For full tour programs, the Group Services staff can arrange anything from transportation and accommodations to lectures, study programs, special events, sightseeing, and meals. The kinds of services Council Travel can arrange include the following:

- conferences and seminars
- educational programs on a wide range of subjects
- political interest programs
- special-interest tours, such as bike tours, ski tours, and so forth
- sport exchanges

Council Charter

Another travel subsidiary of CIEE, Council Charter has been a reliable consolidator for 43 years. It offers direct flights on scheduled and charter carriers between the United States and most major European cities, including Amsterdam, Brussels, London, Madrid, Milan, Paris, and Rome. Council Charter fares, which are open to students and nonstudents alike, have no hidden charges and require no minimum or maximum stay. Council Charter's flexible service provides travelers with a low-cost cancellation waiver allowing cancellation for any reason up to three hours prior to departure; the option of flying into one city and returning from another; continued assistance through its European offices; and frequent departures.

CIEE MEMBERSHIP

At present, more than 225 educational institutions and organizations in the United States are members of CIEE. As members, they may take advantage of CIEE's information and publications services; become involved in CIEE's advocacy, evaluation, and consultation services; and participate in conferences and services organized by CIEE. Membership allows educational institutions and organizations to play a central role in the development and operation of exchanges at a national and international level. Members of the Council on International Educational Exchange are listed in the Appendix (see page 297).

COUNCIL TRAVEL OFFICES

U.S.A.

ARIZONA

- **Tempe**
  East University Drive,
    Suite E
  Tempe, AZ 85281
  (602) 966-3544

CALIFORNIA

- **Berkeley**
  2486 Channing Way
  Berkeley, CA 94704
  (510) 848-8604

- **La Jolla**
  UCSD Price Center
  9500 Gilman Drive
  La Jolla, CA 92093-0076

- **Long Beach**
  1818 Palo Verde Avenue,
    Suite E
  Long Beach, CA 90815
  (310) 598-3338
  (714) 527-7950

- **Los Angeles**
  1093 Broxton Avenue,
    Suite 220
  Los Angeles, CA 90024
  (310) 208-3551

- **Palo Alto**
  394 University Avenue,
    Suite 200
  Palo Alto, CA 94301
  (415) 325-3888

- **San Diego**
  953 Garnet Avenue
  San Diego, CA 92109
  (619) 270-6401

- **San Francisco**
  312 Sutter Street, Suite 407
  San Francisco, CA 94108
  (415) 421-3473

  919 Irving Street, Suite 102
  San Francisco, CA 94122
  (415) 566-6222

- **Sherman Oaks**
  14515 Ventura Boulevard,
  Suite 250
  Sherman Oaks, CA 91403
  (818) 905-5777

COLORADO

- **Boulder**
  1138 13th Street
  Boulder, CO 80302
  (303) 447-8101

CONNECTICUT

- **New Haven**
  Yale Co-op East
  77 Broadway
  New Haven, CT 06520
  (203) 562-5335

DISTRICT OF COLUMBIA

- **Washington**
  3300 M Street NW,
  2nd floor
  Washington, DC 20007
  (202) 337-6464

FLORIDA

- **Miami**
  One Datran Center,
  Suite 320
  9100 South Dadeland
  Boulevard
  Miami, FL 33156
  (305) 670-9261

GEORGIA

- **Atlanta**
  Emory Village
  1561 North Decatur Road
  Atlanta, GA 30307
  (404) 377-9997

ILLINOIS

- **Chicago**
  1153 North Dearborn Street,
  2nd floor
  Chicago, IL 60610
  (312) 951-0585

- **Evanston**
  1634 Orrington Avenue
  Evanston, IL 60201
  (708) 475-5070

LOUISIANA

- **New Orleans**
  Joseph A. Danna Center
  Loyola University
  6363 St. Charles Avenue
  New Orleans, LA 70118
  (504) 866-1767

MASSACHUSETTS

- **Amherst**
  79 South Pleasant Street
  2nd floor, rear
  Amherst, MA 01002
  (413) 256-1261

- **Boston**
  729 Boylston Street,
  Suite 201
  Boston, MA 02116
  (617) 266-1926

Carl S. Ell Student Center
Northeastern University
360 Huntington Avenue
Boston, MA 02115
(617) 424-6665

- **Cambridge**
  1384 Massachusetts Avenue,
  Suite 201
  Cambridge, MA 02138
  (617) 497-1497

Stratton Student Center
MIT W20-024
84 Massachusetts Avenue
Cambridge, MA 02139
(617) 225-2555

MICHIGAN

- **Ann Arbor**
  1220 South University
  Drive, #208
  Ann Arbor, MI 48104
  (313) 998-0200

MINNESOTA

- **Minneapolis**
  1501 University Avenue,
  SE, Room 300
  Minneapolis, MN 55414
  (612) 379-2323

NEW YORK

- **New York**
  205 East 42nd Street
  New York, NY 10017
  (212) 661-1450

New York Student Center
895 Amsterdam Avenue
New York, NY 10025
(212) 666-4177

35 West 8th Street
New York, NY 10011
(212) 254-2525

NORTH CAROLINA

- **Durham**
  703 Ninth Street, Suite B-2
  Durham, NC 27705
  (919) 286-4664

OHIO

- **Columbus**
  8 East 13th Avenue
  Columbus, OH 43201
  (614) 294-8696

OREGON

- **Portland**
  715 SW Morrison, Suite 600
  Portland, OR 97205
  (503) 228-1900

PENNSYLVANIA

- **Philadelphia**
  3606A Chestnut Street
  Philadelphia, PA 19104
  (215) 382-0343

RHODE ISLAND

- **Providence**
  171 Angell Street, Suite 212
  Providence, RI 02906
  (401) 331-5810

TEXAS

- **Austin**
  2000 Guadalupe Street
  Austin, TX 78705
  (512) 472-4931

- **Dallas**
  6923 Snider Plaza, Suite B
  Dallas, TX 75205
  (214) 363-9941

WASHINGTON

- **Seattle**
  1314 Northeast 43rd Street,
    Suite 210
  Seattle, WA 98105
  (206) 632-2448

  219 Broadway Avenue East
  The Alley Building,
    Suite 17
  Seattle, WA 98102
  (206) 329-4567

WISCONSIN

- **Milwaukee**
  2615 North Hackett Avenue
  Milwaukee, WI 53211
  (414) 332-4740

OVERSEAS

FRANCE

- **Aix-en-Provence**
  12, rue Victor Leydet
  13100 Aix-en-Provence
  (33) 42-38-58-82

- **Lyon**
  36, quai Gailieton
  69002 Lyon
  (33) 78-37-09-56

- **Montpellier**
  20, rue de l'Université
  34000 Montpellier
  (33) 67-60-89-29

- **Nice**
  37 bis, rue d'Angleterre
  06000 Nice
  (33) 1-93-82-32-83

- **Paris**
  31, rue St. Augustin
  75002 Paris
  (33) 1-42-66-20-87

  8751, rue Dauphine
  75006 Paris
  (33) 1-43-25-09-86

  16, rue de Vaugirard
  75006 Paris
  (33) 1-46-34-02-90

  49, rue Pierre Charron
  75008 Paris
  (33) 1-43-59-23-69

GERMANY

- **Düsseldorf**
  18, Graf-Adolf-Strasse
  4000 Düsseldorf 1
  (49) 211-32-90-88

JAPAN

- **Tokyo**
  Sanno Grand Building,
     Room 102
  14-2 Nagata-cho 2-chome
  Chiyoda-ku, Tokyo 100
  (81) 33-581-7581

UNITED KINGDOM

- **London**
  28A Poland Street
  London W1V 3DB
  England
  (44) 71-437-77-67

PART ONE
THE BASICS

Chapter 1
THE POSSIBILITIES

*E*verything that follows is meant to convince you to leave the country—to take that giant step toward an experience abroad. We want you to learn about other countries firsthand, to make friends while you're away, to come back wiser and more aware of both yourself and the other inhabitants of our world. We want you to go out, get a taste of life in a different culture, and take a look at the world from a different point of view. There's nothing subtle about our message: we want you to take the plunge.

There are so many possibilities to choose from that the variety of programs is almost overwhelming: sailing the Caribbean, bicycling in Africa, working on an archaeological dig in Israel, living with a family in Japan, working on a community service project in Haiti, going on a wilderness canoe trip in Canada, learning French for a summer in Paris, or spending a whole year in Germany as an exchange student! And those are only a few of the opportunities that await you.

Because the possibilities are so diverse, we've written this book to let you know what's available and to direct you to the people who can help make your trip abroad as exciting as it should be.

This book starts out with the basics—the kinds of things you need to know before you make your choices and pack your bags. The second part of the book consists of specific listings that describe the extraordinary array of available programs. We've grouped these programs into general categories, but you may still want to refer to the index at the back of the book (page 301) to help you in your search. The programs have been indexed by location to help you focus in on a specific country or region. The index also will help you find different types of programs, such as bicycling tours, language study programs, summer camps, or voluntary service opportunities.

A CONVERSATION WITH LISA D.

Lisa D. spent the summer in Switzerland as a participant in AFS's summer homestay program.

Q. Why did you choose this particular program?
A. All the foreign students at my high school who had come on AFS were very interesting, active, and multitalented. It seemed like an excellent group of people to be with.

Q. What were some of the most difficult parts of your experience?
A. Frustration with the language. After about three weeks, I started understanding Swiss German and conversing in High German (I had studied it for three years in school). I had my own Swiss friends by early August (I'd arrived in mid-June), and then I had to leave! Also, the family I lived with was large and noisy, and it overwhelmed me sometimes. I wasn't homesick much, but lonely sometimes.

Q. Did your international experience change you?
A. Yes. It changed my life. It gave me a new perspective on my home community. I grew more independent and sure of myself. All the pressures in the high-school scene didn't seem so important when I got back. I became close to fellow AFS participants from all over the U.S. and spent time at other high schools for AFS weekends my senior year. I understood my parents better after having had other "parents," and I became much more interested in politics, international affairs, and the rest of the world. The best part is having a second home and family abroad for life—"AFS Mom and Dad," five "AFS brothers and sisters,"—in addition to my real family.

Q. Would you recommend this kind of experience to others?
A. Yes, but the student needs to be pretty emotionally stable to make the most of living with a host family. If you mainly want to travel, you should consider a tour instead. I wish I'd gone for a full year instead of just the summer.

Q. What advice do you have for someone about to do the same thing?
A. Expect to experience high highs and low lows while you adjust to the new culture, family, and language. Be outgoing and inquisitive—don't wait for friends and adventure to come to you. And finally, try to speak the language no matter what.

The Realities

This book presents the possibilities—that's what the 207 pages of program listings are all about—but not without important guidelines to help you sort them out. Chances are you'll find a number of programs that interest you; the hard part is finding the one that suits you best. Then again, you may still be wondering if you're ready to go at all. To start with, here's a set of questions for you to ask yourself and then discuss with parents and counselors.

What's the right age for an overseas experience? It's impossible to make a general statement about the best time to go abroad, but we wouldn't be writing this guide if we didn't believe in an early start. Some young people are ready for an independent overseas experience (one without their parents) by the age of 13; some may not be ready for years after that. Assuming you're ready for the experience, there are several advantages to going abroad in high school, such as better preparation for college and a head start in pursuing your new interests.

What kind of program do you want? You can choose a program that emphasizes study, or one that involves travel, outdoor activities, the creative arts, or voluntary service. Just to give you an idea of your options, we've described some of the most common types of programs below. Most actual programs, however, aren't so neatly classified—they mix different elements to provide a fuller experience.

- **Study Abroad:** These programs involve spending time in a classroom learning languages or other subjects, such as the history and culture of a particular country. Study abroad programs can last from a few weeks in the summer to a semester or full academic year, and often involve homestays in the host country. In most countries, but especially in Mexico and Europe, you'll find numerous language schools established to serve foreign visitors—from beginners to advanced students. In the United States, a number of organizations specialize in placing high-school students overseas on academic exchange programs. In the program listings in Part Two of this book, you can find opportunities to study just about any subject area imaginable.
- **Study-Tour:** This category embraces a combination of study and travel, though the quality of study may vary greatly from program to program. Some programs may conduct actual classes with required coursework, while others consist of informal lectures. A number of U.S. universities offering summer study-

JOINING A DIG

Virtually all the archaeological digs that take place around the world throughout the year require the help of volunteers. Often, volunteers must be 18 or over, but some digs accept younger participants. Here are five good sources of information on digs:

- Archaeological Institute of America, 675 Commonwealth Avenue, Boston, MA 02215. AIA publishes an annual *Archaeological Fieldwork Opportunities Bulletin,* which lists excavations all over the world. The booklet costs $10.50 for AIA members and $12.50 for nonmembers. It's published each January.
- Archaeology Abroad, 31-34 Gordon Square, London WC1H 0PY, England. This London-based organization distributes information on digs outside the United Kingdom, in the form of an annual bulletin and two newsletters. The 1992 subscription price was $15. To receive these publications, write to the attention of the Secretary at the above address and enclose a self-addressed envelope, international postal reply coupon, and your check payable to University College London. (See page 37 for information about the international postal reply coupon).
- Council for British Archaeology, 112 Kennington Road, London SE11 6RE, England; (44) 71-582-0494. This organization is solely concerned with archaeological projects in Great Britain. Its bimonthly newsletter, *British Archaeological News,* gives details of digs around the country that require volunteers. Most digs require participants to be at least 16 years of age. The subscription price from the United States is $25. Enclose a self-addressed envelope and international postal reply coupon with your request.
- Israel Antiquities Authority, P.O. Box 586, Jerusalem 91004, Israel. This office publishes a yearly listing of opportunities for volunteers interested in working on archaeological digs in Israel. Available free of charge.
- The Young Archaeologists' Club, Clifford Chambers, 4 Clifford Street, York YO1 1RD, England. This organization specializes in placing students ages 9 to 18 on digs in England and abroad.

tours for credit accept high-school students. Many museums and other cultural organizations offer similar opportunities.

- **Travel Tour**: While this category may seem self-explanatory, there is actually a great variety of options to choose from. Most commercial tour organizers offer the standard sight-seeing packages of museums and monuments. Others make a genuine effort to put you in contact with the people of the country. Needless to say, there's a big difference between a bus tour of major European cities and a bicycle tour through China. Most of the organized tour programs listed here cater exclusively to young people; a few others accept participants of all ages. It's up to you to decide which you prefer.

- **The Arts**: If you're into art or want to learn a craft, you can find all sorts of stimulating possibilities overseas, from fine arts institutes to ceramics workshops. Many art schools in the United States also sponsor their own programs abroad. Filmmaking and writing in England, weaving in Scotland, and painting in France are only a few of the opportunities. Other creative possibilities include programs where you can study acting, music, or dance. How about a drama workshop at Oxford, or a Greek dance program in Athens?

- **Camps**: A number of summer camps abroad bring together young people from all over the world. Surprisingly, they are usually comparable in price to camps in the United States. Like camps in the United States, they usually offer participants a wide range of activities, such as windsurfing, sketching, tennis, horseback riding, and so on. The difference is that overseas camps put you in contact with people from around the world.

- **Sports/Outdoor Adventure**: If you love sports or other outdoor activities, why not meet people who share your interests abroad? In this book you'll find camps and programs that focus on particular sports, such as riding and skiing. Other organizations specialize in wilderness expeditions, such as hiking, mountain climbing, and sea kayaking.

- **Voluntary Service**: People who like the idea of giving something of themselves to the countries they visit find working as a volunteer the perfect solution. Every country has some need for volunteers, and there are many organizations that gather young people from around the world to work together on special projects. The choices may involve upkeep of national parks, restoring historic landmarks, teaching English to refugees, or working on agricultural cooperatives.

Do you want to travel on your own? Maybe the idea of participating in

A Conversation with Melissa K.

Melissa K. spent two months in Japan as part of World Learning Inc.'s Language/Homestay Program.

Q. Were you prepared for your experience?
A. No, of course not, because there's no way to be really well prepared for something so entirely new. I was prepared in the sense that I knew not to bring too many clothes, and I did some research on Japan. I wouldn't be considered an ignorant *gaijin* [foreigner].

Q. What were the most difficult parts of your experience?
A. Just leaving my family and flying to California was difficult. For the first few weeks, having to depend on someone else for direction and understanding—all the waiting and following—was frustrating. Meeting my family and adjusting was frightening and awkward but well worth the trouble.

Q. Did the experience change your perception of yourself?
A. Definitely. Seeing other people live with such a totally different attitude and atmosphere showed me how narrow one's margin of vision is. But I also saw how amazingly similar all humans are.

Q. Did you keep a record of your trip?
A. Yes, and I'm glad I did. There are so many things to remember that it is impossible to recall them all. Pictures are priceless because they can best show to others what you saw. Once in a while now I go back to look at my journal just for fun.

Q. Would you recommend this kind of experience to others?
A. Only to those willing to take risks and adapt to another culture. If you don't go with an open attitude, you gain nothing.

Q. What advice do you have for others about to do the same?
A. Keep your cool. If you become frightened and panic, you can't think. Be patient—don't expect to understand where you're going and what you're doing all the time. Be open-minded always. Be friendly, ambitious, and perceptive. If you're unsure of how to act, watch others. Laugh and laugh and laugh. Don't be afraid to make mistakes—you're expected to make mistakes. If you don't try, you don't learn.

A CONVERSATION WITH PETER G.

Peter spent six weeks on an island in the West Indies working on a voluntary service project sponsored by Operation Crossroads Africa.

Q. Why did you choose Operation Crossroads Africa?
A. I wanted to work to help others, not just myself, and the Third World setting sounded adventurous.

Q. What expectations did you have before you went?
A. I thought that we Crossroaders would build a building or something concrete to "make our mark." In fact, the physical contribution we made was far less significant than the personal impressions we made on people—we showed them that America cares about the people there.

Q. What were some of the hardest parts of your six weeks?
A. Getting along with the seven other Americans in my group, being outgoing and meeting the people of the village, dealing with the poverty, and keeping up with the hard physical labor.

Q. What advice would you give others about to undertake the same kind of experience?
A. Be outgoing and receptive to people of your host country. It's too easy to let your work group of Americans act as an insulation against experiencing a foreign culture. Don't be dainty—roll up your sleeves and get dirty.

an organized program doesn't appeal to you. You may prefer to travel on your own or with a friend. If you do decide to go solo, however, be sure to check Chapter 4 for tips on how to go about it in the best way possible, taking advantage of student fares, youth hostels, and other privileges of your student status. One more suggestion: consider combining independent travel and a program—spend a few weeks at a workcamp or at a language institute and then trek around on your own. Even if you've traveled abroad before, you'll find that starting your trip with a structured program will help you ease into the experience.

When do you want to go abroad? Most students go abroad during summer vacations, but many organizations offer short-term opportuni-

A WORD ABOUT WORKCAMPS

The concept of a workcamp is not as well accepted in the United States as it is in many other parts of the world. The name itself may be a bit of a turnoff for Americans, but the concept is exciting. Workcamps are composed of groups of people from all over the world who come together to gain a broader cultural and social awareness through working on a common project. At a workcamp in Rosans, France, volunteers have restored a tower built in the tenth century; in Germany, volunteers have cleared streams, built fences, and removed refuse from forests. While the minimum age is usually 18, some workcamps accept participants as young as 16.

Workcamp volunteers usually stay for two to three weeks and work in groups of 10 to 20. The work week is usually five days (40 hours) long; in exchange for their labor, volunteers receive room and board. Everyone lives together, sharing meals, dividing chores, and relaxing after work. Some workcamps charge a registration fee, but it is usually quite reasonable. The work may consist of manual labor or social service. No special skills are required, but some workcamps may have a language requirement.

Accommodations, as you would expect, are basic. Volunteers may stay in schools, hostels, churches, or tents. Leisure-time activities are organized by the group as a whole; weekends are usually used for sight-seeing and exploring local cities and towns.

ties that coincide with spring and winter vacations. One of the most popular study-abroad alternatives is the junior year abroad, but there are also many semester-long programs. Consider, too, taking a year off between high school and college. Many students find that the "in-between year" gives them the chance to reflect on their high-school experiences and plan for their college career. Whatever you do, remember that a semester or a full year abroad can seem like a very long time once you're there, so consider the longer-term programs carefully and realistically.

Do you want academic credit for your experience? It's often possible to earn high-school or college credit for participation in many of the programs listed in this guide. If you're planning on studying abroad for an entire year, you'd better make sure that your home school will accept the credit you'll earn abroad. If you decide on taking a language course over the summer, will it help you fulfill possible college language requirements? While receiving academic credit may not seem immediately important to you, it's always good to explore the options. See page 51 for more on this subject.

Where do you want to go? This decision will depend on many things: whether you want to practice a language you're studying now or acquire a new one, whether you want to explore your roots or go to a place that represents a totally new experience for you. Do you want to have your first experience abroad in an English-speaking country? Do you want to concentrate on one country—or even one city in that country—or do you want to cover more territory?

How much are you able to spend? This is a very important consideration, on which your choice of destination may depend. Of course, you'll have to work within a budget, but don't make the mistake of thinking that an international experience is an extravagance or a financial impossibility. Many of the programs listed in this book cost no more than a similar-length stay at summer camp in your home state. And for many of the programs included here, there is full and partial scholarship aid available. There are also lots of creative ways for you to raise money for the kind of trip you have in mind. See page 64 for some specific suggestions.

What do you want to get out of your experience? Once you've decided what it is you want to gain from your trip abroad, you're in the best possible position to make a sound choice from the possibilities available to you. Consider some of these possible goals: increased language proficiency, acquisition of a new language, acquisition of a new skill, the experience of life in another country from an insider's perspective, the chance to see some of the places you've read about, and the opportunity to meet new and different people. Goals can be grandiose, but they can be practical as well. Once you've decided what your goals are, there are no limits on what you can accomplish.

Further Reading

For more program ideas, you may want to consult the following:

Learning Vacations (1989), by Gerson Eisenberg. Peterson's Guides, P.O. Box 2123, Princeton, NJ 08543-2123 ($11.95 plus $4.75 postage). Written mainly for college students and adults, this book includes some programs that are also suitable for teenagers.

Summer Opportunities for Kids and Teenagers (1993). Peterson's Guides, P.O. Box 2123, Princeton, NJ 08543-2123 ($16.95 plus $4.75

ENROLLING IN A FOREIGN SECONDARY SCHOOL

You may want to investigate the possibility of enrolling directly in a school abroad. The U.S. Department of State publishes a pamphlet entitled *Overseas American-Sponsored Elementary and Secondary Schools Assisted by the U.S. Department of State,* which lists schools that receive aid from the Department of State because they meet certain legislative criteria. There are schools that follow basic American curriculum patterns and utilize English as the language of instruction. Copies of the pamphlet are available free from the Office of Overseas Schools, Room 242 SA-29, U.S. Department of State, Washington, DC 20522-2902. For a more comprehensive list of possibilities, consult *Schools Abroad of Interest to Americans,* published biennially by Porter Sargent Publishers, 11 Beacon Street, Suite 1400, Boston, MA 01208; (617) 523-1670. Another useful publication is the *International Schools Directory,* published by the European Council of International Schools (ECIS). The *International Schools Directory* lists ECIS members and 400 other English-speaking independent international schools throughout the world. At press time, the projected cost of the 1993 edition was $30 (including postage). For up-to-date information, contact ECIS, 21B Lavant Street, Petersfield, Hampshire GU32, 3EL, England; (44) 730-268244.

postage). Scattered throughout this directory are some programs that take place outside the United States.

Vacation Study Abroad: The Complete Guide to Summer and Short-Term Study (1992). IIE Books, 809 U.N. Plaza, New York, NY 10017-3580 ($31.95 plus $3 postage). This publication, designed to inform U.S. students of summer study-abroad opportunities, lists programs offered by U.S. and foreign educational institutions in more than 60 countries. Not all programs described will accept teenagers, but many will.

Advisory List of International Educational Travel and Exchange Programs. Council on Standards for International Educational Travel (see page 51).

Teenager's Vacation Guide to Work, Study & Adventure (1991), by Victoria Pybus. Vacation Work, 9 Park End Street, Oxford OXI 1HJ, England; (44) 865-241978. Geared toward the English student, this book lists a great many opportunities throughout the United Kingdom and Europe that also accept U.S. students. Not yet available in the United States, this guide can be purchased directly from Vacation Work for 6.95 British pounds (approximately $13), plus postage. Call or write Vacation Work for ordering information.

Chapter 2
FINDING OUT IF YOU'RE READY

*A*n experience abroad will most likely present you with some demanding emotional and intellectual challenges. Coming to grips with life in a country with unfamiliar customs and manners—not to mention a foreign language—may seem frustrating at times. That's why you need to know how you might react in certain situations. For example, what if you can't understand your host family's dinnertime conversation? Do you retreat into yourself and get angry that they don't try to explain things to you in English? Or do you open up your eyes and ears and try to understand whatever you can? Think hard about yourself and your expectations before you make the decision to go abroad.

THE KIND OF PERSON YOU NEED TO BE

Flexibility and adaptability are the two most important qualities for anyone who wants to go abroad to have. If you don't have these two qualities, you'll be happier staying at home. Just think for a moment of some of the very practical things you will need to adapt to:

1. *Diet.* The foods in the place you're going to visit are likely to be very different from what you're used to eating at home, especially if you travel to countries outside of Europe.
2. *Concepts of time.* From country to country, the day is structured differently. Working hours, meal times, even the concept of

punctuality—all these things are relative to local habits. It may take you a long time to adjust to the new hours.

3. *Sanitary facilities.* Have you ever tried to shower with a hand-held nozzle? Or found yourself in a restroom which consists of nothing but a hole in the floor? How would you comport yourself in a Japanese public bath?

4. *Dress codes.* Articles of clothing most Americans take for granted, like shorts or miniskirts, may be improper in other countries. You might also be surprised to see many students wearing school uniforms.

5. *Etiquette.* Unlike English, many languages have different levels of politeness built into their grammar. Forms of address, greetings, and expressions of gratitude may vary according to such qualities as age or social status. Your relationship with your teachers, for example, may be much more formal than at home. It's safest to err on the side of being overly polite until you get a feeling for where you stand.

6. *Dating customs.* You may be surprised to find out that young people in many other countries consider American teenagers to be somewhat loose. If you stay with a host family, you can probably expect your social life to be more closely supervised than at home.

7. *Numbers.* Do you know your height in centimeters? Because the United States is the only country that hasn't adopted the metric system officially, you'll have to adjust to a different system of weights and measures while abroad. Currency exchange rates may also present a challenge at first. Keeping a small calculator on hand will help you make conversions.

8. *Weather.* Keep in mind that weather patterns differ all over the world. In countries that have rainy seasons, such as India and Japan, you should be prepared for a few wet months. Also remember that in Southern Hemisphere countries, the current season always is the opposite of the one in the North. Make sure you know what kind of weather to expect when you go abroad.

9. *Standard of living.* Depending on where you go, you may encounter poverty unlike any you have ever seen. Even in countries more like the United States, you can expect material differences in the way people live day to day.

To get through these and other adjustments of living abroad, your powers of adaptation must be tempered with a sense of humor. You have to be able to laugh at yourself and at your mistakes. Be patient; don't expect everything to come at once.

To take full advantage of an experience abroad, you'll have to make

ESPECIALLY FOR PERSONS WITH

DISABILITIES

Mobility International, an organization founded in London in 1973 with offices in more than 30 countries to date, has devoted a great deal of energy to making the world of international travel accessible to persons with disabilities. Its office in the United States is Mobility International USA (MIUSA). In addition to its quarterly newsletter, *Over the Rainbow,* MIUSA publishes an excellent book called *A World of Options for the Nineties: A Guide to International Educational Exchange, Community Service and Travel for Persons with Disabilities.* Written by Cindy Lewis and Susan Sygall, the book lists international educational exchange and workcamp programs that accommodate persons with disabilities. Also included are a special section on travel for the disabled, and first-person accounts of young people with disabilities who participated in a variety of travel adventures. As the authors state, ''Their enthusiasm, sense of accomplishment, and matter-of-fact handling of the obstacles they faced are the essence of this book; their message is clear: 'I did it. . . . you can, too.' '' *A World of Options* is available by mail for $16, including postage, from MIUSA, P.O. Box 3551, Eugene, OR 97403.

Other MIUSA publications include *A New Manual for Integrating People with Disabilities into International Educational Exchange, Equal Opportunities in International Educational Exchange,* and *Global Perspective on Disability.* MIUSA also has a videotape series documenting the international experiences of travelers with disabilities.

MIUSA offers its own exchange programs as well as International Leadership programs in countries of Asia, Europe, and Latin America. Check with MIUSA for details. (For information on the exchange programs sponsored by MIUSA, see MIUSA's listing on page 235.)

important decisions for yourself, keep yourself healthy, and budget your money to last the entire time you're away. Along with that maturity must go a sense of independence. You'll be required to handle many living situations that may never arise at home and you're going to be without the advice and counsel of your family and friends. You'll also be on your own in social situations. Don't be shy; introduce yourself. You'll find that most people are as curious about you as you are of them, even if they don't appear to be so at first.

Above all, enjoy yourself. You'll have your ups and downs, periods of homesickness and confusion. But in spite of the trying moments, this will probably be the best time you've ever had.

HOW TO GET YOURSELF READY

There are lots of ways to go about preparing yourself for an international experience. What you need to do is learn as much as you can both about the United States and about the country or countries you're going to visit.

You will find that young people in other countries are often much more politically conscious and historically aware than most of your peers in the United States. Conversation in cafes and at parties is likely to center around politics—both the realities and the philosophies. You will most certainly be asked at some point in your visit about the position of the United States on a number of issues—from Middle East policy to health care at home—as well as to explain past actions of your country.

It's a good idea to prepare yourself for in-depth political discussions. Review your U.S. history. Do you have any idea how relations are between the United States and the countries you're going to visit? Do the two have a history of conflict or cooperation?

One of the best ways to get yourself politically oriented is to read *Great Decisions,* published annually by the Foreign Policy Association. Each year this publication summarizes the background facts and examines different points of view on eight important foreign policy issues confronting Americans. *Great Decisions 1992* ($11, plus $2.50 for postage and handling) and other publications on U.S. foreign policy can be obtained from the FPA, Department SS, 729 Seventh Avenue, New York, NY 10019. Also read *The New York Times,* the *Christian Science Monitor, The Wall Street Journal* and national news magazines.

A now out-of-print book by The Experiment in International Living entitled *Getting the Whole Picture* offers excellent suggestions for getting ready for your trip. The authors suggest that you start by drawing a map from memory of the place you are going, putting in the capital, major cities, rivers, mountains, and so on. Then check your drawing with an atlas. How close did you come? As you begin to find out about the place you are going to visit, the authors suggest getting the answers to the following questions:

A WORD ABOUT THE THIRD WORLD

Undertaking a study program or voluntary service project in a Third World country means that you'll be meeting special challenges. These countries are so different from our own that you must be willing to make even more adjustments than you would for a stay in one of the industrialized nations. But if you believe you're up to the challenge, think seriously about it.

Three-quarters of the world's people live in the developing countries of the Third World. On a study program or service project in one of these nations you can experience a way of life that is really different from your own. You come back with a better understanding of the people and the problems of the *whole* world—rather than just those of the industrialized nations. The experience is valuable preparation for life in a world that is growing increasingly interdependent.

The listings in Part Two of this book include over 60 programs that take place in Third World countries. We refer you, too, to the International Student Identity Card Fund, designed especially to assist students seeking experiences in the Third World (see page 62).

If you are ready to start college or are in college now, you should take a look at CIEE's pamphlet *A Guide to Educational Programs in the Third World.* This publication lists U.S.-sponsored study programs for college students in developing nations. Copies are free and available from CIEE, Information and Student Services Department, 205 East 42nd Street, New York, NY 10017.

1. Who is the leader of the government?
2. Who are some of the famous sports stars, singers, and movie stars?
3. Who are some of the national heroes?
4. How are distances measured? What temperature scale is used?
5. What is the basic unit of currency?
6. What will your clothing size be there?
7. What time do people eat their meals?
8. What are the typical foods for each meal?
9. How do teenagers dress?
10. What do people your age do in their spare time?

A CONVERSATION WITH JONATHAN T.

Jonathan T. spent the summer in Finland as a participant in Youth For Understanding's Family Living Experience.

Q. Were you well prepared for your experience?
A. Yes, but not in the standard sense. The real preparation you need is to realize that most situations cannot be prepared for. Youth For Understanding was very good at convincing me that an open mind is the best preparation of all.

Q. What were some of the most difficult parts of your experience?
A. This is called a "Family Living Experience," and indeed one of the most difficult aspects is getting along with your family. You quickly learn to leave all shyness behind and speak with a frankness and candor virtually unknown in the United States. This is necessary to compensate for communication problems.

Q. Did the experience change your perception of yourself and your country?
A. The experience gave me great self-confidence. It also created great, if unexplainable, patriotism.

Q. What do you wish you'd known before you went?
A. I wish I could have started in the general emotional state in which I ended up. It's an open, innocent, and inquiring state of mind, which seems like the essence of the exchange.

Q. What advice would you give someone about to embark on a similar experience?
A. I'd tell them that an exchange experience is much like running. When you start, everything is awkward; muscles are tight and the body is uncoordinated. Soon, though, you get into your own pace, get warmed up, and things go pretty well. Your ankle or your knee may hurt, but it is terribly satisfying. Toward the end, you become fatigued, but you know you can make it. At the finish line, you're proud of having finished. You're tired, but you also have stronger muscles. Like running, exchange has a long-term effect.

How do you find out the answers to these questions? You can go to the library, talk to someone who has recently returned, talk with a foreign student in your area from that country, look through the newspaper for current events in the country, and get newspapers and magazines from the country (you should be able to find them in any good-sized library, perhaps even at your school). You don't have to become an expert on the country you are going to visit, but you should know enough when you arrive so that your hosts can tell that you are really interested in them. For instance, before you go, listen to some popular or traditional music from that country: it will make a common point of reference that will go far to break the ice in a new situation.

Of course, if you are going to a non-English-speaking country, the more language you can acquire before you go, the better. Check your local library for language tapes; it's important to get used to the sound of a language before you are completely and irreversibly immersed in it. Read books about the country, but don't limit yourself to guidebooks and history. Read some fiction by authors from that country—set the mood for yourself.

One often-overlooked source of information on a country is that country's tourist office in the United States. When you contact a tourist office, be specific about what you want, whether it's information on study, camping, maps, or anything else. Ask if they have any special information packets for young travelers; most tourist offices do.

An excellent series of profiles on more than 100 countries has been put together by Brigham Young University's David M. Kennedy Center for International Studies. Updated yearly, *Culturgrams* are four-page briefings containing information on customs and manners, useful words and phrases, socioeconomic statistics, history and government, travel tips, and maps. They cost $1 each for orders of one to five or 50 cents each for orders of six or more; the complete set of 106 countries costs $40. Copies are available from Brigham Young University, David M. Kennedy Center for International Studies, Publications Services, 280 HRCB, Provo, UT 84602; (801) 378-6528.

Although our emphasis here is on getting ready for your experience, it is important to remember that the "preparation" process must continue when you are in the midst of your experience and even when you return. There should be an evaluation process going on all along the way. While you are away, you should be asking yourself, "How am I doing? Have I made friends? Am I learning the language? Am I an integral part of my group or host family?" When it comes to an international experience, there are challenges and rewards that you must be ready and willing to accept at each step of the way.

WOULD YOU LIKE A PEN PAL?

One time-tested method of making friends abroad is by writing to a pen pal. There are many ways to go about finding a pen pal. Below are the names and addresses of five organizations that will help. We suggest sending a stamped, self-addressed envelope with any requests in order to cover the cost of mailing.

- Afro-Asian Center, P.O. Box 337, Saugerties, NY 12477; (914) 246-7828
- International Pen Friends, P.O. Box 290065, Brooklyn, NY 11229-0001; (718) 769–1785
- The League of Friendship, P.O. Box 509, Mount Vernon, OH 43050; (614) 392-3166
- Student Letter Exchange, 630 Third Avenue, New York, NY 10017; (212) 557-3312
- World Pen Pals, 1690 Como Avenue, St. Paul, MN 55108; (612) 647-0191

FURTHER READING

Coming to terms with another culture requires much mental preparation. In addition to the materials discussed above, a number of other publications can assist you in this task. One good book on the subject of cross-cultural encounters is the *Transcultural Study Guide,* written by Volunteers in Asia, Box 4543, Stanford, CA 94309 ($4.95, plus $1.50 for postage). The staff of Volunteers in Asia, an organization that provides voluntary service and study opportunities in Asia, originally put this book together to help prepare its own participants for their experience abroad, but the book applies to others as well. The *Transcultural Study Guide* takes readers step by step through a series of questions that lead to cross-cultural sensitization and help students learn more about the country they're visiting.

The works of anthropologist Edward T. Hall are recognized as classics in the field of cross-cultural communication. His four basic works are *The Silent Language,* which explores nonverbal communication; *The Hidden Dimension,* which studies the use of space in different

A CONVERSATION WITH MS. SHEPARD

Ms. Shepard is a teacher of German who annually takes a group of students from her high school to Austria through CIEE's School Partners Abroad program.

Q. What can teenagers do to find out if they're ready for an experience abroad?
A. I think they need to know themselves pretty well; they need to ask themselves if they have the maturity and the flexibility to adapt to a totally new environment. But students should be aware that just because they feel they're not ready for a semester or year-long program, it doesn't mean that all study-abroad programs are out of their reach. The School Partners Abroad program, for example, allows students to try a three- to four-week living experience abroad as part of a group from their own school. And because this is an ongoing program at our school, interested students can easily speak with their peers who have already participated to get a better idea of what's involved and whether or not it's right for them.

Q. How do you help prepare teenagers for a trip abroad?
A. I meet with the students once a week beginning four months before the exchange takes place. We go over the language and culture of Austria—from its educational system, history, and politics, to religion and family life. We make plans both for the trip abroad and for hosting the Austrian students in our community.

Q. How does the experience affect those who decide to take part?
A. I'm always amazed at how much the students mature—emotionally and intellectually—as a result of even a brief experience abroad. They return to the U.S. with a much greater sense of themselves and the world around them. It's also interesting to see the impact that hosting foreign students from our partner school can have on the American students who, for whatever reason, do not travel abroad themselves. That's what's really exciting—the school partnership has an effect on the *entire* school.

cultures; *Beyond Culture,* which examines the way particular cultures bind humans to behavioral patterns; and *The Dance of Life,* which analyzes differences in the perception of time among cultures. You should be able to find these books in your library, or they can be purchased as a set for $32.80 (plus $2 postage) from Intercultural Press, P.O. Box 700, Yarmouth, ME 04096; (207) 846-5168.

Intercultural Press distributes a number of other books that deal with overcoming cultural differences, many of them country-specific. Among their titles are *Behaving Brazilian: A Comparison of Brazilian and North American Social Behavior; With Respect to the Japanese: A Guide for Americans; Good Neighbors: A Guide to Communicating with Mexicans;* and *Communicating with China.* Write to the address above for a catalog.

Chapter 3

HOW TO MAKE THE RIGHT CHOICE

*R*egardless of where you learn of a program—in this or in some other publication, or from a friend or teacher—you should scrutinize it carefully. Ask as many questions as you can think of and insist on answers. Ask questions of the program sponsors, past participants, and your guidance counselor. Ask questions about the larger aspects of the program and about the smaller ones. No question, if it's on your mind, is insignificant. Do everything you can to be sure that there won't be any unpleasant surprises when it is too late.

We've put together a number of questions that you should ask. Some you may have thought of already; others may not have occurred to you. All may not relate to the kind of program you're considering, but they should get you started thinking in the right direction.

Who is the sponsor? As you will see, programs abroad are offered by many different types of organizations: educational institutions such as high schools, colleges and universities, and language schools; private, nonprofit agencies such as Youth For Understanding or World Learning Inc.; religious and fraternal organizations; commercial travel agencies; voluntary service organizations; and even individuals. It is important that you know *exactly* who is responsible for the program, and that you find out as much as possible about that person or group. Here are some things to consider:

- Is it a profit-making or a nonprofit organization? Sometimes the distinctions can be unclear, and we feel that it's important to explain them. In this book we list both profit and nonprofit sponsors. Profit-making sponsors are commercial businesses owned by individuals or shareholders. Nonprofit companies gen-

WRITING THE FIRST LETTER

Your first letter requesting information from a program sponsor should be as specific as possible. Be sure to include the following:

- your age and grade in school
- how much time you want to spend abroad
- when and where you want to go
- what you want to do

Many organizations offer more than one program. You can expect to receive a number of printed materials from which you should be able to extract the information you need.

When writing to sponsors in other countries, it's a good idea to include international postal reply coupons, available from your local post office.

Here's a sample you can follow:

Summer Study Abroad   36 Park Way
128 Main Street   Bismarck, ND 58501
Chicago, IL 60616   October 2, 1993

Dear Friend:

I am a sixteen-year-old sophomore attending John F. Kennedy High School in Bismarck, North Dakota, and would like to spend the summer studying Spanish in Mexico. I noted in *Going Places: The High-School Student's Guide to Study, Travel, and Adventure Abroad* that you operate this type of program, and I'd like to find out more about it. Specifically, I'd like to spend the month of July in Mexico, and I am interested in living with a family while I study. Please send me your organization's brochure and an application form.

Many thanks.

Sincerely,
Ellen T.

erally provide services that are seen as being in some way unique or beneficial to society and are not established with the motive of making money. The U.S. government accords nonprofit organizations a special status that exempts them from corporate taxation. This is not to say that profit-making businesses are concerned *only* with making money. There is no guarantee that the services of a nonprofit organization are any better than those of a commercial one; indeed, some are not. But when choosing a program with an educational component, many people feel more assured of a certain earnestness of purpose with a nonprofit group.

- Does the stated sponsor bear full responsibility for the program? Determine whether the sponsor takes care of all aspects of the program or whether it hires other organizations to handle such things as travel arrangements and accommodations. While it's normal for programs that include travel to make group package deals through travel agencies, you should know the exact terms on which such arrangements are made.

- Is the sponsor based in the United States or elsewhere? This could matter if legal responsibility became an issue. If complications involving legal action were to occur, it might be difficult or even impossible to protect your rights as a U.S. citizen in a dispute involving a foreign organization. This is not meant to scare you off; rather, it is just to add a word of caution. If you need to check on the reliability of a foreign-based organization, contact that country's embassy or consulate.

- What is the current financial situation of the sponsoring institution? Ask how the organization finances itself and be sure you know whether it is financially sound. To get this kind of information, ask for the annual report of any organization you are seriously considering. You definitely have the right to know where such an organization gets its money and how it spends that money. You should also know whether or not the organization expects you to do fund-raising as part of your participation.

- What is the reputation of the sponsor? There are several ways to determine this. You can go first to your guidance counselor to see whether he or she has any information, or ask others around your school, such as foreign-language teachers. Check with your state's department of education. To investigate commercial agencies, you can contact your local Better Business Bureau. Any literature that you get from the organization should be carefully scrutinized (see page 45). In the United States, any respectable organization should provide you, upon request, with

WANT TO BE A HOST FAMILY?

All this talk about homestays abroad may start you thinking about the possibility of hosting a foreign student in your own home. Think of the benefits: you'll expose your family to a new culture, possibly a new language; you'll be able to introduce a visitor to the United States; you'll establish a contact with another part of the world that can blossom into follow-up visits and lifelong friendships.

There are many U.S.-based exchange organizations looking for host families. And don't think that only "nuclear families" are eligible—families take on many configurations these days, and a host family needn't be the old formula of mother, father, and 2.4 children.

An entire book has been written on this subject: *The Host Family Survival Kit: A Guide for American Host Families,* by Nancy King and Ken Huff. If you're planning to host a visitor, this book gives excellent advice on how to handle arrivals and departures, cultural differences, children's reactions, the adjustment cycle, and communications. In an appendix, the authors tell how to determine the reliability and quality of any sponsoring organization you consider. Some of their points:

1. Find out whether the organization is known to your principal or guidance counselor.
2. Talk to families who have been hosts for this particular sponsor before.
3. Learn about how the organization works—how it screens students, how it stays in touch.
4. Find out what the arrangements for emergencies are.
5. Meet with local representatives.
6. Find out if the program is designated by the U.S. Information Agency by writing to USIA, Exchange Visitor Program Services, Room 3030, 400 Sixth Street, SW, Washington, DC 20547. Request a copy of their list of designated teenage exchange organizations.
7. Look through the promotional materials and evaluate them.
8. Ask about special services to hosts—for example, counseling, orientation, and so on.

Want to Be a Host Family?

9. Ask about the costs to the students and to the host family.

10. Be sure your family is stable enough to take on another member, and avoid being pressured into any arrangement that might be too stressful.

The Host Family Survival Kit is available for $10.95, plus $2 postage from Intercultural Press, P.O. Box 700, Yarmouth, ME 04096.

Several CIEE-member organizations recruit U.S. families to serve as hosts for foreign students: AFS Intercultural Programs, The Experiment in International Living, International Christian Youth Exchange, Open Door Student Exchange, and Youth For Understanding International Exchange. If you're interested in contacting them, you can find their addresses in the listings that follow, as each of them sponsors programs abroad as well. For a larger list of host-family organizations, contact the Council on Standards for International Educational Travel (see page 51).

---

the names of past participants you can contact by phone or letter. Ask them the kinds of questions the sponsor might not be able to answer—the day-to-day, nitty-gritty kinds of things. Your parents might want to talk to the parents of the past participants as well.

Who are the leaders? We have a category in our listings called "supervision" because we consider this an important part of any program. Find out how leaders are chosen. Beware, in particular, of leaders who are chosen purely for their ability to recruit participants—those who get a free trip or commission in return for registering a certain number of students, for example. This may not always be a negative feature of a program, but we think it's an aspect to consider. An outstanding leader is essential to a positive international experience. Find out what the organization's requirements are for their leaders, and keep the following questions in mind:

- How mature are the leaders? Leaders should be mature enough to command respect. They should be wise and resourceful, yet also able to identify with their younger companions.
- How knowledgeable are the leaders? Leaders should be familiar with the country or countries to be visited. They should know the

language and have a good understanding of the culture and customs.

- How dedicated are the leaders? Leaders should be ready and willing to devote almost 24 hours a day to the job. Any leaders who are pursuing their own studies or interests should be suspect.

How will you interact with the host culture? Some of the programs in this guide will immerse you in the life of the host country; with others, you will see the life of the country you visit from a greater distance. You can rightfully expect fuller immersion with a semester-long study abroad and homestay program than with a three-week tour of six countries. This is not to say that the tour is necessarily less worthy; for some, it can be a valuable introduction to other countries. But if a program claims that cultural immersion is one of its aspects, the following questions should be asked:

- How much help will you get developing cross-cultural understanding? If it's a study program you're investigating, does the curriculum include courses that focus on the host culture, or are you expected to discover such things for yourself? Make sure to find out exactly how you will come into contact with local people and how you will be involved with the everyday life of the country or countries you visit. Some of the weakest programs effectively insulate themselves against the host culture; they could as easily take place in Topeka, Kansas, as in Paris, France. If there's no true cross-cultural experience, if you're living, studying, and spending leisure time only with other Americans, why go to the trouble and expense of going abroad?

What are the living arrangements? Where will you be living? There are lots of possibilities. You may be staying in youth hostels, dormitories, hotels, pensions (the European term for guesthouses), tents or barns, or with families. Just be certain there are no surprises and that you know before you go what to expect in the way of accommodations.

- Are living arrangements included in the cost of the program, or are you expected to pay extra for accommodations? Is the living situation arranged at all, or do you have to fend for yourself?
- Will you be living alone or with a group? With Americans only or with people from other countries?
- If you're hoping to interact with young people your own age from the countries you visit, deluxe hotels are not the way to go. But if you know you're the kind who is miserable without your

A CONVERSATION WITH MRS. F.

Mrs. F.'s daughter spent two months in Chile as an AFS program participant. Here are some thoughts from a parent's point of view.

Q. Was the trip your idea or your daughter's?
A. It was entirely her idea. At first when she came to me and told me she was applying for a scholarship to go to Chile, I didn't think much about it, since I thought the possibility was remote. When she did in fact have the opportunity offered, I got a bit nervous.

Q. What made you nervous?
A. I'd never been anywhere out of the country, and the only time she'd spent away from home was a week at her aunt's house. Even then I worried. She was going to a new country, to a place where she didn't know the language—I was nervous about the political aspect too.

Q. What convinced you?
A. The AFSers who came to my home for the family interview. They talked about their experiences and turned my thinking around.

Q. What was the most difficult part for you while she was away?
A. I wasn't prepared for the fact that I wouldn't hear from her for such a long time. I didn't know that mail was so delayed in Chile—she was in a remote village—and it was five weeks before I got a letter. I tried to call, but there was only one line and it was always down.

Q. How did it all work out?
A. Very, very well. She definitely achieved a sense of independence. She felt she learned a lot, not only about Chile, but about her own country as well from the other AFSers from other parts of the United States. She had such a good time that she wants to go to Japan this year with the same program.

comforts, how wise would it be to sign up for a workcamp where you have to sleep with four other people in a hastily converted village school?

- Many of the programs listed in this book include a homestay as part of their experience. The homestay option is an incomparable opportunity to share in the day-to-day life of a family in another country. However, this possibility generates its own set of questions.

How are homestays arranged? Who selects the participating families? Is it someone from the sponsoring organization or is this task performed by another agency?

- What criteria are used to select the families?
- Do program representatives visit with the families before they're accepted and during the participant's stay? (Obviously, if the answer is no, this is an automatic red light.)
- Are the families compensated? Are they paid by the participant or the sponsor or compensated in any other way for extra costs during the participant's stay? Distinguish between a real homestay and a stay in a family-owned guesthouse.
- Are you given the name and address of the family before you leave home? This is a real plus; making a connection ahead of time, perhaps sending a picture of you and your family and a word or two about yourself, is an excellent way to begin.
- What provisions have been made in case you do not get along with your family? Be sure there's someone to help if this happens. Experienced program sponsors have told us that most misunderstandings are cultural, not personal, and can be worked out, but there must be someone available to help work them out.
- Will there be someone your age in the family? This is not always possible. If there is no one of the same or nearly the same age, be ready and willing to make an effort to make friends outside of the family and realize that it will require resourcefulness and an outgoing personality.
- Will you be expected to return your host family's hospitality? Some of the best homestay experiences arise from exchange programs, in which your own family agrees to invite a member of your host family abroad for a stay in the United States. Strong friendships between the two families often result from this sort of arrangement, but playing host requires much thoughtful preparation.

What about money? Most programs in this book charge a fee for participation. Be sure you know what that fee includes, and what it doesn't. This should be *clearly* stated in the sponsoring organization's literature, and their representatives should be more than willing to supply the information. If not, it's another red light.

- Find out whether international transportation is included, and if it is, whether it's from your hometown to the host country or, as is more likely, from one designated U.S. city (such as New York or Los Angeles) to the host country.
- Compare the transportation costs with regularly scheduled fares. If they are much higher, ask why.
- Find out how much of your in-country travel will be covered. Once you leave the airport, will you be on your own, or does the fee include ground transportation to your ultimate destination? What about local daily transportation, say between your home-stay and the school you may be attending?
- Are all meals and lodging covered? Will you be expected to pay for any weekend or evening excursions on your own?
- Is there an application fee in addition to the program fee? Pay attention to disclaimers in small print about possible increases due to inflation or fluctuation in exchange rates. If airfares are hiked, will there be a surcharge?
- How much spending money will you need to bring? Individual needs differ, but the sponsors should certainly be able to give you some idea of typical personal expenses, as well as advice on how far you can expect your dollar to go with the current rate of exchange. This is a good question to ask past participants, too.
- What, if any, insurance is provided? A responsible sponsor should be sure that all participants are covered by health and accident insurance. This does not mean that they must necessarily provide the coverage, although some do; they may simply provide information about insurance and then require proof that you have insurance. *Be sure that you don't leave the United States without being fully insured!*
- What if you cancel? Be sure to find out what the arrangements are for refunding your money in case of an unavoidable cancellation or if an emergency forces you to come home before the program is completed.
- What about official papers? If a visa or other official government permit is necessary, are you responsible for securing it or will your program sponsor do it for you?

How much contact will you have with other students or representatives of your program? Are you part of a group, or are you left to fend for yourself?

HOW TO READ AN ADVERTISEMENT

In the course of compiling *Going Places,* we have come across advertisements, posters, and brochures that provide loads of flash and little substance. You really do have to be on the lookout for copy that is meant to tantalize but is, in fact, misleading.

Here is the text of an imaginary advertisement*:

Spend Your Summer in Sunny Spain!

1. Live in a Medieval Castle or with a Local Family
2. Learn Spanish at a Renowned Academic Institution
3. Outstanding Faculty
4. International Student Body
5. Academic Credit Available
6. Limited Enrollment—All Ages Eligible
7. Inclusive Charge
8. Write to the Director of Admissions, P.O. Box 000, Cambridge, MA

Let's take this mock advertisement line by line and see what it really does and does not say.

First, the emphasis seems to be on spending the summer in sunny Spain. Not an unappealing idea, of course, but if your objective is to learn the language, will that be accomplished? How serious does the program sound if it uses as its hook a travel brochure's eye-view of Spain?

Line 1: A medieval castle sounds great, but how close is it to the place where you will study or to town? Are there places to eat nearby? It may be a castle, but how has it been converted? Will you sleep crammed in with six other students? And what about the host family? Is it going to turn out, in fact, to be someone who simply wants to make some extra money by having an American boarder?

Line 2: Just what is this renowned academic institution? Is it a university? Why isn't it named? Some overseas universities *do not* have regular classes during the summer, so what is probably referred to here is a special course for foreigners—not a regular university class. Whenever the ad or brochure uses the words "recognized" or "accredited" to describe a learning institution, find out exactly who does the recognizing and accrediting.

How to Read an Advertisement

Line 3: This reference to outstanding faculty needs to be explained carefully in any brochure. The teachers' names, titles, and affiliation should be given. This phrase is much too vague.

Line 4: Get specifics on this. The students who are categorized as coming from France may actually be sons and daughters of U.S. parents working abroad. Find out how many countries are really represented.

Line 5: This vague reference to credit is of little use, since the transfer of credit is such an individual matter. Whether or not you can get credit is something that only you can find out. You should, however, ask for the sponsor to give you a list of institutions who have granted credit for the program in the past. This will be excellent ammunition if you need to approach your own guidance counselor to request credit.

Line 6: How selective is this organization? What are the standards for limited enrollment? Are there, indeed, standards? And if all ages are eligible, how will you like being together with people much younger or older than yourself? If some are working for credit and others aren't, will that affect the seriousness of the work?

Line 7: "Inclusive charge" is much too vague. This is where the small print comes in. Find out exactly what is included and get an estimate of the total expenses, whether or not they are included.

Line 8: The actual name of a responsible person would be better here. When the backup brochure arrives, it should list (besides the director or faculty) a board of advisers, trustees, and so on. Don't let the Cambridge address mislead you into assuming that the program is affiliated with Harvard. Remember that anyone can get a post office box anywhere.

[*] Based on an article by Lily Von Kemperer, which appeared in the NAFSA Newsletter (1976) entitled "How to Read Study Abroad Literature."

- How much of your time is scheduled? A good program will strike a comfortable balance between scheduled time and free time. Particularly in the case of travel tour programs, ask for itineraries. Free time is important, but unless you know exactly what you want to do, you may end up feeling you've wasted some of that time.
- What kind of support system will be available to you? This is a question parents will certainly want answered in detail. How

much help will you get once you are thousands of miles from home? Is there someone available at all times in case of emergency? Whom can you go to if you're having trouble with your studies or having a hard time making friends? Is there someone you can talk to if and when you're feeling homesick? Independence is a wonderful quality, and one to be nurtured during an experience abroad, but there must be someone to turn to when help is needed.

SOME SPECIAL CONSIDERATIONS FOR STUDY PROGRAMS

Travel tours of foreign countries, homestays, and voluntary-service participation can be enormously educational, but these are not, formally speaking, study programs. A study program for which you expect to receive academic credit must conform to the educational standards of your home school system, which means it should include graded coursework, tests, reports, and other evaluative devices. Remember, if you want to receive credit for your study-abroad experience, you will have to make most of the arrangements yourself. First you should find out whether students who have gone before you on the program have received credit and where. Then check with your own counselors at your school to determine whether foreign credit will be accepted. Below are some questions to ask specifically of study programs. Much of what follows is based on *Criteria for Evaluating Study Abroad Programs* published by NAFSA: Association of International Educators.

Where will you study? Will you be enrolling in a foreign high school? Will you be in classes with other Americans or with local students? Some programs may lead you to believe you're going to study in a foreign university, but if it's a summer program, beware. Make sure that country's academic calendar actually includes summer sessions. If not, you will probably be in a course designed for foreigners and have little chance to interact with local people. Is that what you want?

What about the sponsor's academic reputation? How long has the sponsor been operating a study program? Does the sponsor oversee all aspects of the program (budget, staff appointments, curriculum planning, recruiting, and selection) or are some subcontracted? Beware of any so-called sponsor that is involved only in recruitment.

What are the admission requirements? Some programs are highly selective, but for some you need only to show some signs of life—and pay the fee—to be accepted. If you want a high-quality program, you are going to have to meet some very specific standards. As part of the screening process, a sponsor should be doing whatever it can to determine your maturity, adaptability, and your earnestness of purpose as well as your ability to meet the more tangible application criteria such as grades or study prerequisites. In other words, ask yourself if the sponsors are as careful about choosing their participants as you are about choosing a sponsor.

What are the objectives of the program? The objectives of any valuable study program sponsor should be clearly stated in any printed material it distributes. The description of the objective should be detailed and precise—not a meaningless list of clichés about international understanding. What you really need to look for are the ways the sponsor plans to accomplish its goals. Do the curriculum, the place of study, and the extracurricular activities seem to fit in with the objectives, or are there inconsistencies? A good study program will balance academic learning with cross-cultural contact. It will offer study opportunities that wouldn't be available to you at home.

What kind of preparation is provided? How well are participants prepared for the experience? Another signal of the sponsoring institution's seriousness is the type of orientation it offers. The best orientation materials do two things: (1) they provide information and (2) they guide the prospective participants toward finding their own information. (There's more about the specifics of getting ready in Chapter 4.) Although it may be geographically impossible to spend a great deal of time with your group before you leave, there should be some kind of predeparture and postarrival orientation, certainly more than just a batch of materials sent by mail. There should also be some sort of prereturn orientation that addresses problems of coming home and suggests ways to use the international experience to best advantage once you've returned.

How good is the curriculum? Does the curriculum take advantage of the physical, human, and cultural resources of the host country? Have the sponsors been creative in their use of the foreign setting?

What size will classes be? This will give you an idea of the kind of individual attention you can expect.

Are there adequate academic resources? What are the classroom activities? Is there an adequate library? Are there language labs? Are there

A CONVERSATION WITH JESSICA G.

Jessica G. spent an academic year in Rennes, France, as part of School Year Abroad.

Q. What did you do to get yourself ready for the experience?
A. I read *The Ugly American,* and I spoke in French to anyone I could find who spoke French, and to my family—who don't speak French—and my cat. To read is important, but to *speak*—or at least to practice speaking—is paramount.

Q. What were some of your most difficult experiences?
A. Having ravioli on Thanksgiving was hard, and so was having to share a room with a little sister; the rare—and terrible—misunderstandings between my French mother and myself were hard. However, all of those seem trivial in comparison with the emotional strain of missing those you love. I often felt more alone than I ever had before.

Q. Did the international experience change your perception of yourself? Of your country? Of others? How?
A. If my perception changed at all, it made me wary of making broad, sweeping, blundering generalizations. Of myself, I hope I gained a measure of independence and strength of character. Of my country, I felt its international influence. And I learned what it feels like to be American; one can only do this in an environment where most people are *not.*

Q. What do you wish you had known before you went?
A. I wish I knew in September what I knew in December—that perfunctory academics should take a back seat to first-hand cultural *experience.* I decided to stop saying no to family activities in order to study. That was the best decision I made all year. You can read about it when you get home; you have to *live* it while you're there. And try not to worry about school.

Q. Did you keep a record of your trip?
A. I kept a journal until I ran out of paper—which was a lame excuse—and I wrote long letters home to my mother. She has a postcard from every place I visited, and I have a poster collection. And I also took about a million color slides, which are a *joy*—I recommend them.

A Conversation with Jessica G.

Q. What advice would you give to someone about to do what you did?

A. Go with an open mind, open eyes, and an open heart, but by all means *go!* Embrace the opportunity: talk with locals, travel, eat the food, drink the wine, get involved, believe in yourself, and know that everyone that has come before was afraid, too. Don't worry—but dare to dive in! This could be the best year, nine months, six weeks, or whatever, of your life. It was for me.

---

studios or practice rooms if the program emphasizes fine or performing arts? Are there local libraries or resource centers that will also be available to you?

What is the language of instruction? You will, of course, need to be quite proficient in the foreign language to be able to absorb regular subject matter. Be sure you're not going in over your head.

Are the language requirements realistic? Are appropriate language courses available to beginners? What about the library attached to the learning institution: Does it have materials suited to your proficiency?

How are grades reported? Grades should be reported to students, and it should be possible to have transcripts sent to your own school. If the grading system at a host school is different from the one at home, which is almost always true, a table for converting the grades should be included.

What will the faculty be like? If you're not attending a local high school, where do the faculty members come from? What are their qualifications? How were they chosen? In the written materials the sponsors send you, the faculty members should be named, along with their academic affiliations, their degrees, and the subject areas in which they teach. Find out from past participants whether teachers are approachable, involved with learning, enthusiastic about their subject matter, and knowledgeable about the country in which they teach, or whether they tend to be pedantic and remote.

What about the resident director? Who is he or she and what kind of prior experience does he or she have? Is the resident director knowledgeable about the host country, fluent in the language, sensitive to

GETTING CREDIT

Before you make any commitments to a particular program, decide whether or not you want to get academic credit for your international experience. Many of the programs in this book can earn you credit—not just the study programs, but voluntary service and travel as well.

The best way to approach the topic of credit is to sit down with your guidance counselor as long a time before your trip as possible and discuss the possibilities. Some semester- and year-abroad program sponsors have had a great deal of experience in this area and can give you advice on how to go about it. Be sure to find out *exactly* what your school or district needs in order to accept credit. Some will accept a letter from the principal of the school you'll attend; others want a fully translated transcript. You must be sure to get clear guidelines on any necessary requirements from your counselor. If you're going to study for a semester in France, for instance, you should certainly be able to get credit for language, but getting credit for the math you may study while there will be trickier.

When you approach your guidance counselor about credit, emphasize the enrichment aspect of an international experience. In general, the schoolwork abroad is more rigorous than that in the United States; most high-school classes abroad are almost the equivalent of courses in our first and second years of college.

Some programs listed in this book have credit-granting arrangements with specific colleges and/or universities so that your experience can be translated into college credit. Ask whether this is a feature of the program you're considering.

students' needs? Does he or she understand the special needs and background of American students? Does the resident director have regular office hours? Is he or she readily accessible?

We hope the above list of questions hasn't overwhelmed you. As we mentioned at the beginning of the chapter, not all questions apply to all programs. Use what is most helpful to you. For a bit more on choosing a program, refer to a booklet put out by the Council on Standards for International Educational Travel, the *Advisory List of International Educational Travel and Exchange Programs*. Revised annually, the *Advisory List* includes programs that have earned what is essentially CSIET's

A CONVERSATION WITH TERESA C.

Just one month after her graduation from high school, Teresa C. went off for a year to Tampere, Finland, as a participant in an International Christian Youth Exchange program.

Q. What did you expect to gain from your experience?

A. Before I left I had no clearly defined expectations. I knew that the time was going to be one of intense self-awareness, and I looked forward to a period of personal growth in the area of self-understanding, ability to relate to others, ability to adapt, and possibly develop more defined goals for my future. I was not, however, at all certain how all of this was going to miraculously happen. I was also looking forward to learning the Finnish language—especially since I had heard many stories about how difficult it is, and the challenge of learning it intrigued me.

Q. What was the hardest part of your experience?

A. The language barrier was sometimes overwhelming. It was a chore every single morning to decide to continue to work on this impossible language and not just to give up. Another real hard time that I experienced was the first time I caught a cold abroad. It seemed then that the distance between me and home grew greater than ever and problems loomed larger than ever. Also difficult was that first month when I had to start from scratch and make friends in a foreign community in a foreign language. The final difficult time was coming home. I had adapted by the end of my year and came to feel such a part of my new situation that I did not want to leave.

Q. How did your experience change your perception of yourself and the United States?

A. I have become able to accept my personal shortcomings better, which I believe is the first step in overcoming them. It was also quite eye-opening to view my country from the outside instead of always from the inside. I was able to see its role in the world today once I was able to get out and view it in a more detached way.

Q. What do you wish you had known before you went?

A. That makes me laugh! I wish I had known not to take so many clothes. I also wish I had known what a profound difference the year would make in my life.

A Conversation with Teresa C.

Q. Did you keep a record of your trip?
A. We were advised to keep a daily journal throughout the year, but I didn't. I have some writings, but they're at irregular intervals. I regret not having been more faithful in this, but I do have photos, clippings, ticket stubs, brochures, and other memorabilia saved from the year.

Q. Would you recommend that others do what you did?
A. One hundred and ten percent yes! Of course, I realize that not every person's year will be like mine; I feel very fortunate that mine was so positive. Nevertheless, I feel that the experience to be had from a year abroad is invaluable in today's world. And the self-reliance and self-identity that comes with the territory are necessary tools in the path to maturity. Before the exchange can have a positive effect on a person, though, that person must want to have a positive learning experience. One should under no circumstances be pressured or forced into an undertaking such as this.

"seal of approval." The book is available from CSIET, 3 Loudoun Street SE, Leesburg, VA 22075; (703) 771-2040. Call for the cost of the book.

Now that we have given you some guidelines for evaluating a program, you must take the next steps yourself. Use these questions to scrutinize each and every program you consider, whether it appears in this guide or not.

Whether you plan to go abroad on your own or as part of a group, there are some travel necessities that you'll have to take care of yourself. Before going into the essentials, we'll refer you to another CIEE publication, *Student Travels,* a free 48-page travel magazine especially for high-school and college students. This new magazine has replaced CIEE's *Student Travel Catalog* and includes in-depth articles and travel tips, all from a student's perspective. It will also keep you up to date on the lowest student airfares and student services offered by Council Travel, CIEE's travel division.

THE ESSENTIALS

Your Passport

To enter just about any country other than Canada or Mexico, a U.S. citizen needs a passport, and for some countries, a visa as well. A passport, which serves as proof of citizenship, is issued by your own country's government.

Passports for U.S. citizens under 18 are valid for five years from date of issue and cost $30. For people 18 and over, passports valid for 10 years cost $55. An execution fee of $10 is charged for first-time applications.

For your first passport, you must apply in person at either (1) a U.S. post office authorized to accept passport applications; (2) a federal, state, or county courthouse; or (3) one of the passport agencies located in Boston, Chicago, Honolulu, Houston, Los Angeles, Miami, New Orleans, New York, Philadephia, San Francisco, Seattle, Stamford, or Washington, D.C. Between March and August the demand is heaviest, and the process takes longer than at other times of the year. The State

Department advises travelers to apply between August and December, when demand is lowest. In any case, apply several months before departure, as it generally takes at least three weeks to process a first-time passport application and even longer during the peak travel season. If you're going to need visas, allow yourself even more time.

To apply, you'll need to bring proof of U.S. citizenship. This can be a certified copy of your birth certificate, naturalization certificate, or consular report of birth abroad. In addition, you must have proof of identity, such as a valid driver's license or student identification (not a Social Security or credit card). You'll also need two recent, identical photographs two inches square (most vending machine photos are not acceptable). The photos may be color or black and white, but must be taken against a white background. The distance between your chin and the top of your head may not exceed one and three-eighths inches. Most photo shops will know what you need. Finally, you must complete form DSP-11, "Passport Application."

You may apply by mail and avoid the $10 execution fee if (1) you have had a passport issued within 12 years of the new application; (2) you are able to submit your most recent passport with the application; and (3) your previous passport was not issued before your 18th birthday (that's the clause that eliminates most of our readers). In addition to sending your previous passport and two new passport-size photographs, you must complete form DSP-82, "Application for Passport by Mail."

If you lose your passport in another country, you'll need to get a replacement at a U.S. embassy or consulate. Before leaving, make a photocopy of the pages in your passport with your photo, number, and date and place of issue. You should also have with you some other form of identification, such as a valid driver's license or student identification. If you carry along two extra prints of your passport photo, it will make the replacement process faster.

Remember that a number of countries will not permit visitors to enter and will not place visas in passports which have a remaining validity of less than six months. If you return to the United States with an expired passport, you are subject to a passport waiver fee of $80.

Non-U.S. citizens with permanent residency in the United States but without a valid passport from another country can apply for a U.S. travel permit. This permit functions much like a passport and can be obtained from the Immigration and Naturalization Service in the state where the applicant resides. Note, however, that requirements for obtaining visas with travel permits are usually different from those that apply to U.S. citizens. Non-U.S. citizens—whether traveling with a travel permit or a valid passport from another country—will have to consult the embassy or consulate of the country they want to visit to obtain the appropriate visa requirements.

If you have further questions, write to Passport Services, Department of State, Washington, DC 20524 or call (202) 647-0518 for a recorded message on passport applications.

Visas

A visa is an endorsement or stamp placed in your passport by a foreign government, giving you permission to visit the country for a specific purpose and a specific period of time. Visa requirements differ from country to country. To study in any foreign country for longer than a few months, you will most likely need a student visa. In most cases, you'll have to obtain your visas before leaving the United States. Apply directly to the embassy or nearest consulate of the country you plan to visit. Travel agents sometimes help with visas; program sponsors may assist as well. Passport Services at the U.S. Department of State *cannot* help you get a visa for travel to a foreign country.

Most countries charge a processing fee, which usually isn't very much but can sometimes be quite expensive. Many also require proof that you will leave the country by a certain date (a round-trip air ticket usually suffices). *Foreign Visa Requirements,* a U.S. government publication, lists entry requirements for U.S. citizens in most countries. Single copies are available for 50 cents from the Consumer Information Center, Department 454, Pueblo, CO 81009. However, because entry requirements can change at a moment's notice, the best source of information is still a country's embassy or consulate.

Since the visa is usually stamped directly onto one of the blank pages of your passport, you'll need to submit your passport along with a visa application form to the embassy or consulate of each country you plan to visit. Acquiring a visa may take several weeks, so it's wise to start the process early, especially if you need to get more than one.

Customs

As you probably know, you'll have to go through U.S. Customs on your return to the States. You can bring back $400 worth of goods free of duty, the tax usually charged for imported goods. However, the U.S. government prohibits the entry of certain articles and imposes import fees or duties on others. For the lowdown on customs procedure, read *Know Before You Go,* available from the U.S. Customs Service, P.O. Box 7407, Washington, DC 20044; (202) 566-8195.

STAYING WELL

You'll want to try to stay as healthy as you can while you're away. Even a head cold can be a real misery when you're far from home. Here are a few things to keep in mind:

1. Make sure your insurance covers medical care abroad.
2. If there are any prescription drugs that you use frequently, bring them with you in clearly marked bottles. It's wise to take along a copy of the prescription as well, for customs purposes.
3. Visit the dentist before your trip.
4. If you wear glasses or contact lenses, bring an extra pair and a copy of your prescription as well.
5. Take a compact first-aid kit with you: adhesive bandages, aspirin or aspirin substitute, antiseptic, motion-sickness pills, and sunscreen should be the basics.
6. Find out if you need to get any inoculations.
7. Eat well. The erratic hours and excitement of foreign travel make it even more important than ever to practice good nutrition.
8. Rest up before you go.

Health

Some countries require certificates of vaccination for inoculation against yellow fever and cholera. For others, certain inoculations are recommended even if not required. Check your medical records to make sure that your measles, mumps, rubella, polio, diphtheria, tetanus, and pertussis (whooping cough) immunizations are up to date. The Centers for Disease Control has an International Traveler's Hotline for determining whether any special vaccinations are needed to visit a country: (404) 332-4559.

The two greatest threats to travelers' health today are diseases against which you *cannot* be inoculated: diarrhea and malaria. The most common causes of traveler's diarrhea and other gastrointestinal ailments are parasites and other organisms to which your body isn't accustomed, but which may be common to the water supply and certain foods, especially fresh produce, of the countries you're visiting. Malaria is spread through the bite of the female anopheles mosquito. Some travel agents and tourist bureaus won't tell you about the malaria risk in certain countries for fear that you'll go elsewhere. Most types of malaria can be prevented, but you must begin taking antimalarial drugs *before* you arrive in the infected area and must continue taking them after you leave.

One organization that has been working to alert travelers about the risks of malaria and other health problems worldwide is the International Association of Medical Assistance to Travellers (IAMAT). IAMAT is a nonprofit organization with centers in 450 cities in 120 countries. Members of IAMAT (there's no membership fee, but a donation is welcome) receive a pocket-size dictionary listing these centers, a world immunization chart, and various other publications that alert travelers to existing health problems throughout the world. Contact IAMAT at 417 Center Street, Lewiston, NY 14092; (716) 754–4883.

As always, when traveling you should be aware of the risk of contracting AIDS (acquired immunodeficiency syndrome). Don't let exaggerated or distorted information alter your travel plans, but be aware of the risks and prepare ahead. Be aware that some countries may require HIV (human immunodeficiency virus) antibody tests before they'll grant a visa for an extended period of time; tourists staying for 30 days or less are usually exempt. You might want to be tested before you depart; do so only at a center that offers pre- and post-test counseling and allow two weeks for the testing process. While traveling, remember: the best way to deal with AIDS is through knowledge, foresight, and action—not ignorance and fear.

The Centers for Disease Control has issued the following advisory: "AIDS has been reported from more than 130 nations, but adequate surveillance systems are lacking in many countries. Because HIV and AIDS are globally distributed, the risk to international travelers is determined less by their geographic destination than by their individual behavior. HIV infection is preventable. There is no documented evidence of HIV transmission through casual contacts; air, food, or water routes; contact with inanimate objects; or through mosquitos or other arthropod (insect) vectors. HIV is transmitted through sexual intercourse, blood or blood components, and perinatally (at birth) from an infected mother. Travelers are at increased risk if they have sexual intercourse (homosexual or heterosexual) with an infected person; use or allow the use of contaminated, unsterilized syringes or needles for any injections, e.g. illicit drugs, tattooing, acupuncture, or medical/dental procedures; or use infected blood, blood components, or clotting factor concentrates."

There are several things that you can do to avoid contracting the human immunodeficiency virus (HIV). First and foremost, bring condoms and/or dental dams with you. You may not have access to these items in certain parts of the world, and conditions, manufacturing, and storage of condoms in other countries may be questionable. More importantly, use them—even if you are aware of the HIV status of your partner. Remember, testing HIV negative does not necessarily mean that a person has not been in contact with the virus. If you do need a blood transfusion, try to ensure that screened blood is used. If you are concerned about needing a blood transfusion while abroad, contact others in your academic program or traveling group; you can arrange with those that have your blood type to be blood donors if necessary. For more information, write CIEE, 205 East 42nd St., New York, NY 10017, for a free copy of Council Travel's brochure, *AIDS and International Travel,* which explains ways to avoid contracting the disease when you're abroad. Copies are also available free of charge from any Council Travel office. Another resource for information is the Centers for Disease Control AIDS Hotline: (800) 342-AIDS.

There are a number of helpful books written on the subject of staying well as you travel. The following books are recommended reading for overall health issues. You won't need to consult all of them, but do try to look through at least one.

- *The Pocket Doctor,* by Stephen Bezruchka, an emergency doctor with extensive travel experience in Asia, is a slim, pocket-sized publication written especially for travelers. You can order it from The Mountaineers Books, 1011 S.W. Klickitat Way, Suite 107, Seattle, WA 98134, for $3.95 plus $2 postage and handling.
- *Staying Healthy in Asia, Africa, and Latin America,* by Dirk Schroeder, is basic enough for the short-term traveler yet complete enough for someone living or traveling off the beaten path. The book is also quite small in size, making it very portable. Order it from Volunteers in Asia, Box 4543, Stanford, CA 94309, for $7.50 plus $1.50 postage.
- *The International Travel HealthGuide,* by Stuart Rose, is updated annually and published by Travel Medicine, 351 Pleasant Street, Suite 312, Northampton, MA 01060; (413) 584-0381. Its 400 pages include country-by-country immunization, health, and safety listings. It also has chapters on AIDS, travel and pregnancy, traveling with disabilities, and a directory of clinics that offer pre- and post-travel medical services and consultation. The 1992 edition costs $16.95. You can find it in good bookstores, or order it from the publisher (include $3 postage).

Some general advice: Make sure you're in good general health before setting out. Go to the dentist before you leave on your trip, have an extra pair of eyeglasses or contact lenses made up (or at least have your doctor write out your prescription), and if you take along any prescription drugs, pack them in clearly marked bottles and have the prescription with you in case a customs officer asks for it.

Safety

Leaving the United States is not dangerous in and of itself. In fact, travelers will encounter few countries where the crime rate—especially the frequency of violent crime—equals that of the United States. But it is important to remember one thing: while traveling, you will be recognized as a foreigner. To some, this means you will be a novelty; to others, a rube. You must be aware and thoughtful at all times, because you can no longer rely on your instinctive knowledge of what may be considered unsafe, insulting, or provocative. This doesn't mean that you should not explore or stray off the tourist-beaten path. It does mean that you should be aware of your passport and money at all times and take along a good guidebook that will give you a rough idea of the situations you will be getting yourself into. Try to determine areas to avoid alone or at night and try to avoid arriving in strange cities late at night unless you have a confirmed place to stay and a secure means of getting there. You can't control everything that happens to you—at home or abroad— but you can sway the odds.

Women especially should be aware of situations in which they might be harassed, molested, or robbed. When traveling, there is not only the usual burden of sexism to deal with but also the fact that, as a recognizable American, you will be treated according to stereotypes of U.S. women, who are thought in some parts of the world to be promiscuous, immodest, and wealthy. Good advice for women travelers can be found in *Women Travel: Adventures, Advice, and Experience,* published by Prentice Hall Travel as part of its *Real Guide* series. For each country, the book lists suggested styles of dress, valuable contacts, as well as tips from other women travelers.

If you're planning a trip to a spot where a political problem has existed for a while or just flared up, a reliable source of information is the Citizens Emergency Center (CEC) operated by the State Department in Washington, DC. This center will inform you of any State Department travel advisories that warn travelers of danger and recommend taking special precautions, or in more extreme cases, postponing travel to certain countries or regions. Recorded travel advisories can be obtained anytime from a push-button phone by calling (202) 647-5225. If you're using a dial phone, call between 8 A.M. and 10 P.M., Monday through Friday, or between 9 A.M. and 3 P.M. on Saturday.

Insurance

Check to see whether your medical and accident insurance policies are valid when you are traveling outside the United States. You should never underestimate the importance of being insured when traveling abroad. If you purchase an International Student Identity Card (see next section), you will automatically receive basic medical insurance for travel outside the United States, valid from the time of purchase until the card's expiration date. Also included is a toll-free emergency hotline number for travelers needing legal, financial, or medical assistance.

You should also investigate the various plans for baggage and flight insurance. Baggage or personal effects insurance covers damage to or loss of your personal belongings while traveling. Flight insurance covers the cost of your fare if you are unable to take a flight you have already paid for. One insurance package, Trip-Safe, provides a variety of options which may be purchased in any combination for any period from one month to one year. You can find details in *Student Travels* (see page 54), available free from CIEE, 205 East 42nd Street, New York, NY 10017. Trip-Safe insurance can also be obtained at any Council Travel office.

International Student Identity Card

Each year, nearly two million student travelers obtain the International Student Identity Card. This card is internationally recognized as proof of student status, and it's your key to discounts and benefits in every part of the world. Any student—junior high, high school, college, university, or vocational school—who is at least 12 years old and enrolled in a program of study leading to a diploma or degree is eligible. The card is issued by the International Student Travel Confederation (ISTC), made up of student travel organizations in 74 countries around the world. The Council on International Educational Exchange is the U.S. member of the ISTC.

Although the services of ISTC members vary from country to country, holders of the International Student Identity Card can usually expect to receive student discounts on transportation and accommodations, and reduced admission to museums, theaters, cultural events, and other attractions. Probably the best-known discounts are the student fares on international flights. Cardholders can save up to 50 percent of commercial fares on the same routes. For sample student fares, see "Student and Youth Airfares" (page 71).

Even in countries where there is no ISTC member, the card is often recognized as proof of student status. We advise following the "it can't hurt" theory: always show your International Student Identity Card and

A WORD ABOUT THE INTERNATIONAL STUDENT IDENTITY CARD FUND

The International Student Identity Card Fund provides travel grants to high-school and undergraduate students participating in educational programs in the developing nations of Africa, Asia, and Latin America. Students involved in any type of educational program including study, work, voluntary service, internship, and homestay programs are eligible for funding.

Established in 1981, the fund is supported by the sale of the International Student Identity Card in the United Sttes as well as by private donations. Awards are made twice each year: in April for programs beginning between June 1 and December 31, and in November for programs beginning between January 1 and July 15 of the following year. Awards are for the minimum cost of transportation to and from the program site. Past recipients have undertaken such projects as the following:

- studying rural development in Zimbabwe
- teaching English in China
- working with a community health project in Jamaica
- studying social service agencies in Guatemala
- creating a photo essay on the black educational system of South Africa

Proposals are accepted only from students either attending a CIEE member institution or participating in a program sponsored by a CIEE member (see page 297). Awards are determined according to the educational merit of the proposal and the financial need of the applicant. Information and application forms are available from the CIEE's Information and Student Services Department, 205 East 42nd Street, New York, NY 10017. Deadlines for applications are March 31 and October 31.

ask if there are any discounts available—whether it's for a trolley ride, entrance to a museum, or a night in a hotel.

Besides the student discounts, the International Student Identity Card provides basic medical insurance. All students who buy the card in the United States receive automatic coverage while they're abroad for as long as the card is valid. Also available to cardholders is a toll-free hotline to the Traveler's Assistance Center, whose multilingual staff offers worldwide assistance in medical, legal, and financial emergencies.

To obtain the International Student Identity Card, submit a passport-size photo and proof of student status. High-school students can prove student status with a photocopy of a report card or a letter from a principal or guidance counselor on school stationery. The card can be ordered through the mail from CIEE, 205 East 42nd Street, New York, NY 10017. You can also pick it up at any Council Travel office (see page 8) or any of more than 450 U.S. issuing offices authorized by CIEE. (High schools are also eligible to issue the card. If a faculty member or administrator at your school is interested, have him or her write to CIEE's Information and Student Services Department at the address above.)

The 1993 card costs $15 and is valid for 16 months, from September 1, 1992, to December 31, 1993. For an application form, and more information, ask for CIEE's free publication *Student Travels.* Keep in mind that it takes two to three weeks (and longer in the peak seasons of December and April through June) to process a card through the mail.

International Youth Card

Nonstudents under the age of 26 are eligible for the International Youth Card, a document sponsored by the Federation of International Youth Travel Organizations (FIYTO). FIYTO member organizations in 41 countries offer many of the same discounts and benefits that holders of the International Student Identity Card receive. International Youth Cards issued in the United States through CIEE also carry the same insurance and traveler's assistance benefits as the International Student Identity Card described above. For more information on the International Youth Card, contact CIEE or any Council Travel office (see page 8).

Youth Hostel Card

Staying at youth hostels is one of the best and most inexpensive ways to meet fellow travelers. In order to take advantage of the more than 6,000 hostels in 70 countries affiliated with Hostelling International—formerly the International Youth Hostel Federation—you must usually show a membership card. Some hostels, but not all, will accommodate nonmembers for a higher fee. Hostel membership cards are available in the United States from American Youth Hostels offices and from Council Travel offices. If you're under 18, the membership fee is $10; for ages 18 to 54, it's $25. A family membership, which includes children under the age of 18, is $35. See page 75 for more on hostels.

For the full rundown on hostels, what they're like and where they're located, check Hostelling International's *Guide to Budget Accommodations.* This is a two-volume set: Volume 1 covers Europe and the Mediterranean; Volume 2 covers the rest of the world ($10.95 each plus $3 postage per book). You can purchase them from any Council Travel office (see page 8) or from American Youth Hostels, P.O. Box 37613, Washington, DC 20013-7613; (202) 783-6161.

FINANCING THE TRIP

There are lots of creative ways by which you can raise money for your trip. There's no trick to fund-raising. To some extent it involves luck, but to a much greater extent it involves approaching—in an organized fashion—as many persons, organizations, religious groups, businesses, and charitable organizations as possible about assisting you.

If you are embarking on a voluntary service project especially, religious organizations may be sympathetic to your cause. Perhaps you could arrange to do a presentation when you get back in return for any help they can give.

Community groups may also be willing to help; contact neighborhood associations, community newspapers, radio and TV stations, the Lions Club, the Elks Club, the Kiwanis Club, the Rotary Club, and your local Chamber of Commerce. These groups, too, might like something in return—a slide presentation or an article for their newsletter.

Support can also come from your schoolmates. Organize your friends for some kind of fund-raiser—a bake sale, a car wash, a spaghetti dinner, or a dance.

Try putting up posters or putting an ad in the local newspaper offering to do odd jobs—car washing, baby-sitting, serving at parties, or dog walking.

If you're going on a study or service program in the Third World, remember CIEE's International Student Identity Card Fund (see page 62). In addition, some of the programs included in this book offer scholarships. Be sure to ask about the possibilities.

Don't let the financial aspects of going abroad stand in your way. If you are determined to go and are resourceful, you will be able to raise the funds.

Money

The best way to carry money abroad is in traveler's checks. The most common are American Express, Citicorp, Thomas Cook, and Visa. Most traveler's checks cost one percent of the total dollar amount you're buying; that is, you'll be charged one dollar extra for every hundred dollars you buy. Holders of the International Student Identity Card are eligible for a wavier of this service charge at participating dealers.

Most banks, except in the smallest towns and villages, will convert traveler's checks in dollars to local currency. Avoid changing money in hotels or restaurants; the rate won't be as favorable as at a bank or official exchange shop. For free conversion tables, write to Swiss Bank Corporation, Advertising and Public Relations, 4 World Trade Center, Box 395, Church Street Station, New York, NY 10008, and ask for *Travel Tips and Currency Guide.* For the latest information, however, simply consult the foreign exchange listings in any good financial paper, such as *The Wall Street Journal.*

You'll want to have some local currency with you when you first arrive in a country. Although there are exchange offices in most air, ship, or train terminals, it's a good idea to change some of your dollars before you leave the United States.

Carry your money and traveler's checks in a safe place, such as a money belt, but don't keep all your valuables in one place. Put your passport in an inside pocket, your traveler's checks in a money belt, and so on. Keep a separate list of the numbers of your credit cards and traveler's checks so that if they're lost or stolen, you can report them more easily. You should also give a copy of that list to someone at home to put in a safe place.

If you need to have money sent from home, you can use American Express money orders. Traveler's checks in denominations of $50 can be sent to you within three days. Note: Even if your bank has overseas branches in the country you visit, it probably won't automatically transfer your money overseas unless you have a special account. However, if you have a bank credit card, you should be able to withdraw cash from automated teller machines (ATMs) around the world. Check with your local branch before you go.

Mail

While you're away, you'll certainly want to receive mail from home. If you're not sure what your exact address will be, have your mail addressed to Poste Restante (General Delivery) at the central post office of the cities you'll be visiting. American Express cardholders can have mail sent to local American Express offices overseas. For a list of offices abroad, call American Express at (800) 528-4800. Make up a list of mailing addresses before you go to tell your friends and family where and when they can reach you.

Drugs

Many Americans traveling abroad assume that buying or carrying small amounts of drugs cannot result in arrest. This is simply *not true*! Americans have been jailed abroad for possessing as little as one-tenth of an ounce (three grams) of marijuana. Penalties for drug violations are severe in foreign countries, including pretrial detention for months or even years and lengthy prison sentences without parole. Many countries do not permit bail in drug-trafficking cases. Beware of the person who asks you to carry a package or drive a car across the border. You might unknowingly become a narcotics trafficker. Remember, when you are traveling abroad, you are not protected by U.S. law. You are subject to the laws of the country in which you are traveling.

To learn more about the facts, send for the brochure *Travel Warning on Drugs Abroad,* available free with a stamped, self-addressed envelope from the Bureau of Consular Affairs, Room 5807, Department of State, Washington, DC 20520.

TRAVELING ABROAD

Now that you've begun the process of getting your passport, visas, and other necessary items, it's time to think about making your travel arrangements. Which airline will you fly? Where will you be staying? How much will you get around once you're abroad? You'll have many possibilities to choose from; to find the ones that are best for you, plan ahead. Good research and planning will help you make the most of the time you have and can make a big difference in keeping your costs low.

If you live near a Council Travel office, your research will be a bit easier. Council Travel is a full-service travel agency that specializes in providing services for students and other budget-minded travelers. There are 38 of them in the United States, as well as a number in Europe and Asia (see list on page 8). Most are located near university campuses. All are staffed by trained personnel who can answer your questions about student discount airfares, rail passes, and other ways to save money while traveling. CIEE's other travel subsidiary, Council Charter, is discussed later in this chapter.

Whether or not you live near a Council Travel office, your research should begin with a copy of *Student Travels,* available free of charge at

PACKING

One good packing method is to fill your backpack or suitcase with what you think you'll need, then take out half of what you've packed and leave it home. Although it's hard to believe, it works. Pack and then walk a mile with your suitcases, backpack, or whatever you'll be carrying and feel how heavy it gets. Now imagine schlepping that load from the airport to the hotel, or trying to squeeze through a crowded train car corridor. When you get back from the walk, you'll probably want to eliminate whatever you can from the bags. Looking back on a trip, most people think they brought more than they needed. You're going to want to buy a few things once you're abroad, so leave some extra space for whatever you pick up along the way. Climate, local custom, and the type of program will, of course, affect your choice of what to bring. The following should suffice for a few months abroad during the spring or summer:

> two pairs of pants
> three shirts or blouses
> one or two sweaters
> two or three skirts
> one raincoat or jacket
> one outfit for more formal occasions
> one week's worth of socks and underwear
> one bathing suit
> one pair of shorts
> one pair of walking shoes or sneakers
> one pair of dress shoes

Be sure that the clothes you take are easy to care for; dry cleaning is enormously expensive in most countries. Plan to dress comfortably, but be sensitive to the customs of the country you'll visit. For example, in most countries, don't wear shorts except when you're involved in sports, and always have proper coverings for visits to places of worship. Talk to someone who has recently returned for the best advice.

Council Travel offices and at many study-abroad offices and international centers at colleges and unversities, or by mail from CIEE. Besides the in-depth articles, its 48 pages are filled with information on travel basics, including air fares, car-rental options, and rail-pass plans. Take a look at it before going to a travel agency to make sure you're getting what you want at a reasonable price. Remember, research really is the only way to make your overseas experience an economical one.

Getting There

Over the last several years, the airline industry has seen a number of changes—not uncommon in an industry that's always in a state of flux. In general terms, international airfares remain highly competitive and prices for tickets to some international destinations are actually falling.

Before you begin researching fares, you'll need to make a few decisions about your trip. You should have a rough idea of your general itinerary, your travel budget, how many stopovers you plan to make, what time of year you plan to travel, and the length of time you plan on staying. Most people travel during the summer, but those who have more time on their hands should keep in mind that there are "low" and "high" seasons for travel, during which prices are accordingly lower and higher. The low season lasts roughly from January to March and the high season from June 15 to September 15. The period between April 1 and June 15 is sometimes called the "shoulder" season, with prices somewhere between high- and low-season fares. Depending on the airline, you may find either low or shoulder fares from September 15 to January.

Remember that many bargain airfares are limited in availability and must be purchased far ahead of your departure date. Be aware, too, that although some advertised fares may be lower than others, there are usually certain restrictions attached that you'll learn about only by reading the fine print. As you do your research, keep in mind that inexpensive fares abound; they just require a certain amount of investigation, flexibility, and a good deal of creative planning. Let this be your guiding principle when it comes to airfares: the more conditions attached to a certain fare, the cheaper it's going to be.

If you use a travel agent, select one who is interested in selling budget travel. Many agents simply don't find it worthwhile to search through their computer data bases on your behalf in return for the small commission a budget fare earns them. Those agents who don't normally devote a good deal of time to reading and studying bargain fares won't be of much help to you. To get an idea of available bargains, or to locate budget travel agents, check the Sunday travel sections of large metropolitan newspapers such as *The New York Times, The Chicago Tribune,*

A CONVERSATION WITH JANET W.

Janet W. spent six weeks in Luxembourg as part of 4-H's International Youth Exchange Program.

Q. What expectations did you have?

A. I wasn't really sure of what to expect from my experience. The constant use of the word "experience" made me nervous. It was never a trip, exchange, or visit—always an "experience." Now that I'm back and have had time to think about it, no other word really fits. It *was* an experience.

Q. What was the most difficult part of your experience?

A. For me, the hardest part of the trip was changing families. We stayed with each family for about two and a half weeks—it doesn't seem like long, but once you get into it the time really flies. Even harder than changing families was getting sick away from home.

Q. Did the international experience change your perception of yourself?

A. I learned that I could depend on myself more than I thought I could.

Q. Would you recommend this kind of experience to others?

A. Yes! Not only would I recommend it, but I'd offer to carry luggage for anybody who's going on an exchange.

Q. Any advice for someone about to embark on a similar experience?

A. Pack light, be prepared for anything and everything. Mail can take from one to two weeks to get to Europe. Have your parents and your friends write to you about a week before you leave; you'll feel more at home, and it will take some of the "sick" out of "homesick." And don't worry too much. If you spend twenty-four hours a day worrying about your camera being stolen or your money or whatever, you aren't going to have a good time and you aren't going to learn anything.

A CONVERSATION WITH AMY D.

Amy D. spent a year studying in Barcelona, Spain, as part of the School Year Abroad Program.

Q. What expectations did you have before you went?
A. I truly believed that Spain would be a different world. In fact, I discovered that living in Barcelona had *much* in common with life here. Many students I met in Barcelona were people who had a lot in common—interests, attitudes—with people I knew in this country.

Q. What was the most difficult part of your experience?
A. Without a doubt, coming back to the U.S. I hate to sound like a cliché, but I really did do a *lot* of growing up, and returning to the same school, the same friends, even the same family was very hard.

Q. Would you recommend this kind of experience to others?
A. *Definitely!* It is an experience that in some way or another will be meaningful to anyone.

Q. What advice do you have for others?
A. I guess the best advice I could give is what was told to me before I left—"Expect the unexpected." Anything can happen during an experience abroad. It's very easy to attach yourself to the other American students you'll meet wherever you are and spend all your time hanging out talking about all the great things back home. Take some chances.

The Los Angeles Times, and *The Washington Post.* Usually, these are full of ads for competitive airfares and contain the latest travel information in columns or feature articles. Budget travel agents also advertise heavily in weekly papers such as the *Village Voice* and *L.A. Weekly.* When searching for airfare bargains on your own, here are the options you're most likely to encounter:

- *Economy Fares.* The term "economy," when applied to airfares, is always relative to first- and business-class seating. That is, it's a euphemism for a regular coach-class ticket. There's really nothing economical about it. You should be able to find less expensive fares, but if you are making reservations at the last minute, an economy fare may be your best—or only—option.

- *Special Promotional Fares.* Promotional fares pop up sporadically, usually as part of a "quick sale" strategy that airlines use to fill seats during slow periods. At press time, the ailing airline industry had been issuing bargain fares to European cities with unprecedented frequency. One drawback to these fares is that they usually require the traveler to act immediately rather than plan an itinerary ahead of time. Many are also restricted to certain dates, usually in the low season. But if you have the luxury of flexibility, or if you find a deal on a flight that happens to fit your schedule, a promotional fare can be a dream come true.

- *Advance Purchase Excursion (APEX) Fares.* APEX fares are between 30 and 40 percent lower than regular economy class. Since low fares seem to go hand in hand with restrictions, however, beware of minimum and maximum stay requirements, cancellation and change penalties, and stopover restrictions. You must also purchase your ticket anytime from 7 to 30 days in advance. "Super" APEX fares are somewhat cheaper than regular APEX but are in effect on a limited number of routes.

- *"Last Minute" Youth Fares.* Almost every major carrier has replaced its old "standby" fares with what we call "last minute" youth fares. These are available usually to passengers 12 to 24 years of age on a one-way or round-trip basis, but must be booked within three days of departure.

Student and Youth Airfares While the least expensive airfares usually carry the most restrictions, special youth and student discounts are the exception to the rule. For those who are eligible, student/youth fares can cut as much as 50 percent off regular economy fares. Besides the low cost, student/youth fares have few of the restrictions that apply to most budget airfares, and are valid on regularly scheduled flights of a number of major airlines. In order to qualify for most student/youth airfares, you must have either the International Student Identity Card (see page 61) or the International Youth Card (see page 63).

Most student and youth fares are the result of special contracts made between student travel agencies and the airlines, and are generally not sold directly by the airlines themselves. In fact, most airline ticketing offices will not have information about them. To find out about student/youth fares, check with Council Travel or any other agency that specializes in student and youth travel. Listed below are sample round-trip fares available during the spring and summer of 1992:

Route	Round-Trip
New York/London	$390
Los Angeles/Tokyo	$1,198
Chicago/Frankfurt	$730
London/Paris	$130
Boston/Mexico City	$470
Bangkok/Hong Kong	$330

We can't predict what prices will be by the time you read this book. For starters, look through *Student Travels* (see page 54), or ask for Council Travel's *Airfare Updates,* which provides the latest information on nearly every type of international airfare.

Consolidator Tickets and Charter Flights A charter flight is one in which a tour operator reserves a plane to fly a specific route on certain dates. This arrangement allows charter companies to offer tickets at a discount. Consolidators offer a similar service. When airlines can't fill seats, consolidators buy extra tickets at a discount, then sell these discounted tickets to the public.

Keep in mind that consolidators and charter companies work with airlines. If you book with a charter company, be sure to find out what airline you'll be flying on. Also ascertain the exact arrangements that have been made between the airline and the company selling you the ticket. Before purchasing your ticket, ask for a copy of the contract; operators are by law required to supply you with one when you book a charter. Know your rights and responsibilities beforehand to avoid headaches later.

Consolidator and charter tickets are usually nonrefundable and cannot be changed. However, this isn't true for all companies. If you book with Council Charter, for example, tickets are at least partially refundable as long as you cancel before your scheduled departure from the United States. Council Charter return flights can be changed in Europe for a fee of $75. You can also purchase a trip cancellation waiver, which guarantees a full refund if you cancel anytime up to your scheduled check-in time. Another feature that makes Council Charter unique is its mix-and-match plan, which lets you fly into one city and return from another. Although the actual cities served vary slightly from year to year, Council Charter's destinations generally include Amsterdam, Brussels, London, Lyon, Madrid, Malaga, Nice, Paris, Rome, and other European cities. Council Charter flights depart from Boston and New York, with low-cost add-on fares from a variety of other U.S. cities. Here are some sample round-trip fares from 1992:

Route	Low Season	High Season
New York–Paris	$438	$498
Boston–Brussels	$438	$618
New York–London	$358	$498
New York–Rome	$498	$798

For more information contact a Council Travel office (see page 8) or call Council Charter's toll-free number: (800) 800-8222.

Getting Around

Your international flight will only be the first step in your journey. If you plan to spend all of your time in just one city, you'll probably make use of local public transportation, such as subways, trams, or buses. But if you plan to travel more extensively, you may have a wide variety of transportation options available to you, including planes, trains, buses, cars, and boats, or even bicycle or foot.

Before you go, think about these options. Consider such things as geography, scenic interest, efficiency, and price. You may find, for example, that an overnight ferry between two points, while not as fast as a plane, is much less expensive and more interesting. In many countries, buses are faster and cheaper than trains, although they may be somewhat less comfortable. Consult a good guidebook to get an idea of how you'll get around. You should also get a good map of the country as well as detailed street plans of any cities you'll be visiting. If you can't find these in a store near you, contact the country's tourist board in the United States, or try bookstores that carry travel literature (see For Further Information on page 77).

By Air If you are going to be doing any air travel in another country, be sure to ask about student/youth fares. To be eligible you need to have an International Student Identity Card or International Youth Card (see pages 61 and 63). Student fares on many routes can be booked at any Council Travel office (see page 8). Many of the more popular routes, such as London–Paris, Rome–Athens, and Paris–Tel Aviv, fill up early, so do your planning, calling, and booking as soon as possible.

In some countries, foreign travelers can obtain special air passes that entitle them to a certain number of flights during a specified period of time. For example, in Brazil, a vast country with limited roads and railways, an air pass provides an economical and convenient way to get around. The Brazil Air Pass allows five stopovers within Brazil for three weeks for $440. Air passes for most countries must be purchased before departure from the United States. To see if special air passes are available for a particular country, contact the country's tourist bureau or the office of its official airline.

By Train Traveling by train in other countries is a totally different experience from traveling by train in the United States. In many parts of the world, rail travel is much more common than it is here. Train travel gives you the chance to meet and talk to the locals and to see some scenery as well. Most national rail systems, such as BritRail and Japan Railways, offer rail passes good for travel over a certain period of time. Young people traveling to several countries in Europe may want to consider the following rail bargains:

- *Eurail Youthpass:* Anyone under age 26 can purchase this pass for unlimited second-class travel in 17 countries. One month is $470, two months is $640.
- *Eurail Youth Flexipass:* Also available to anyone under 26, this pass is good for 15 days of travel within two months and costs $420.
- *BIJ Tickets:* Sold under the Transalpino, Eurotrain, and Twentours names, BIJ tickets (Billets Internationaux de Jeunesse) can save anyone under 26 up to 50 percent off second-class fares for international trips within Europe and Morocco. Tickets are valid for two months (six months for Turkey and Morocco), allowing free stopovers in other countries along a direct route. Tickets must be purchased from specified agents, usually student travel organizations, located throughout Europe.

Eurail also offers several passes without age restriction, including the standard Eurailpass good for 15 days to three months of unlimited travel; the Saverpass for groups of two or three travelers; various Flexipasses; and the European East pass for travel through eastern Europe. Eurail passes can be purchased in the United States through Rail Europe, 226-230 Westchester Avenue, White Plains, NY 10604; (914) 682-5172, or (800) 345-1990 outside New York, New Jersey, and Connecticut. Council Travel (see page 8) is also an official distributor of Eurail passes as well as most other national rail passes. If neither has what you're looking for, try the tourist board of the country you plan to visit.

By Bus Bus travel isn't as popular in Europe as it is in the States, but in other parts of the world—in Latin America, Asia, and Africa—buses (and such variations on buses as minivans and flatbed trucks) are the most popular forms of transportation. In some areas, buses are virtually the only means of reaching certain destinations. While bus travel in most countries is already inexpensive, many countries also offer youth fares as well as passes good for travel over a certain period of time. Consult the national tourist office of the country you plan to visit.

By Boat Most people think of travel by boat as something from a bygone era. Nevertheless, lake, river, and maritime connections are still vital in many parts of the world. Hovercraft shuttle across the English Channel; hydrofoils connect the Mediterranean coasts of Europe and North Africa; steamers navigate the Amazon and the Nile; ferries link the East Asian countries of China, Korea, Taiwan, and Japan. If you're traveling with a Eurail pass, you're eligible for discounts on a number of European ferry routes. The International Student Identity Card (see page 61) is also good for special rates on English Channel and Mediterranean sailings. Contact a Council Travel office (see page 8) for details.

By Bicycle It's easy to take your bike along with you—the airline will tell you how to get it ready for the trip. You can also rent or buy one when you get there. In fact, many national rail systems offer their own special bike rental deals, allowing you to alternate travel by train and bike. Bicycle touring is a great way to see the country up close and at your own pace, stopping at will and choosing your own route. A number of organizations sponsor group tours abroad (see the Outdoor Activities section). If you want to go it alone, find out whether the country you're visiting has any cycling clubs; they should be happy to provide you with information.

Lodgings

If you're going abroad on an organized program, lodgings will probably be arranged for you. Otherwise, looking for places to stay will be your own responsibility. With a little bit of resourcefulness, you won't have to put too big a dent in your budget. You can always consult one of the many guidebooks for budget travelers, but remember that even the most up-to-date guides usually reflect prices from at least the year before. Once you've arrived in a place, if it's a city of any size at all, the local tourist office can give you names and addresses of inexpensive hotels; some will even phone ahead to book your room. Local members of the International Student Travel Confederation (see page 61) should be able to offer some help; many, in fact, run their own student hotels. Below are described two options especially for youth and students.

Youth Hostels Hostelling International and its network of hostels offer low-cost accommodations to members (for membership information, see page 63). Originally designed for hikers and cyclists, hostels now welcome all sorts of travelers. They can be found in major cities as well as in remote, scenic spots. Accommodations are usually dorm style, in which you share a room with fellow travelers. Many hostels, however, have a limited number of private rooms which couples or small groups can share at a slightly higher price. The hostel provides you with a bed, pillow, and blanket, and you provide your own sleep sack (a sheet folded over and sewn up on three sides) or rent one from the hostel. Sleeping bags are generally *not* allowed except in remote, rustic hostels that cater primarily to hikers. Many hostels have specific regulations. Almost all require that you help with a small domestic chore, such as sweeping out the bunk room. Most hostels have evening curfews and limit the length of stay to three consecutive days, unless you have made special arrangements ahead of time. Many also have a lockout system that requires all guests to stay out for most of the day, usually from 10 A.M. TO 5 P.M. If you don't mind these restrictions, youth hostels are great places to meet fellow travelers, trade stories and information, and plan what's coming next.

Student Hostels Don't confuse these with youth hostels. They're usually located in university dorms and are open only during vacation periods. Often a student restaurant is attached or nearby. Local members of the International Student Travel Confederation can point you to the nearest one.

Meeting the People

Getting to know the local people should be one of your goals as a traveler. Probably the best way to accomplish this goal is to stay with a family. In the listings, you'll find a number of organizations that specialize in homestay experiences. Depending on the organization, the homestay may last anywhere from a week to a full year. One thing we must reiterate here: If you choose to participate in a homestay program, make sure to find out how the sponsoring organization selects host families. If you suspect that an organization's host families participate only to make some extra money, you'd do better to look elsewhere.

If you'd like to spend a short time with one or more hosts while you travel, you may want to become a member of SERVAS. SERVAS puts travelers in touch with host families and individuals who invite SERVAS members into their home for a two- to three-night stay. Applicants to SERVAS are interviewed by local area representatives and, if accepted, receive an introductory letter to people in the area they'll be visiting. The rest is up to the traveler and the host to arrange. The U.S.

KEEPING TRACK

After returning from a trip, many people regret not having kept a careful record of their experience. Don't make that mistake. Keep a journal, take photographs; you might even carry a small tape recorder to record conversations with the friends you make. (Some people also enjoy sending recorded letters home instead of having to write.)

Bring an address book in which to record the names and addresses of the people you meet along the way. You'll want to contact them again or give their names to other friends who are headed in their direction. If you jot numbers and addresses on bits of napkins and corners of envelopes, you're probably going to lose them.

Another good idea is to compile a scrapbook filled with ticket stubs, postcards, advertisements, matchbook covers, and maps. You can even make a collage out of these things and hang them on your wall to evoke memories. Whatever you do, months or years after your trip you'll appreciate having something around to show your friends and remind you of the great time you had.

SERVAS Committee is located at 11 John Street, Room 706, New York, NY 10038; (212) 267-0252.

For those who want to visit local families without staying the night, most countries have organizations that specialize in short-term get-togethers. You may be invited to someone's home for dinner or just a few hours of conversation over tea. Contact the official tourism office of the country you plan to visit to see if such a service is offered.

FOR FURTHER INFORMATION

The purpose of this book is to provide you with a listing of organizations that sponsor programs abroad, as well as to guide you in selecting the right program and preparing for your international experience. To be truly prepared, however, you'll have to do a lot more research on your own. One good source of general information on over 75 different countries is *Work, Study, Travel Abroad: The Whole World Handbook*, compiled by CIEE and published by St. Martin's Press. The 11th edition (1992–93) costs $12.95 and is available from Council Travel offices and bookstores, or by mail from CIEE (include $1.50 book-rate postage or $3 for first class). If the handbook doesn't give you the specific information you need, at least it will tell you where to get it.

You'll probably need a good guidebook. The drawback of most guidebooks, of course, is that they're read by thousands of other travelers. There's always the danger that low-cost hotels, once listed, will suddenly raise their prices, or that those quaint little restaurants will be invaded by hordes of American travelers like yourself—just what you want to avoid! Don't depend on guidebooks every step of the way; after all, the fun of travel is exploring new things on your own. Still, a guidebook can help you get your bearings. When selecting a guide, it's important to look for one that doesn't just list the addresses of hotels and restaurants, but that attempts to give you a good feel for the territory and the people you'll be visiting.

The *Let's Go* series, produced by Harvard Student Agencies and published by St. Martin's Press, is written by students for students. Packed with budget travel information, there are *Let's Go* guidebooks for most European countries as well as Mexico, Israel, and Egypt. They're available at most bookstores, as well as from Council Travel offices or by mail from CIEE.

Prentice-Hall Travel publishes another good series called *Real Guides*. While they aren't always as budget-minded as the *Let's Go* guides, they offer a better historical and cultural introduction to the countries they cover and make more of an effort to understand contemporary attitudes. *Real Guides* also offer a wider array of titles, including countries in Asia, Africa, and South America.

If you really want to get off the beaten path while staying on a tight budget, there are two publishers you should definitely check out: Lonely Planet Publications and Moon Publications. Lonely Planet *Travel Survival Kits* cover countries throughout the Americas, Africa, Asia, and the South Pacific. Its *On a Shoestring* guides cover wider regions for those planning to visit several countries in a given area, such as Southeast Asia or West Africa. If you don't see these books in your local bookstores, ask for a catalog from Lonely Planet, Embarcadero West, 155 Filbert Street, Suite 251, Oakland, CA 94607-2538; (800) 275–8555. Moon Publications also covers many nontraditional destinations with its *Moon Handbooks*. You can receive their catalog by writing to 722 Wall Street, Chico, CA 95928, or by calling (800) 345-5473.

If you want a larger selection of titles, a number of travel bookstores publish mail-order catalogs: Travel Bookstore, 1514-North Hillhurst Avenue, Hollywood, CA 90027; Hippocrene Books, 171 Madison Avenue, New York, NY 10016; Forsyth Travel Library, 9154 West 57th Street, P.O. Box 2975, Shawnee Mission, KS 66201; Wide World Bookshop, 401 Northeast 45th Street, Seattle, WA 98105; and Traveller's

A SHORT CHECKLIST

Here's a list to help you in preparing for your trip. Check off the boxes to make sure you have the following essentials:

Passport
Visas
International Student Identity Card
Insurance coverage
Traveler's checks, a safe place to keep them, and a copy
   of their numbers to leave at home
Air tickets
Rail passes
International Youth Hostel Card

Are you all set? Go!

Bookstore, 75 Rockefeller Plaza, New York, NY 10019. All of the above also distribute maps.

There are also a few good magazines for travelers in search of a real cross-cultural experience. One of the best, *Great Expeditions,* publishes accounts of off-the-beaten-path journeys all over the world and includes great advice from its writers. Letters from traveling readers also help to make this magazine an excellent source of timely first-hand information. A yearly subscription (four issues) costs $18. Contact *Great Expeditions* at Box 18036, Raleigh, NC 27609; (800) 743-3639. Another interesting magazine, *Transitions Abroad,* is geared primarily toward people looking for long-term employment or volunteer opportunities overseas, as well as university students who want to study abroad. However, each issue contains valuable information for anyone planning an experience abroad of any length. A yearly subscription of six issues costs $18. Write to Transitions Abroad Publishing, 18 Hulst Road, P.O. Box 344, Amherst, MA 01004.

Chapter 5
COMING HOME

*B*efore you go, you should think about one last thing: coming home. You probably feel there's no reason to worry about this, especially now, but there are adjustments to make when you come home as well as when you go abroad. Just as preparation helps make your trip easier, thinking ahead helps to ease the transition when you return home.

Returnees often report they feel strange coming home from abroad. You also may feel uneasy after you come home, and wonder why. After all, home is home, and you know how people act in your own culture. But remember, you have traveled or lived somewhere else for a while—several months, a year—and probably tried very hard to adapt to a different culture and to accept that culture's ways of doing things. When you come back, you may forget that you are seeing home a little differently from before. Your perspective now is not an exclusively American one but the perspective of an American who has had a cross-cultural experience.

Not surprisingly, the person who becomes most comfortable in the new culture and has an intensely positive experience will probably have the hardest time coming home. If you have been speaking another language, your English may even be rusty. On the other hand, the person who travels with a group of American friends or eats mostly at McDonald's or Pizza Hut probably won't have a sufficiently different experience to find coming home very difficult.

Assuming that you *have* immersed yourself in another culture, at least in some small ways, you have to be ready to deal with not only some jet lag, but also some culture lag. Many returnees feel confused and disoriented, which is understandable if just yesterday they were in

This chapter was written by Angene H. Wilson, Professor, College of Education, and Associate Director, International Affairs, University of Kentucky. Professor Wilson is also a volunteer for Youth for Understanding.

A CONVERSATION WITH JACKIE W.

Jackie W. spent one week in Kenya and six weeks in Botswana as a participant in 4-H's International Youth Exchange Program.

Q. What was the hardest part of your experience?
A. For me, coming back and readjusting was the hardest part, no doubt. I remember thinking that nobody understood me and what I had just gone through.

Q. Why was coming home so difficult?
A. When I first came back, I was frustrated at how little people knew about Botswana and even Africa in general. It was difficult to break through stereotypes. I had to play teacher when telling them about my experience. I would tell stories about the people in the village I was staying in. I found that many people were excited to hear my stories and even asked lots of questions about the village and its people. But it was nearly impossible to communicate the depth of my experience and how it had changed me.

Q. How did the experience change you?
A. My whole outlook on life is different. It also made me want to someday go back to Botswana or Africa for a longer period of time and do some volunteer work.

Q. Would you recommend this kind of experience to others?
A. Yes. I would hesitate to recommend a trip to Botswana to just anybody, but I would definitely encourage anyone to travel if they have the opportunity.

the cloud forest in Costa Rica or walking along the river Seine in Paris. But after a while they get back their rhythm and start to feel like they're home again. Perhaps the transition was easier in the old days when people traveled slowly on ships!

Besides the culture lag, there are other reasons for feeling strange at home. Living or traveling in another country is a special experience, and you may feel like a special person as an exchange student or international workcamp volunteer. Being an American abroad is a novelty; it may be hard to readjust to ordinary life back home and also to being an ordinary person in the home culture.

Those who like adventure may adjust more easily overseas but less quickly at home. Abroad, there always seems to be a new place to explore or a new person to meet or a new challenge to overcome. At home, everything might seem just as it was when you left.

You might also find it frustrating to try to talk about your trip to people back home. Returnees say they get tired of the same old questions, such as "How was your trip?" or "Did you have fun?" You will probably be annoyed by what seem superficial questions, because the places you have been and people you have met are important to you and can't be described in just a few words. It's hard to remember that you once had to look on the world map to find the Caribbean island where you were going to take part in a workcamp. It's hard to remember that you knew little about Switzerland except that it was home of the Alps, before you spent the summer there as an exchange student. It's also discouraging if the places you lived in or traveled to overseas are rarely or never covered in your local newspaper, which makes it difficult to find news about them after you return.

Many returnees see educating others as part of their role. They have figured out ways to answer questions that challenge other people's stereotypes and to teach other people some of what they have learned. Some show pictures to help their friends visualize the country. Of course, it's still hard for people who have not had your experience to really understand what you're feeling inside, but you can help them see things in a different light.

Sometimes returnees have a slide party for family or friends and serve international dishes. Other ways to involve friends include inviting them to attend international activities at school or to see foreign films. You can also get to know new exchange students at your school and introduce them to your friends.

Of course, some people simply may not be interested in other cultures. In that case, there's not much you can do. You may want to tell everyone about what you've done, but it's important not to brag. Bring up your experience in a natural way when the opportunity arises in conversation.

Also remember to show interest in events that occurred while you were away; your younger brother's baseball team championship, your friends' beach party, and so on. If you show that you care about the activities of friends and family, they'll be more willing to share your experiences. (They may even stay awake during most of your slide show.)

What about your parents? One research study of high-school students returning from a homestay program abroad indicates that an experience abroad has a direct and usually positive impact on relationships with family. In communication with parents, returnees reported greater closeness, greater equality in the relationship, greater appreciation for parents, and a smoother and more open relationship.

What about school? Many schools have international clubs you can join to meet others who have traveled, as well as international students. Foreign-language clubs may offer a chance to keep up your new fluency in a second language. Sometimes these clubs sponsor international dinners, talent shows, or other activities. Members of these clubs can be helpful by organizing a buddy system for new international students.

Lots of returnees find they want to help build bridges between cultures as well as tell people about their experiences when they come home. Befriending a new international student who may be an immigrant, a refugee, or an exchange student is one way to do this. Since you're familiar with the nervous, confused feeling that foreign students have, go out of your way to talk to, eat with, or help students who are new.

Returnees may also find opportunities to be helpful in their wider communities. Many are inspired to act as tour guides for school groups visiting from other countries, to teach English to Spanish-speaking neighbors, and generally to provide assistance to new community members from outside the United States. Bridge building doesn't have to be limited to people of the country you visited. You will probably feel generally more interested in people of other cultures and more understanding of what it is like to be a stranger in a new culture.

Here is a list of things you can do when you return from a trip abroad:

- Go to a reentry program after you get back if the organization you go overseas with has one. If not, get together with other students who have had similar experiences to talk. Remember that feeling strange is normal.
- Throw a party for your family and friends and share your pictures and international food.
- Tell people about other cultures based on your own experience when they ask you questions. You can be a teacher!
- Keep in touch with new friends overseas.
- Make new international friends back home.
- Find international organizations to participate in, such as Amnesty International or Oxfam.
- Make presentations about your experience to a class at school, younger students in elementary school, and community groups.
- Invite an international student to your home for Thanksgiving or become a host family for an exchange student.
- Start a dream fund to save money for your next international experience.

With a little planning, you can feel enthusiastic not only about going abroad, but also about returning and using your newfound skills and knowledge at home. Don't make the mistake of thinking the experience is over when it's only beginning. Your adventure abroad doesn't have to end. If you maintain your new contacts, interests, and awareness, the experience can last a lifetime.

Part Two
The Programs

HOW TO READ THE LISTINGS

*I*n this book, you will find a wide range of program possibilities—programs based in the United States and overseas, programs run by nonprofit organizations and those run by profit-making firms, programs that emphasize study and others that offer touring, camping, sports, or voluntary service. To make your search for the one that's right for you easier, we've organized the program listings into seven sections:

- Study Abroad
- Language Study
- Creative Arts
- Organized Tours
- Work/Volunteer
- Outdoor Activities
- Homestays

Of course, some organizations do not fit neatly into a category; a number of them offer more than one type of program. In these cases, we've provided a complete description of the organization and its programs only in the section that reflects what seems to be the organization's main focus. For example, you'll find all the offerings of AFS Intercultural Programs—including volunteer, homestay, and outdoor activities programs—listed in the Study Abroad section, since most of its programs emphasize study. However, to make things easy for you, we have cross-referenced the organizations offering multiple programs in all the appropriate sections. Browsing through the Outdoor Activities section, for example, you'll come across references to organizations described in other sections of the book. You can also refer to the index, which lists programs both by location and by type.

The fact that an organization is listed here is no guarantee that its programs are flawless. You must be sure to apply the evaluation techniques we outlined in Chapter 3 to the programs in this book, as well as to any others you encounter. There are, however, a few programs that we *can* vouch for—programs that are sponsored by members of the Council on International Educational Exchange. Check the description to see if the organization is a CIEE member. CIEE-member programs are all operated on a nonprofit basis; they include some of the largest and best-established international exchange programs available. As part of the membership review process, they have undergone the scrutiny of the CIEE Membership Committee, which has examined their programs and services as well as their organizational structure. As members of CIEE, they have demonstrated an interest in maintaining high standards and a willingness to contribute to the development of the field of international exchange.

Format for the Listings

We've tried to distill the material we received from each sponsor and present it in a format that will give you a feel for what each program is really about. Organizations are listed alphabetically in each section. Within each listing, the information is broken down in this way:

- *The sponsor:* Some background about the organization that offers the program—when it was founded, what its stated goals are, what other organizations it may be affiliated with.
- *The program:* What the sponsor has to offer—the duration of the program, when and where it takes place, and what it involves.
- *Orientation:* How the organization prepares participants for the experience.
- *Supervision:* The type and amount of supervision offered by different organizations vary greatly. Some programs do not supervise participants outside the classroom or do much beyond handling program logistics. This does not mean that the program is better or worse than a more closely supervised one, but it should help tell you whether the program is the type you're looking for.
- *Services for persons with disabilities:* Specific services for participants with disabilities. Some programs do not have any specific policy and simply consider applicants on a case-by-case basis.
- *Requirements:* Age, academic, and language requirements, as well as other qualifications that the sponsors are seeking from applicants.
- *Living arrangements:* Whether participants live in a tent, with a

local family, or in a first-class hotel. Where room and board are included, we've sometimes distinguished between half-board and full board. Half-board includes breakfast only; full board includes breakfast and dinner.

- *Finances:* How much the program will cost, what the fees include, and whether scholarship aid is available. For foreign-based organizations, we've converted local currency into U.S. dollars using exchange rates valid in 1992.
- *Deadline:* The date by which applications must be received to be considered for the program.
- *Contact:* Wherever possible, we give a specific name and that person's title, so that your letter of inquiry won't get lost in a pile of mail.

Not every listing has every heading; for some programs, a few of the items may not apply. Whenever information about a program appears within quotation marks, it is a direct quote from the sponsor's promotional material.

Remember, we've only summarized the programs in this book. Finding out all the information you need is up to you.

STUDY ABROAD

*I*n this section, you'll find a wide range of study-abroad options, whether you want to study for an academic year, a semester, or even just a few weeks during the school year. Most of the institutions or organizations in this section are based in the United States and offer programs especially designed for Americans.

Courses are usually taught in a classroom, and in some cases by a foreign instructor in the language of the country. Many of the programs, however, offer the option of courses taught in English. Students can learn about a variety of topics, including the country's history, culture, and language.

Many of the study-abroad programs also involve homestay or organized tours before, during, or after the study experience. Individual students can enroll in most of the study programs described, but a few involve school-to-school exchanges—a group of students (and teachers) from one school exchanges with a group from a school abroad.

ACCENT
814 Mission Street, Suite 201A
San Francisco, CA 94103
Telephone: (415) 512–8191

The sponsor: Accent is a commercial agency that plans and coordinates academic programs in conjunction with U.S. colleges and universities.

The program: Accent offers summer and semester programs in Florence and Stresa, Italy; Nice and Paris, France; Heidelberg, Germany; and Madrid, Spain.

Orientation: Predeparture orientations and intensive on-site orientations are offered.

Supervision: The student-teacher ratio is usually 10 to 1.

Services for persons with disabilities: Accent encourages participation by persons with disabilities to the extent that host institutions can accommodate their needs.

Requirements: Students should be at least 17 and have completed their junior year in high school.

Living arrangements: Students generally have a choice between residence halls, homestays with local families, or private apartments.

Finances: Costs for summer programs range from $2,100 to $3,300; semester programs from $3,400 to $4,400. The fee includes instruction, housing, orientation, excursions, and partial board.

Deadline: Varies according to program.

AFS INTERCULTURAL PROGRAMS
313 East 43rd Street
New York, NY 10017
Telephone: (212) 949–4242 or (800) AFS–INFO

The sponsor: The AFS idea originated with volunteer ambulance drivers who served in World War I and II and then established an international exchange program for secondary-school students in 1947. Originally called the American Field Service, AFS is "dedicated to peace through the promotion of worldwide intercultural learning experiences for secondary-school students, young adults, and families from all walks of life." It offers international exchanges including homestays for secondary-school students and special programs for young adult professionals in the field of education. This nonprofit organization is a member of CIEE.

The program: AFS offers choices in more than 50 countries:

- *Semester Program:* Young people may spend five months attending local secondary schools in any of 10 countries.

- *Year Program:* Young people may spend a year attending local secondary schools in any of 37 countries.
- *Summer Programs:* AFS offers 8- to 10-week summer placements in 30 countries. These include the following:

> *Summer Homestay:* Students immerse themselves in the local culture by living with a host family.
>
> *Language Study/Homestay:* Choose among Spanish, French, German, or Japanese. In Latin America and Japan, participants live with host families while attending classes during the day. Participants in Europe receive two to three weeks of language training at a university campus or in a youth hostel preceded or followed by a homestay.
>
> *Cultural Studies/Homestay:* Students live with host families and participate in group activities such as museum visits, nature studies, historic restoration, and excavations.
>
> *Outdoor/Homestay:* This program in Australia and New Zealand includes a five-week homestay with school attendance. In a two- to three-week group experience, students participate in such activities as map reading, bush and river skills, navigation, rock climbing, canoeing, and camping.
>
> *Soviet Youth Camp:* Participants from the United States, Japan, and countries of the former Soviet Union combine language and culture studies with structured discussions about global issues. Past camps have been held in Alam-Ata, Kazakhstan, and Odessa, Georgia.

Orientation: AFS provides orientations on a local and national basis before departure, as well as an orientation once the participants have arrived.

Supervision: AFS maintains national offices in each host country. Host families are visited by local staff during the participant's stay. Travel and orientation periods are conducted by staff and assisted by AFS volunteers.

Services for persons with disabilities: AFS welcomes disabled candidates. Participants are placed in appropriate accommodations.

Requirements: Although specific requirements vary, AFS programs generally are open to high-school students. Most programs require a 2.7 GPA.

Living arrangements: The homestay is integral to the AFS experience. Host families are carefully screened and receive no remuneration. AFS staff visit host families at least once a month.

Finances: The fees vary from program to program. Costs range from $2,495 to $5,395. The fee includes international transportation and living expenses. Financial aid is available.

For returnees: More than 25 U.S. colleges and universities offer scholarships specifically for AFS returnees, and another 16 offer financial aid based on need to any AFS returnee admitted to their institution. A listing of participating schools called *AFS: The College Connection* is available from AFS's New York headquarters.

Deadline: Rolling admissions.

Contact: AFS (address above). Be sure to indicate any special interests you may have; new programs are being developed all the time.

ALEXANDER MUSS HIGH SCHOOL IN ISRAEL (AM/HSI)
3950 Biscayne Boulevard
Miami, FL 33137
Telephone: (305) 576–3286 or (800) 327–5980

The sponsor: Established in 1972, AM/HSI sponsors short-term academic programs in Hod Ha'Sharon, Israel. AM/HSI works in cooperation with public and private schools in the United States, the Israeli Ministry of Education, and the Mosenson Regional High School in Israel.

The program: There are five sessions. Four sessions are eight weeks long and occur during the school year, beginning in September, November, February, and April. The fifth session is a seven-week summer session starting in late June. The curriculum concentrates on the history of Israel from ancient to modern times, using the historical sites in Israel as classrooms. The basic disciplines of mathematics, science, and foreign language are also taught. Classes are conducted on campus and at the related historical sites.

Supervision: The full-time staff, consisting of Americans who are permanent residents of Israel, provides student supervision. There is one teacher for every 18 students.

Services for persons with disabilities: Because more than 50 percent of the program involves strenuous hiking to ancient sites, the program does not often accommodate persons with physical disabilities.

Requirements: Students must be high-school juniors or seniors, have a minimum 2.5 GPA, and be recommended by their home school.

Living arrangements: Students stay in coed dormitories.

Finances: The fee ranges from $3,375 to $4,550, depending upon session dates. Included are tuition, room and board, international airfare, and ground transportation in Israel.

Deadline: Applications should be sent in at least two months prior to departure. Classes are often booked to capacity two to four months prior to departure.

Contact: Admissions Department (address above).

AMERICAN ASSOCIATION OF TEACHERS OF GERMAN (AATG)
112 Haddontown Court 104
Cherry Hill, NJ 08034
Telephone: (609) 795–5553

The sponsor: AATG is a nonprofit professional association of teachers of German in the United States from the elementary to the college level.

The program: Each summer AATG sponsors a four-week travel/study program to Germany in cooperation with the Pedagogical Exchange Service, a German government agency. Participants live with German families and attend *Gymnasium* classes (*Gymnasium* is the German equivalent of American high school). Organized field trips are included, and often the host families plan excursions as well.

Supervision: An American teacher of German is available to help with trips, act as a liaison with German school authorities, and provide personal counseling.

Services for persons with disabilities: Provisions may be made according to the disability involved.

Requirements: Applicants must be high-school students at least 15 years old with at least two years of German and the recommendation of a German teacher.

Living arrangements: The families chosen to host the students have a son or daughter about the same age as the American visitor. The entire four weeks is spent with the host family.

Finances: The fee of approximately $1,700 includes round-trip airfare, room and board, excursions, insurance, and classes.

Deadline: April 1.

Contact: Helene Zimmer-Loew (address above).

AMERICAN FRIENDS OF THE COLLÈGE LYCÉE CÉVENOL INTERNATIONAL
c/o Moses Brown School
250 Lloyd Avenue
Providence, RI 02906
Telephone: (401) 272–5158

The sponsor: The Collège Lycée Cévenol International is a boarding school located in the village of le Chambon-sur-Lignon, in France. It was founded in 1938 by two pacifists, pastors from the local parish. The goal of the Collège Lycée Cévenol International is "to foster world peace and global understanding by bringing together students from many different places and cultures." The American Friends of the Collège Lycée Cévenol International is a nonprofit organization made up of former students, workcamp participants, and ministers. It was founded in 1946 and is staffed by volunteers.

The program: The Collège Lycée Cévenol International, situated on a 30-acre campus that was once a family farm, offers an academic-year program, a summer school, and a workcamp. The school year runs from September to June. The student body and faculty are international and the curriculum is that of the standard French *lycée*. Fifteen or twenty countries are usually represented. The summer school combines language study with tennis, horseback riding, swimming, team sports, workshops (woodwork and drawing), performing arts (music, drama, film), and excursions to the surrounding countryside. The workcamp takes place in July, and participants from all over the world work together on a project that might involve remodeling building interiors, painting the outside of a building, landscaping, or doing farm or forestry work. Each day includes time set aside for a language course; evenings are reserved for group activities.

Supervision: During the summer and academic-year programs, there is one teacher for every 10 students, and resident counselors live in the student dorms. The workcamp has one or two group leaders responsible for limited supervision of 20 volunteers.

Requirements: For the school-year program, students should be 13 to 18 years old with two years of French. The summer school accepts students from 12 to 18 years old with some French-language background; for the workcamp, a minimum age of 17 and some knowledge of French is required. International Baccalaureate preparation is available (some courses in English).

Living arrangements: Students live together in dormitories with two or three students per room. There are resident counselors in each dorm. "The Collège Cévenol seeks to promote a simple life, where students learn the importance of helping one another, of working together with shared responsibilities. All students are expected to help with campus chores in the dorms or dining hall."

Finances: The school year program costs approximately $2,200 per trimester, with travel and vacation expenses extra. The summer school requires payment in francs (approximately $1,140, depending on the length of the session). The fee for the workcamp is $110 plus $25 for insurance.

Deadline: May 15 for school year and summer program, May 1 for workcamp.

Contact: Anne W. Burnham (address above).

AMERICAN HERITAGE ASSOCIATION
P.O. Box 425
Lake Oswego, OR 97034
Telephone: (503) 635–3703

The sponsor: American Heritage Association is a nonprofit organization which, since 1957, has provided intercultural and experiential educational programs. The organization is a member of CIEE.

The program: American Heritage Association offers programs for secondary-school students that include international homestay/travel programs and school-to-school exchanges. Groups of students travel to Europe, Asia, and Mexico on programs custom-designed to suit their needs. The emphasis in all programs is on education, using travel as a tool. Students and their adviser are required to participate in a training course during the academic year preceding travel.

Orientation: An orientation at a weekend camp is held six weeks prior to departure. In addition, students must participate in a series of predeparture meetings required of each group.

Supervision: An adviser stays with the group during the program. The student-teacher ratio is 10 to 1.

Services for persons with disabilities: Each participant with a disability is handled individually.

Requirements: Participants usually are between 13 and 18 years old. Students are accepted based on personal and educational motivation, participation in group preparation including orientation, satisfactory medical examination, attention to program deadlines, satisfactory transcript, and references.

Living arrangements: For most of the time, participants stay in local homes but might also be housed in hotels or youth hostels.

Finances: Program costs vary depending on itinerary and activities. The average cost for a 30-day program in Europe is $2,700, which includes round-trip airfare, all meals and lodging.

Deadline: For spring programs, applications should be submitted by December 31; for summer programs, the deadline is February 15.

Contact: Eloise Mark, Director, Secondary Programs (address above).

AMERICAN INTERCULTURAL STUDENT EXCHANGE (AISE)
7720 Herschel Avenue
La Jolla, CA 92037
Telephone: (619) 459–9761

The sponsor: AISE is a nonprofit educational foundation dedicated to fostering better international understanding and appreciation through language education and cultural exchange.

The program: AISE sponsors four types of homestay programs:

- *High-School Year in Europe/Australia:* Students spend a semester in Australia or France or an academic year in Australia, Denmark, Finland, France, Germany, Norway, Spain, Sweden, or Switzerland.
- *Five-week Summer Homestay Program:* Students live with a host family for five weeks in Denmark, Finland, France, Germany, Italy, Norway, Spain, or Sweden.
- *Five-week Summer Language and Homestay Program:* Students live with a host family in either France or Spain and attend language classes three hours a day, five days a week.
- *Six-week Summer Homestay/Adventure:* Students live with a host family for four weeks in Sydney or Melbourne, Australia. Students fly to Cairns for a nine-day adventure/safari in the area of the Great Barrier Reef.

Orientation: For short-term programs, written materials on country and experience are sent to the student prior to leaving. For academic-year programs, students receive orientation in New York or Los Angeles. A week-long orientation is held upon arrival overseas.

Supervision: All programs have an escort for the international flight. During the student's stay abroad, supervision is the responsibility of the host family.

Services for persons with disabilities: Students with physical disabilities are accepted on program.

Requirements: Participants should be 15 to 18 years old. For year-long programs to France, Germany, Spain, and Switzerland, students need a minimum of two years of language study. All students must be in good health.

Living arrangements: For all programs, students live with a local family and participate in the family's daily life.

Finances: Costs for academic programs vary from $4,300 to $4,900, including room and board, orientations, round-trip international transportation, and health and accident insurance. The five-week summer homestay program costs $2,500, including homestay (room and board), round-trip transportation from New York City, health insurance, escorts, and supervision. The five-week summer language/travel homestay program costs $3,200 and includes homestay, language lessons, day trips, round-trip transportation from New York City, health insurance, escort, and supervision. The six-week summer program in Australia costs $3,300. If the student's family hosts an AISE student the same year the student goes abroad, $250 is deducted from the program cost.

Deadline: April 1 for school year and summer programs; October 1 for Australia (February departure).

Contact: Kathy Cohrs, Director, American Student Division (address above).

ASPECT FOUNDATION
26 Third Street
San Francisco, CA 94103
Telephone: (800) 879–6884

The sponsor: ASPECT Foundation is a nonprofit educational foundation that has offered year-long study programs for Americans and international students since 1979.

The program: ASPECT's *Ambassador Program to Germany* places students in high schools in and around Hamburg for a 10-month period lasting from mid-August to mid-June. Participants live with local families. An excursion to Berlin is also included.

Orientation: Participants receive an overnight predeparture orientation in San Francisco as well as a welcome orientation upon arrival in Germany.

Supervision: Each student is handled individually by the host family. Professional staff in Germany and the United States are available for support or emergency assistance.

Services for persons with disabilities: Each case is handled individually.

Requirements: Students must be at least 15 years old and sophomores, juniors, or seniors in high school. Participants must have had two years of any foreign language and a 2.5 minimum GPA.

Living arrangements: Students live with host families for their entire stay.

Finances: The program cost is $4,995. This fee includes escorted international airfare, host family placement, staff support, orientations, Berlin excursion, and insurance.

Deadline: Rolling admissions.

ASSE INTERNATIONAL STUDENT EXCHANGE PROGRAMS
228 North Coast Highway
Laguna Beach, CA 92651
Telephone: (800) 333–3802

The sponsor: Affiliated with the Swedish and Finnish ministries of education, ASSE was founded in 1976 to provide student exchange between Sweden and the United States. In the last decade it has expanded to include exchanges with Australia, Canada, Czechoslovakia, Denmark, Finland, France, Germany, Great Britain, Iceland, Italy, Mexico, the Netherlands, New Zealand, Norway, Portugal, Spain, and Switzerland. ASSE believes that "through cultural exchange programs and homestay programs a greater international understanding is achieved among people and countries."

The program: There are three choices for U.S. students going abroad with ASSE:

- *The Academic Year Abroad:* This program consists of 10 months in Australia, Canada, Czechoslovakia, Denmark, Finland, France, Germany, Great Britain, Iceland, Italy, Mexico, the Netherlands, New Zealand, Norway, Portugal, Spain, Sweden, or Switzerland. Participants leave home in August (for Northern Hemisphere destinations) or mid-January (for Southern Hemisphere destinations) and attend school for the academic year.
- *Summer Abroad.* If you can't get away for a full year, ASSE sponsors a summer program from early July through mid-August in Czechoslovakia, Denmark, Finland, France, Germany, Iceland, Italy, the Netherlands, Norway, Portugal, Spain, Sweden, and Switzerland. Students live with a host family in which at least one member speaks English.
- *Language Adventure:* Another summer possibility, this 28-day program takes place in France (the Riviera), Germany (Berlin), or Spain (Madrid), and combines a homestay, intensive lan-

guage and culture study, and excursions for sight-seeing, shopping, or recreation.

Orientation: All three programs include orientation—a half day for the summer programs, a full day for the year-long program—prior to departure. For students going to a non-English-speaking country for the academic year, an intensive 8- to 10-day language training and culture orientation is included.

Supervision: Students receive supervision from a volunteer community representative.

Services for persons with disabilities: ASSE will accommodate students with disabilities on an individual basis.

Requirements: Students must be 15 to 18 years old. Applicants for the year program must have at least a B average; summer applicants must have a C+ average. The organization looks for participants with emotional maturity, intellectual curiosity, and an outgoing disposition, among other characteristics. All participants must be interviewed and must supply letters of recommendation, an autobiographical essay, transcripts, and a health form. There is no language requirement.

Living arrangements: Each program provides a homestay experience.

Finances: The Year Abroad program costs $2,600 to $4,600 and includes round-trip airfare (excluding Canada and Mexico programs), insurance, accommodations, school placement, and supervision. The Summer Abroad program ranges from $1,600 to $2,200. Scholarships are available.

Deadline: April 1 for Northern Hemisphere destinations. August 1 for Southern Hemisphere destinations.

Contact: William J. Gustafson, President (address above).

BRILLANTMONT INTERNATIONAL SCHOOL
Av. Secretan 16
CH 1005 Lausanne
Switzerland
Telephone: (41) 21-3124741
Fax: (41) 21-208417

The sponsor: Brillantmont, founded in 1882, is accredited by the European Council of International Schools and the New England Association of Schools and Colleges and is a member of the Swiss Federation of Private Schools. It offers two curricula—one prepares students for entrance to an American or European university, and the other is a school of languages. The school is coeducational, both boarding and day. Situated in the center of Lausanne, Brillantmont overlooks Lake Geneva and the Swiss Alps.

The program: Students can attend the year-long program from mid-September to the end of June or the summer program in July and August. The school offers programs at the 9th- through 12th-grade levels. Four programs are offered:

- *The American High School Program*, which is the equivalent of 9th through 12th grades in the U.S. educational system
- *The British Section,* which prepares students for the IGCSE (International General Certificate of Secondary Education) and Advanced (A) Level of the Cambridge Board Examinations
- *The Language Program,* which includes English, French, German, Italian, or Spanish
- *The Commercial Program* in French with emphasis on languages

Classes have an average enrollment of 15 students and are in session from 8 A.M. to 4 P.M., five days a week. The school also offers instruction in the following subjects at an additional cost: art, art history, music history, current affairs, mass media, photography, modern or classical ballet, cooking, drama, piano, guitar, flute, horseback riding, and tennis. A variety of sports activities is available. Optional excursions are organized for weekends and school breaks. The summer program includes French language study, a variety of sports and cultural activities, and optional sewing and cooking courses.

Supervision: Supervision is provided by the instructors during the day and by house mistresses and resident teachers at night.

Requirements: Brillantmont accepts girls and boys between the ages of 13 and 18.

Living arrangements: Students live in the five main buildings, which are divided according to age groups. There are two to three students housed in each room. Students are encouraged to speak French.

Finances: One year of schooling and boarding costs 35,500 Swiss francs (approximately $26,250). A deposit of 6,000 Swiss francs (approximately $4,500) is required to cover extra expenses such as private or extra lessons, clubs, students' supplies, excursions, pocket money, health insurance, and laundry. The summer program costs 960 Swiss francs (approximately $720) per week and includes all required and optional classes, excursions, cultural activities, and room and board, but does not include pocket money. The application fee is 30 percent of tuition, which is deducted from the final account when full payment is made.

Deadline: May for the year program. There is no deadline for the summer program.

Contact: Mrs. F. Frei-Huguenin, Principal (address above).

BRITISH AMERICAN EDUCATIONAL FOUNDATION (BAEF)
135 East 65th Street
New York, NY 10021
Telephone: (212) 772–3890

The sponsor: Founded in 1966, The British American Educational Foundation is "dedicated to fostering a continuing exchange of ideas, educational techniques, philosophies, and values between the two major English-speaking nations of the world."

The program: BAEF's *Scholars' Program* places juniors, seniors, and high-school graduates from the United States into British boarding schools. The program lasts a full academic year. According to BAEF, "our young Americans learn important lessons from Britain's enduring traditions. At the same time, they themselves carry their own strengths and American vitality to the English schools, giving the future leaders of Britain a firsthand, in-depth, personal experience of an American's perspectives and values." Since its founding, BAEF has placed about 600 U.S. students in British schools.

Orientation: Upon arrival in London, participants are given a two-day orientation.

Supervision: Students are supervised by their school housemasters during term. They are assisted in making holiday plans by the BAEF's London Director.

Services for persons with disabilities: Students with disabilities will be accommodated according to each school's facilities.

Requirements: Applicants must be high-school juniors or seniors between 16 and 18 years old. They should have verbal SAT scores of at least 500 and are required to have a personal interview.

Living arrangements: Participants live at the schools in which they are placed. Schools are usually divided into "houses," and all the students in one "house" live together for their entire school experience. Until recently there were only a few coed schools in the United Kingdom, but their numbers are growing and girls are now accepted in the Sixth Form (the last two years of high school) at some of the more traditional British schools. In some of these schools the girls have their own house, in some they live in coed dormitories, and in others they live with faculty families.

Finances: Although the cost varies from school to school, the approximate fee for an eleven-month term with round-trip transportation between New York and London is $20,000. Scholarships are available.

Deadline: It's best to apply earlier, but applications can be accepted until May of the year you plan to leave.

Contact: N. S. Bauer, Executive Director (address above).

BUTTERFIELD AND ROBINSON

For information on Butterfield and Robinson and its study-abroad programs, see its listing in the Organized Tours section of this book, page 202.

CET

For information on CET and its study-tour programs in China, see its listing in the Organized Tours section of this book, page 203.

EF FOUNDATION
1 Memorial Drive
Cambridge, MA 02142
Telephone: (800) 447–4273

The sponsor: EF Foundation is a nonprofit organization dedicated to promoting intercultural understanding through student exchanges. Since 1979, over 20,000 high-school students from 28 countries have participated in the organization's academic homestay programs around the world.

The program: EF Foundation participants can spend an academic year or semester in Australia, France, Germany or New Zealand. In each country, participants attend a local school and live with local families.

Orientation: The programs have an optional, introductory component—a language and culture camp—held in each of the host countries. At the camps, students receive instruction in the language and culture of the country.

Supervision: Each exchange student is assigned to one of EF Foundation's local area representatives abroad. These representatives serve as a liaison between the students and the families and schools and are available to offer advice and encouragement.

Services for persons with disabilities: EF Foundation will attempt to accommodate most persons with disabilities by handling cases individually, placing disabled participants in appropriate programs.

Requirements: Applicants should be between the ages of 14 and 18, and have above-average grades. The program in France requires two previous years of language study.

Living arrangements: EF Foundation students live with families that have been selected by area representatives. Families choose the student that best suits their interests, personalities, and life-style.

Finances: For the full-year program, the fee is approximately $4,500 for the European countries, and $5,200 for a year in Australia or New Zealand. The semester program costs $4,200 for Europe, and $4,900 for Australia or New Zealand. Fees vary depending on domestic airport, and include round-trip airfare, ground transportation to the host family, orientation materials, family placement, school placement, tuition, ongoing supervision, and a free subscription to *The Exchange* newsletter.

Deadline: April 1 for programs beginning in the fall; September 1 for programs beginning in January.

Contact: Outbound Program Director (address above).

EUROVACANCES
Bogenstrasse 20
D-2000 Hamburg 13
Germany

The sponsor: Eurovacances is a nonprofit organization that has been organizing international student exchange programs between German and American youths since 1979. Based in Germany, Eurovacances has offices in Australia, Colombia, and the United States.

The program: Eurovacances offers two types of programs: a summer language program and a semester or academic year abroad. In the semester- or year-abroad program (from August to January or June of the following year) students live with German host families throughout Germany and attend local high schools or colleges. An excursion to Berlin is included in the full-year program. Students are expected to become fully integrated family members. The summer language program (four weeks in July and August) provides 80 hours of intensive language instruction, daily activities, and an excursion to Berlin. Students live with families around Hamburg.

Supervision: There is a regional representative and school official in the area.

Requirements: Participants must be at least 15 years old. The maximum age is 18, but older students may be accepted.

Living arrangements: Participants on the semester/year program live with German host families throughout Germany; on the summer language program they live with host families in the Hamburg area.

Finances: Fees are $1,600 for the summer program, $1,700 for the semester program, and $2,500 for the full-year program, including room and board with the host family, counseling, meetings, the Berlin excursion (full-year and summer programs only), and insurance. Participants must make their own flight arrangements to and from Germany. Partial scholarships based on merit and need are available for the semester and full-year programs.

Deadline: For summer, May 15; for semester or year, June 15.

Contact: Margaret L. Johnson, Executive Director, Eurovacances Youth Exchange, P.O. Box 175, Brockport, NY 14420.

THE EXPERIMENT IN INTERNATIONAL LIVING

For information about The Experiment in International Living and its study-abroad program, see the listing for World Learning Inc. in the Homestays section of this book, page 294.

FIELD STUDIES COUNCIL (FSC)
Central Services
Preston Montford, Montford Bridge
Shrewsbury SY4 1HW
England
Telephone: (44) 743–850674
Fax: (44) 743–850178

The sponsor: Founded in 1943, the Field Studies Council is an independent charity whose purpose is to promote the philosophy of conservation through "environmental understanding for all."

The program: FSC operates 12 centers throughout England and Wales where students participate in short-term residential field courses on a variety of environmental topics. Courses involve geography, history, and science and include such subjects as ecosystem management, food webs and food chains, settlement patterns, and organic pollution. While most participants on FSC programs come as part of a British school group, individuals are also welcome.

Supervision: The student-instructor ratio is 20 to 1; instructors are responsible for the students' daily supervision.

Services for persons with disabilities: All are welcome. Two centers are equipped with ramps and special rooms.

Requirements: The minimum age is 15.

Living arrangements: At some centers, students live in dormitories; at others, they stay with local families or at local inns.

Finances: The fee varies depending upon the length of the course. The basic cost for a one-week program is 150 British pounds (approximately $280), which includes room and full board.

FULBRIGHT-GESELLSCHAFT
Frankstrasse 26
500 Cologne 1
Germany
Telephone: (49) 221-214091
Fax: (49) 221-212930

The sponsor: In 1967 the Cologne Center for Teachers in Service Training and the Society of German-American Academic Exchange merged and became the Fulbright Society–German-American Cultural Exchange. The main function of this nonprofit organization has been to promote student exchange between the United States and Germany.

The program: U.S. high-school students study in Germany for a semester (three to six months) or a full academic year. There is also a three-week program during Easter. All programs involve living with a family that has a boy or girl approximately the same age as the participant and attending daily classes at their host school. U.S. participants must be willing to host a German exchange student in return.

Orientation: Preparatory seminars are held for the exchange students.

Supervision: Participants on the Fulbright-Gesellschaft programs are expected to "integrate into the families and to accept family roles like members." Group leaders are responsible "at all times for the welfare and discipline of their students." There's a program representative available in case of emergency.

Services for persons with disabilities: Fulbright-Gesellschaft places no limitations on disabled students who can fully participate in the program.

Requirements: Participants must be between the ages of 14 and 18 and have had at least three years of language study.

Living arrangements: Participants live with families in Germany.

Finances: Costs vary according to the program.

Contact: Write to the above address or contact German-American Cultural Exchange, 12801 Saddlebrook Drive, Department CS, Silver Spring, MD 20906; (301) 946–8708.

FUTURE FARMERS OF AMERICA (FFA)
5632 Mount Vernon Memorial Highway
P.O. Box 15160
Alexandria, VA 22309–0160
Telephone: (703) 360–3600

The sponsor: Founded in 1928, FFA is a nonprofit organization of students who are involved in the study of agriculture, agribusiness, and agriscience. FFA has been involved in international exchanges ever since its first exchange with the Young Farmers Clubs of England and Wales in 1947.

The program: FFA's *World AgriScience Studies* (WASS) program offers one-year exchanges in Australia, Finland, Germany, New Zealand, and Sweden. Students have the opportunity to live with a host family and also attend school while in their host country.

Orientation: There is a three- to four-day orientation at the beginning of the program as well as a debriefing session at the end.

Supervision: In every country there's a staff person who is responsible for the participants. Staff members are all natives of the host country with previous experience in international exchange.

Services for persons with disabilities: Every effort will be made to fully include persons with disabilities in all phases of the FFA WASS program. The orientation site is completely accessible for physically disabled participants.

Requirements: Participants must be between 15 and 19 years old and have a sincere interest in agriculture or previous experience in farming or an agriculturally related field.

Living arrangements: Students live with farm families; they usually have their own room.

Finances: European programs cost $3,100; programs in Australia and New Zealand cost $3,600. The fee includes international transportation, orientation, room and board, and insurance. Full and partial scholarships are available.

Deadline: April 1 for Europe; October 1 for Australia and New Zealand.

Contact: WASS Program Coordinator (address above).

GERMAN-AMERICAN PARTNERSHIP PROGRAM (GAPP)
Goethe House New York
666 Third Avenue, 19th Floor
New York, NY 10017
Telephone: (212) 972-3960

The sponsor: GAPP is a student exchange program between paired U.S. high schools and German secondary schools. In the United States, the program is administered in conjunction witih Goethe House New York. In Germany, the program is administered by the Pedagogical Exchange Service in Bonn. The program has been operating for nineteen years. GAPP serves to promote German instruction in U.S. high schools and to improve participants' understanding of the culture and civilization of the host country.

The program: GAPP matches U.S. schools with German schools and facilitates the exchange. Exchanges are possible at any time of the school year, but most take place at Easter time, when the Germans come to the United States, and in the summer, when U.S. citizens go to Germany. As a rule, the exchange lasts four weeks, three of which are to be spent with host families at the location of the partner school. The format of GAPP is flexible—the teachers and their groups make their own arrangements with the help and advice of GAPP. The most important feature of the program is that U.S. students stay in the homes of their German peers and attend school with them, and vice versa.

Supervision: The program is coordinated by the sponsoring teachers at U.S. and German schools, usually teachers of German and English, respectively. The coordinators and the teachers chaperoning groups of 10 to 20 students are responsible for the planning and the execution of the exchange and for preparing the participants for the experience.

Services for persons with disabilities: GAPP accommodates many participants with disabilities, including participants with physical, learning, or mental disabilities.

Requirements: Only U.S. schools in which German is offered can take part in the program. Students are expected to have a basic knowledge of their partners' language. School attendance of 10 to 12 days is required in the host country. Schools usually exchange on an annual or biennial basis; each group must serve as hosts for the other.

Living arrangements: U.S. students live with German host families;

when the German students come to the United States, they stay with the families of the group members.

Finances: Participants pay their own costs (airfare, spending money, overland travels). GAPP does not charge a fee. Teacher subsidies and group grants are available.

Deadline: No set deadline. Deadline for grants is April.

Contact: Sabina Margalit (address above).

GORDONSTOUN INTERNATIONAL SUMMER SCHOOL
Elgin
Moray IV30 2RF
Scotland
Telephone: (44) 343–830798
Fax: (44) 343–830074

The sponsor: In 1991, 250 students from 27 countries participated in Gordonstoun, an international summer school offering a program involving academics and recreation.

The program: The 24-day program offers courses in July and August in computer studies, British history, and French language. Courses are interspersed with recreational activities including sailing, sports, and a six-day adventure program based at an old Highlands shooting lodge.

Orientation: All students take course tests in their chosen subject so that they can be assigned to an appropriate group.

Supervision: Staff members supervise students. There is one instructor for every two students.

Requirements: Students must be 11 to 16 years old.

Living arrangements: Students stay in dormitory houses at the school.

Finances: The fee is 2,040 British pounds (approximately $3,880) for the all-inclusive 24-day course, not including travel expenses.

IBEROAMERICAN CULTURAL EXCHANGE PROGRAM
  (ICEP)
13920 93rd Avenue NE
Kirkland, WA 98034
Telephone: (206) 821–1463

The sponsor: This nonprofit organization was founded in 1970 with two objectives: "to enhance foreign-language teaching and study programs and to foster mutual international and intercultural understanding and respect." To meet these broad objectives, ICEP sponsors homestay programs in Bolivia, Costa Rica, Guatemala, and Mexico.

The program: Program choices include homestay programs lasting five weeks, three months, a semester, or an academic year. Each program consists of three basic parts: a preexperience orientation, a homestay, and a reentry orientation. The preexperience orientation, held in Mexico City or Miami, involves two days of training in intercultural communication and preparation for the family homestay. From the orientation session participants travel to their homestay. "Host families consist of educated, cultured people who are interested in young people and the promotion of good will between their country and the U.S." At the end of the homestay, participants return to Mexico City or Miami for a reentry orientation before returning to the United States. Programs coinciding with the academic calendar in the foreign country include a school experience. "In an ICEP school experience, you are likely to be the only American student, or one of very few, in a Spanish-speaking culturally authentic environment." Participants are often asked to help teach English in the schools they attend and are expected to tutor members of the host family or their friends.

Supervision: There are program coordinators and local representatives in each participating city.

Services for persons with disabilities: ICEP accepts participants with disabilities, provided they submit verification from a physician that the disability would not preclude successful participation in the program.

Requirements: Programs are open to 15- to 18-year-olds. Short-term programs in Mexico are open to those 15 to 20 years old. Participants must have two years or the equivalent of Spanish, the recommendation of a Spanish teacher, and have "demonstrated responsibility, maturity, good character, and academic ability."

Living arrangements: "The families selected are as representative of the middle class as possible. Within the middle class, though, there is a very wide range. Some houses are rather humble by most U.S. standards, and some are luxurious." Participants are accepted as a family member and are expected to do their share of the household chores.

Finances: Fees range from $725 for six weeks to $2,100 for a full year.

This includes orientation, ground transportation to the homestay, and homestay arrangements. Airfare is not included.

Deadline: Three to four months before start of the program.

Contact: Bonnie P. Mortell, President/Executive Director (address above).

INTERNATIONAL CHRISTIAN YOUTH EXCHANGE (ICYE)
134 West 26th Street
New York, NY 10001
Telephone: (212) 206–7307 (voice/TTY)

The sponsor: ICYE has been a leader in international exchanges since its establishment as a German-American exchange program in 1949. Motivated by a sense of responsibility and service to all humanity, ICYE today has become a federation of 31 autonomous national committees. Because each country exchanges with all the others, young people from all parts of the world experience an exchange year together in each host country. The organization is also a member of CIEE.

The program: ICYE's *Year Abroad* program begins in late July and lasts a full year. The countries involved are Austria, Belgium, Brazil, Bolivia, China, Colombia, Costa Rica, Denmark, Finland, France, Germany, Ghana, Honduras, Iceland, India, Italy, Japan, Mexico, New Zealand, Nigeria, Norway, Poland, Sierra Leone, South Korea, Spain, Sweden, Switzerland, and Taiwan. Participants live with families, attend high school, and participate fully in the life of the host country. ICYE's stated goal for the program is to "help participants become sensitive to problems of national and worldwide issues, and encourage commitment to act on new understandings both during the exchange year and beyond."

ICYE also offers high-school students the opportunity for voluntary service projects lasting four to six weeks in a number of countries like Africa, Latin America, and Europe. Service projects include construction of medical clinics and schools in Third World countries, as well as other projects in Northern Hemisphere countries.

Orientation: Before leaving the United States, participants attend a weekend introductory conference held on the regional level, followed by a short conference in New York. Topics covered include an introduction to ICYE, goals and expectations for the year abroad, questions and answers about the host country, and workshops in crisis management, cultural adaptation, and so on.

Supervision: A local representative of ICYE is always available to give assistance and support once the participant is abroad. ICYE's national structure and its volunteer network, organized on a regional level, are also aimed toward working with and helping participants.

Services for persons with disabilities: ICYE has a teletypewriter (TTY) for communication with the hearing impaired. All program events are accessible to disabled participants. ICYE also surveys all participating countries annually on the possibilities for sending and receiving disabled persons.

Requirements: Applicants must be at least 16 and juniors in high school. Although language ability is not required, it is beneficial. Basic language courses are offered during orientation in the host country.

Living arrangements: Participants live with a host family for the entire year or with several families in different parts of the host country.

Finances: The fee of $4,750 for the year-abroad program covers international travel to and from the host family, the departure conference and additional conferences in the host country, language training, medical and liability insurance, and room and board. Participants must pay the travel costs from their hometown to New York (point of departure). International voluntary service projects range from $500 to $2,600. Some scholarship aid is available.

Deadline: Applications are accepted and screened monthly beween December 15 and April 15; thereafter, applications are accepted on a space-available basis.

INTERNATIONAL EDUCATIONAL NETWORK (IEN)
3001 Veazey Terrace, NW
Washington, DC 20002
Telephone: (202) 362–7855

The sponsor: IEN was founded to improve the quality of math and science education in this country. IEN faculty consists of mathematicians and scientists from the United States, Europe, and Russia. "These educators not only share their knowledge with the students, but also introduce them to the challenging and competitive atmosphere of the scientific laboratory."

The program: IEN has one summer institute in Long Island, New York, and one abroad in Moscow, Russia. The program features formal and informal discussions with distinguished American and Russian scientists, as well as math and science courses. IEN offers what it calls a "spectacular camp environment with many opportunities to enrich your skills and appreciation of the scientific adventure."

Supervision: The student-leader ratio is 12 to 1.

Requirements: Students 13 to 18 are eligible. Selection criteria include PSAT, SSAT, and SAT scores when available as well as transcripts and a nomination by the applicant's math or science teacher.

Living arrangements: Students live two to a room in dormitories.

Finances: The cost for the U.S. session is $1,725 and the Russian session is $1,825. This includes room, board, tuition, and transportation. Transatlantic airfare to Moscow is not included. Some financial aid is available.

Deadline: May 15.

Contact: Linda Leimenstoll, Program Coordinator (address above).

INTERNATIONAL SUMMER INSTITUTE
P.O. Box 843
Bowling Green Station
New York, NY 10274
Telephone: (212) 747–1755

The sponsor: The International Summer Institute is a nonprofit organization founded in 1984 by parents and faculty of three New York City high schools for the academically talented: Stuyvesant, Bronx Science, and Brooklyn Tech.

The program: From July through August, the International Summer Institute brings academically talented students together from around the world. Programs are held in the United States as well as in China, France, Japan, Russia, and countries of eastern Europe. Students participate in sports, academic programs, and travel tours.

Orientation: Students participate in an orientation seminar.

Supervision: There is one group leader for every 10 students.

Services for persons with disabilities: The International Summer Institute has accommodated wheelchair-bound participants and students with impaired eyesight in the past.

Requirements: Students must be between 13 and 18 years old with high academic standing.

Living arrangements: Students live in dormitories, hotels, and with host families.

Finances: Costs range from $1,995 to $2,995, including airfare. Scholarships are available.

Deadline: May 1.

Contact: Dr. Carl Berkowitz, Executive Director (address above).

IRISH AMERICAN CULTURAL INSTITUTE
2115 Summit Avenue
College of St. Thomas (#5026)
St. Paul, MN 55105
Telephone: (612) 647–5678

The sponsor: The Irish American Cultural Institute, a nonprofit foundation with members throughout the United States and 26 countries, is dedicated to "preserving and promoting Irish culture. It is nonpolitical, nonreligious, and nonsectarian."

The program: Each summer the Institute sponsors a program called *Irish Way,* which involves five weeks of study, travel, and homestay in Ireland. *Irish Way* participants are based at King's College in Dublin, and at St. Brendan's College in Killarney, County Kerry. The campuses have facilities to accommodate a wide range of sports activities. A typical day for *Irish Way* participants includes breakfast followed by an Irish history class, a sports class, an Irish folk dance and music class, an Irish literature lesson, lunch, an Irish studies discussion, an Irish-language class, horseback riding, swimming or free time, supper, and then an evening activity, such as a movie, a group talent show, or skits. Students spend a total of three weeks between the two campuses, split by a week-long homestay with an Irish family. The program ends with a five-day tour of the country. The staff of *Irish Way* is made up of certified Irish secondary-school teachers assisted by college-age alumni and Irish Studies students.

Orientation: Predeparture information is provided by mail. Orientation sessions are held in some cities before departure.

Supervision: Certified secondary-school teachers and college and graduate students are responsible for the daily supervision of participants. Student aides stay with the participants in the dormitories.

Requirements: Applicants should be in 9th through 12th grade, have "reasonable grades, hopefully some experience of an Irish nature, and a good recommendation from a counselor or principal."

Living arrangements: Participants live on the King's and St. Brendan's campuses in large dormitories; boys and girls live in separate dorms. For the homestay part of the trip, they are placed with families throughout Ireland—a small town, a farm, or a city. During the five-day tour, participants stay in hotels.

Finances: The fee is $2,050, which covers books, tuition, travel within Ireland, some entertainment, room and board, and laundry expenses. Airfare is not included. Some financial aid is available.

Deadline: May 15, but earlier application is recommended.

Contact: Irish Way (address above).

KW INTERNATIONAL
159 Ralph McGill Boulevard NE, Room 408
Atlanta, GA 30308
Telephone: (404) 524–0988

The sponsor: Founded in 1972, this nonprofit organization encourages and supports international Christian education at two college-preparatory schools in India.

The program: KW International offers year-long programs at the following schools:

- *The Woodstock School:* A boarding school that offers teenagers the chance to take courses in Indian culture, history, music, art, and literature; to take part in an extracurricular program which includes music, hiking, field trips, drama, sports, and social service; and to join the school's five-week winter tour of India. The school is located on a steep hillside on the outskirts of Mussoorie, a city of 10,000 that grows to 80,000 in summertime.

- *Kodaikanal International School Study Program:* This school is located in the southern Indian hill station of Kodaikanal, three hours from Madurai. Courses include an intensive academic program combined with courses on Indian life and culture, extra-curricular activities as above, and the chance to live with a host family during winter vacation.

Supervision: All school events and field trips are chaperoned.

Services for persons with disabilities: KW International does not discriminate against disabled persons; however, it advises that mobility within the schools and travel throughout India may be difficult for a physically disabled participant.

Requirements: Both programs are suited to high-school students in the 10th and 11th grades. There is no language requirement.

Living arrangements: Students are housed in a dormitory that is rustic but comfortable. Two to four students share a room and all students eat in a central dining room.

Finances: The fee of $8,500 includes tuition for two semesters, room and board, field trips, vacation hospitality, and a winter tour of India. Airfare is not included. Scholarships are available based on need.

Deadline: April 15.

Contact: Jane Cummings, Executive Director (address above).

MUSIKER STUDENT TOURS

For information on Musiker Student Tours and its study-abroad program in England, see its listing in the Organized Tours section of this book, page 210.

NACEL CULTURAL EXCHANGES

For information about Nacel Cultural Exchanges and its study-abroad program, see its program listing in the Homestays section of this book, page 287.

NATIONAL 4-H COUNCIL
International Programs
7100 Connecticut Avenue
Chevy Chase, MD 20815
Telephone: (301) 961–2869

The sponsor: The National 4-H Council is devoted to supporting and expanding youth development programs. The largest out-of-school educational program in the United States, 4-H promotes clubs and activities designed to help young people "learn by doing." (The Four *H*s stand for head, heart, hands, and health.)

The program: The International 4-H *Youth Exchange Ambassador* program is a four- to six-week travel-study seminar and homestay program which takes place in June and July. The countries offered vary each year but have included Australia, Botswana, China, Costa Rica, Denmark, France, Germany, Greece, Israel, Italy, Jamaica, Kenya, the Netherlands, Spain, Switzerland, Taiwan, Thailand, and the United Kingdom. All 4-H ambassadors live with host families, learn the language, participate in study seminars, and pursue special activities. Study seminars include natural resources, water quality, camping, biking, foods and nutrition, trade, economics, agriculture, housing, and the fashion industry.

Orientation: A two- to four-day national predeparture orientation is held at either the National 4-H center in Maryland or in the departure city—New York, San Francisco, or Miami.

Supervision: All 4-H *Ambassador* programs operate under the supervision of a group leader who has experience with youth and expertise in the subject material.

Services for persons with disabilities: Each case is handled individually.

Requirements: Participants must be between 15 and 19 years old, in good health, and interested in rural living. There are language requirements for participation in some countries.

Living arrangements: Participants live with host families who are selected by cooperating youth program staff in the host country.

Finances: The program fee varies from $2,000 to $4,000, depending upon the country, and includes transportation, room and board, and all program-related expenses.

Deadline: April 1.

Contact: Apply through your local Extension Office, State 4-H Office, or the National 4-H Council at the address above.

NATIONAL REGISTRATION CENTER FOR STUDY ABROAD (NRCSA)

For information on NRCSA and its study-abroad program, see its program listing in the Language Study section of this book, page 173.

NORTH AMERICAN FEDERATION OF TEMPLE YOUTH (NFTY)

For information on North American Federation of Temple Youth and its study-abroad program, see its program listing in the Organized Tours section of this book, page 211.

NORTHFIELD MOUNT HERMON SCHOOL
Northfield, MA 01360

The sponsor: Northfield Mount Hermon School is an independent boarding school founded in 1879. The school is a member of CIEE.

The program: Northfield Mount Hermon offers summer study-travel programs in France, Spain, and China, as well as a marine biology course in the Caribbean.

- *French Language and Culture:* This course begins with an intensive four-day language course and orientation, followed by a three-week homestay in Arcachon on the Atlantic coast. Morning classes concentrate on language, history, art, and the regional economy. There are a number of excursions and activities scheduled. The final week is spent touring le Périgord and Paris.
- *Spanish Language and Culture:* Students begin the program with two days of intensive language classes in Burgos, then move on to Valladolid, where they spend three weeks attending morning classes while living with Spanish families. After the homestay, the group spends five days visiting different Spanish villages and sites. The final four days are spent in Madrid. Both the French and the Spanish programs focus on family life; afternoons are usually kept free so that students may participate in family activities. At the end of each homestay, students are required to present an independent project in French or Spanish.
- *Chinese Language and Culture:* At the heart of this seven-week program is a five-week stay at Fudan University in Shanghai. Students take classes in Mandarin Chinese and in various aspects of Chinese culture. Many excursions are planned during

this time. At the end of the program the group travels to northern China and spends a final few days in Beijing. The program offers an insider's view of China, seldom seen by American visitors.

- *Marine Biology Course:* The course takes place on Grand Cayman Island in the Caribbean. The course starts with a 12-day period of orientation at the school and continues with four weeks of diving and marine biology explorations on Grand Cayman Island. The diving program leads to scuba certification.

Orientation: Students spend two to three days at the Northfield Mount Hermon campus for "intensive predeparture preparation." Both the Spanish and French programs include several days of language instruction in the host country before the homestay begins. The China program includes an orientation in Hong Kong before departure to Shanghai.

Supervision: Group leaders are responsible for daily supervision of students, including "teaching, advising, counseling, and disciplining." There is one group leader for every 10 students.

Requirements: Students in the French, Spanish, and Chinese programs must be entering at least 11th grade. Participants must have a minimum of two years of language instruction for the programs in France and Spain. There is a minimum of one year language instruction for the China program. For the marine biology course, applicants must have completed the 10th grade and at least one year of high-school biology.

Living arrangements: Students live with local families in France and Spain. At Fudan University, students stay in an international dormitory in Shanghai.

Finances: Cost for the language programs is $4,900, which includes transatlantic airfare, room and full board, tuition, and excursions. The marine biology and scuba program costs $4,400, which includes round-trip airfare, room and board, and textbooks; eiqupment rental is not included. Financial aid is available.

Deadline: For China program: February 15. For other programs: rolling admissions.

Contact: For language programs: Eleanor D. Johnson, Director of International Programs, (413) 498–3290. For marine biology program: James B. Ward, Director, Summer School, (413) 498–3251 (address above).

OPEN DOOR STUDENT EXCHANGE
250 Fulton Avenue
P.O. Box 71
Hempstead, NY 11551
Telephone: (800) 366–OPEN or (212) 485–7330

The sponsor: Open Door Student Exchange, founded in 1964, is a non-profit corporation with programs for United States and overseas high-school students in more than 30 countries around the world. Open Door's executive staff in New York is supplemented by a network of state co-ordinators and area representatives throughout the United States. One or more overseas directors are located in each of the participating countries. Open Door is a member of CIEE.

The program: Open Door offers summer homestays, a semester or academic year abroad, or a number of special programs including the *High School Journalism Program* in Latin America, the *Congress-Bundestag Vocational Program* in German, *Work Experience Programs* in Eastern Europe, and *Thirteenth Year Abroad* for high-school gradu-ates. Open Door students participate in a number of excursions arranged by the overseas directors. United States students take part in the daily lives of their host families.

Orientation: All Open Door programs include both predeparture and postarrival orientation.

Supervision: All Open Door programs are supervised by on-site over-seas directors.

Requirements: High-school students between the ages of 15 and 18 are eligible. There is no language requirement for summer programs (ex-cept the *Latin American Journalism* program). Semester and academic year abroad programs in French-, German-, Russian-, and Spanish-speaking countries require two years of language study with a B average or better. For other countries, students must show language aptitude and interest. School recommendations are required for all applicants.

Living arrangements: Homestays are an integral part of all programs. Overseas staff and volunteers recruit host families and supervise the students during the exchange experience.

Finances: Summer homestay program costs range from $2,200 to $3,500, depending upon the destination. Semester programs cost $3,200 to $4,500. Academic year programs cost $4,200 to $4,400. Fees include international travel, travel within the host country, orientations, and insurance. Not covered are pocket money, visas, and transportation in the United States between home and the city of departure.

Deadline: April 15.

RAMAPO COLLEGE OF NEW JERSEY
505 Ramapo Valley Road
Mahwah, NJ 07417
Telephone: (201) 529-7463

The sponsor: Established in 1969, Ramapo College of New Jersey is a state-supported, coeducational, four-year college of liberal arts, sciences, and professional studies. It is a member of CIEE.

The program: Ramapo College offers a number of summer study-abroad programs, some of which are open to high-school juniors and seniors. Among these programs are an Italian language and culture course in Urbino, Italy, and an archaeological dig at Tel Hadar, Israel.

Supervision: Courses are taught by Ramapo College professors and local faculty.

Services for persons with disabilities: Ramapo College accepts persons with disabilities.

Requirements: Requirements vary from program to program.

Living arrangements: Accommodations vary from university dormitories to hotels to kibbutz housing.

Finances: Costs for most programs range from $2,000 to $3,000. Prices usually include round-trip airfare, room and board, local transportation, and excursions.

Contact: Summer Study Abroad Programs, Study Abroad Office (address above).

ROTARY INTERNATIONAL
1560 Sherman Avenue
Evanston, IL 60201-3698
Telephone: (708) 866-3000

The sponsor: Rotary Clubs exist worldwide and are dedicated to an ideal of service. The first Rotary Club was established in 1905; together there are more than 23,000 clubs in 167 countries.

The program: The *Youth Exchange* program offers two types of exchanges: a full academic year and a short-term stay of several days to several weeks. The full-year program includes a stay with three to four families and attendance at a school in the host country. The short-term programs usually take place during vacation periods and are sometimes arranged as international youth camps. Both short- and long-term exchanges can be arranged for disabled students. Programs are sponsored by individual Rotary Clubs and districts.

Supervision: Each student on the long-term program has a Rotarian counselor from the local host Rotary Club. Short-term programs are led by volunteers who are appointed by the Rotary Clubs or districts involved.

Services for persons with disabilities: Persons with disabilities are encouraged to participate.

Requirements: Participants must be 15 to 19 years old, but their parents need not be Rotarians. Applicants are chosen by a sponsoring club on the basis of a written application and a personal interview.

Living arrangements: These vary for short-term programs; long-term students live with host families.

Finances: Arrangements vary. Participants pay their own travel, insurance, and other costs. For long-term exchanges, the host Rotary Club provides a small monthly allowance and usually pays tuition fees for required academic programs. The host families provide room and board.

Contact: For information on opportunities in your area, contact your local Rotary Club.

ST. GEORGE'S SUMMER SESSION IN FRANCE

For information on St. George's Summer Session in France, see its program listing in the Language Institutes section of this book, page 177.

ST. STEPHEN'S SCHOOL
Via Aventina 3
00153 Rome
Italy
Telephone: (39) 6-575-0605
Fax: (39) 6-574-1941

The sponsor: St. Stephen's School was founded more than 28 years ago. It is a nondenominational, coeducational, English-speaking college-preparatory school in Rome.

The program: St. Stephen's operates in the style of the traditional American boarding school: the academic year is divided into two semesters from September to June. The curriculum prepares students for the American high-school diploma in addition to offering a full range of Advanced Placement examinations and the International Baccalaureate diploma. St. Stephen's takes advantage of its location in Rome, and field trips and informal excursions are a regular feature of school life. In addition, there are two educational trips during the school year to various places in Italy.

Orientation: Each semester begins with a short orientation program for all new students.

Supervision: Students are supervised by resident faculty members.

Requirements: St. Stephen's School is open to students 13 to 18 years old in the 9th to 12th grades. All instruction, except languages, is in English.

Living arrangements: Of the 145 students at St. Stephen's School, approximately 35 are full-time boarders. Accommodations are in dormitory-style rooms.

Finances: The academic year costs approximately $13,000 for day students and approximately $19,300 for boarding students. Limited financial aid is available.

Deadline: Applications are accepted throughout the year.

Contact: The Registrar (address above).

SCHOOL PARTNERS ABROAD
Council on International Educational Exchange
205 East 42nd Street
New York, NY 10017
Telephone: (212) 661–1414, ext. 1234

The sponsor: School Partners Abroad is administered by the Council on International Educational Exchange, which has been involved in secondary-school partnerships for 20 years. Approximately 3,000 students participate in inbound and outbound exchanges each year.

The program: School Partners Abroad matches American secondary schools with counterpart schools in Costa Rica, France, Germany, Great Britain, Italy, Japan, Russia, and Spain. The program is designed as a curricular resource to complement foreign language and social studies class-work. Linked schools are encouraged to communicate frequently; to exchange letters, photos, slides, videos, and curricular materials; and to plan for the program highlight—a three- to four-week annual reciprocal exchange of students and teachers. During each short-term exchange, American students and teachers participate fully in the life of the host school abroad, attending regular classes, joining in extracurricular activities, and living with the families of local students. Similarly, through the experience of hosting overseas students and faculty, U.S. schools benefit from a rich variety of formal and informal encounters in the classroom, local homes, and the surrounding community.

Orientation: Group leaders attend an orientation session once a year. In addition, extensive written materials are sent to group leaders and participating students throughout the year in preparation for both the hosting and sending programs.

Supervision: Group leaders are designated by the participating schools; they are full-time teachers or administrators, with foreign language ability and experience in international education. The average ratio of students to leaders is ten to one.

Services for persons with disabilities: Every effort will be made to accommodate students with disabilities.

Requirements: Applicants must come from participating schools. They should be 15 to 17 years old, high-school sophomores to seniors (although mature freshmen are eligible), with two years of language study for French- and Spanish-speaking countries. A junior-high-school program is also available for seventh and eighth graders.

Living arrangements: Participants live with local families for the duration of the school hosting program (one student per family). While on field trips, participants are accommodated in student hotels.

Finances: Costs vary from $600 to $2,000, depending upon destination. The fee includes international airfare, domestic transportation in the host country, full room and board, insurance, International Student Identity Card, group leader's fee, excursions (where applicable), and program materials. A grant from the German government's Foreign Office is available to students of German.

SCHOOL YEAR ABROAD
Phillips Academy
Andover, MA 01810
Telephone: (508) 749–4420
Fax: (508) 749–4425

The sponsor: This program, founded in 1964, is sponsored by Phillips Academy, Phillips Exeter Academy, and St. Paul's School. Faculty from these schools supervise the program; the headmasters form the Board of Trustees. School Year Abroad is a member of CIEE.

The program: School Year Abroad is a year-long academic program in Barcelona, Spain, and Rennes, France, that gives students the advantage of living in a foreign culture "without sacrificing progress in their schools at home or strong preparation for college." Every year, 55 students go to Spain and 60 go to France. Each student lives with a host family and participates fully in the life of the family and the community. Students take five courses. Classes are taught in both English and French or Spanish by American and native teachers. The sponsors emphasize that "*School Year Abroad* is not just travel abroad—it is not 'the grand tour.' It is a year of serious academic study in an unfamiliar environment." School Year Abroad organizes school trips during the year. Those in France travel to Normandy, Paris, and Provence; in Spain, students go to Toledo, Segovia, and Madrid as well as to several important cities near Barcelona.

Orientation: During the summer before the school year starts, orientation begins via the mail. The first week abroad is devoted to orientation as well.

Supervision: Resident directors are selected by a committee of representatives from the sponsoring school. They act as teachers and counselors and are responsible for daily supervision.

Services for persons with disabilities: School Year Abroad treats each case individually. It has accommodated participants with extremely poor eyesight and other physical disabilities in the past.

Requirements: Participants may come from any secondary school. They must be entering the 11th or 12th grades and must have a minimum of two years' language training and a good academic record. Among the less tangible requirements are "a concern for others and demonstrated maturity." Admission is very competitive.

Living arrangements: Homestays are an integral part of the *School Year Abroad.* According to sponsors, "Students live with butchers, shopkeepers, and postal employees as well as doctors, lawyers, and landed gentry." Most but not all host families have children; more than half have a child the same age as the *School Year Abroad* student.

Finances: The 1992–93 fee of $17,500 includes room and board, instruction, 14 to 19 days of group travel within the host country, and counseling. Although students must pay their own airfare, *School Year Abroad* arranges group travel, and 96 percent of the students choose to go with the group. Scholarships are available; one-third of the students receive financial aid up to full tuition.

Deadline: March 1, but flexible.

Contact: Woodruff W. Halsey II, Executive Director (address above).

STUDIO ART CENTERS INTERNATIONAL (SACI)

For information on SACI, see its program listing in the Creative Arts section of this book, page 195.

UNIVERSITY OF KANSAS

For information on the University of Kansas and its Croatian language and culture program, see its program listing in the Language Study section of this book, page 182.

UNIVERSITY OF NEW ORLEANS
Lakefront
New Orleans, LA 70148
Telephone: (504) 286–7455

The sponsor: The University of New Orleans, through the Office of International Study Programs in cooperation with the Honors Program, operates two credit programs for qualified high-school students, including graduating seniors. The school is a member of CIEE.

The program:

- *The European Experience* is a general introduction to European studies that includes travel to five countries with visits to London, Cambridge, Normandy, Paris, Strasbourg, Munich, Salzburg, Venice, and other cities. Students earn six hours of college credit during a five-week summer school in Innsbruck, Austria.
- *The Glories of France* is an intensive language program that also includes study of French culture and civilization. Students may travel to Nice, Monaco, Avignon, Albi, the Loire Valley, Chartres, Paris, and many other cities. During a four-week summer school in Montpellier, France, students may earn up to nine hours of credit in language, based on an advanced standing exam, and three hours of credit in civilization.

Orientation: *The European Experience* begins with a prestudy tour during which orientation takes place. Orientation for *The Glories of France* is upon arrival at Montpellier.

Supervision: Faculty and staff members from the university accompany each program and are responsible for its operation.

Requirements: For *The European Experience*: ACT composite score of 24 or combined SAT of 1,000; B average in high-school courses; recommendation from school counselor or principal. For *The Glories of France*: two years of French, with a 3.25 average; higher than B average in high-school courses; letter of recommendation from a French teacher.

Living arrangements: Participants live in university dormitories, with faculty and/or staff members housed in the same facility.

Finances: The approximate cost, not including airfare, is $3,000 for The European Experience and $2,000 for *The Glories of France*. Fee includes travel in Europe, tuition, room, and most meals.

Deadline: April 15. Late applications are accepted if space is available.

Contact: Marie Kaposchyn, P.O. Box 569, International Study Programs, Division of International Education (address above).

WORLD EXPERIENCE (WE)
2440 South Hacienda Boulevard
Suite 116, Department EE
Hacienda Heights, CA 91745
Telephone: (800) 633–6853

The sponsor: "Founded in 1977, World Experience strives to forge links of friendship, support, and understanding among students, families, and communities through a personally guided program of sharing. WE believes that the sensitive awareness of cultural differences, developed when students and families live together, results in mutual respect for each culture."

The program: WE offers one- and two-semester programs in Australia, Brazil, Bulgaria, Chile, Colombia, Czechoslovakia, Denmark, Ecuador, Estonia, Finland, France, Germany, Hungary, Japan, Mexico, New Zealand, Panama, Russia, Spain, Thailand, Uruguay, and Venezuela. WE also offers homestay-language programs in Japan, Russia, and Spain.

Orientation: All students attend an orientation before departure and after arrival in the host country.

Supervision: Directors and representatives in each host country are available to offer assistance. Many are volunteers who have sent their own children abroad and/or have hosted students in their families.

Services for persons with disabilities: Homes are sought with medically educated parents. In the past, persons with chronic illness such as diabetes, asthma, and allergies have been accommodated.

Requirements: Participants must be from 15 to 18 years old. Programs in France, Germany, and Spain require two years of language with above-average grades. All students should have above-average academic ability.

Living arrangements: Participants live with host families. They have their own bed, but may share a room with a family member of the same sex. They are expected to abide by the same rules as other teenagers in the family, and share the same responsibilities.

Finances: The one-semester program ranges from $2,500 to $3,600; the two-semester program ranges from $2,550 to $4,400; the summer program ranges from $1,215 to $2,585. Variations on price depend on the destination. Transportation and visa costs are extra, and in some cases there are additional private-school fees on the one- and two-semester programs. Insurance is provided, and financial aid is available if need is proven.

Deadline: March 1 to April 1 for the Northern Hemisphere; October 1 to December 15 for the Southern Hemisphere; May 1 for the summer language program.

Contact: Bobby J. Fraker, President/CEO (address above).

WORLD LEARNING, INC.

For information about World Learning, Inc., and its study-abroad program, see its listing in the Homestays section of this book, page 294.

YOUTH EXCHANGE SERVICE (YES)
4675 MacArthur Court, Suite 830
Newport Beach, CA 92660
Telephone: (714) 955–2030 or (800) 848–2121

The sponsor: Founded in 1974, YES is a nonprofit organization that organizes international teenage student-exchange programs.

The program: YES operates a homestay exchange program in which students can spend the academic year or second semester in countries of Asia, Europe, or Latin America. The program offers the opportunity to live with local families and attend local schools. YES also seeks families and schools to serve as hosts for students visiting the United States.

Orientation: Orientation sessions are provided before departure and after arrival.

Supervision: Local representatives are available for counseling, orientation, and supervision.

Services for persons with disabilities: Students with disabilities are accepted provided YES can find "the right host family."

Requirements: Students must be 15 to 18 years old.

Living arrangements: Students live with host families.

Finances: Academic-year programs cost $3,500; second-semester programs cost $2,900. Fees do not include transportation.

Deadline: May for academic-year programs, October for second semester.

YOUTH FOR UNDERSTANDING (YFU) INTERNATIONAL EXCHANGE
3501 Newark Street NW
Washington, DC 20016
Telephone: (202) 966–6800 or (800) 424–3691

The sponsor: YFU began as a post–World War II effort to reestablish ties between the United States and Germany. It is dedicated to promoting international understanding and world peace through the exchange of young people in 30 countries around the world. Since 1951, YFU has placed more than 150,000 high-school students. The organization is a member of CIEE.

The program: YFU offers programs that last a full year, a semester, a summer, or one month.

- *Overseas Year Program:* Participants spend an academic year in Argentina, Australia, Belgium, Brazil, Chile, Denmark, Ecuador, Finland, France, Germany, Italy, Japan, Mexico, the Netherlands, New Zealand, Norway, Paraguay, Spain, Sweden, Switzerland, the United Kingdom, Uruguay, or Venezuela. During their stay, they live with host families and attend school. High-school or college credit may be arranged.
- *Overseas Semester Program:* Students live with families and attend school from July to January in Argentina, Brazil, Denmark, Finland, France, Mexico, Russia, Spain, the United Kingdom, or Uruguay; or January to July in Argentina, Australia, Brazil, Chile, Denmark, Finland, Japan, and New Zealand.
- *Overseas Summer Program:* This homestay program involves all the countries listed under the year-long and semester programs plus China, Poland, and Greece. Participants live with host families and participate in a variety of YFU-sponsored activities.
- *Sport for Understanding (SFU):* This exchange is built "around the excitement and camaraderie of sport." Participants choose any of 30 sports, including swimming, basketball, field hockey, gymnastics, and tennis. The group forms a team, usually 12 to 16 students, that travels to a host country for a stay of about four weeks. They are hosted by a sport club and its coaches. Choices of location vary.

Orientation: Cross-cultural orientations are provided on a regional basis, and orientation materials are periodically mailed to YFUers before they leave.

Supervision: YFU has area representatives wherever there are participants backed up by a support/counseling system coordinated through regional, national, and overseas offices. *Sport for Understanding* participants are accompanied by leaders who are experienced in coaching and education and have had international experience. There is one coach for every 10 to 12 students.

Services for persons with disabilities: YFU consults its contacts in the applicant's preferred country to make sure they will be able to deal with the particular disability.

Requirements: YFU programs are open to students 14 to 18 years of age. Language proficiency is required for some of the year and semester programs and for the summer program in French-speaking countries. There is no language requirement for the one-month tour program or for *Sport for Understanding.*

Living arrangements: The heart of YFU's summer, semester, and school-year programs is the host family living experience. As a family member the student learns firsthand about the host country and culture in a way not afforded the average tourist. In many cases a member of the host family has participated in a YFU exchange to the United States.

Finances: Fees include international travel, room and board, but do not include travel to the point of departure. Participants are responsible for their own insurance. The cost of the year program is $4,640 to $4,980; the semester program, approximately $4,380 to $4,980; the summer program, $2,080 to $3,590; and the *Sport for Understanding* program, $2,350 and up. Scholarship aid is available.

Deadline: Varies with program.

LANGUAGE STUDY

*M*ost study-abroad programs include an element of language study, but some programs concentrate primarily on languages. Some U.S. organizations, colleges, and universities sponsor language programs abroad, but the majority of available opportunities are offered by language institutes that specialize in the instruction of foreign students.

Language institutes generally offer instruction at all levels, from beginning to advanced. Most of the programs involve "intensive" instruction of at least three to four hours on a daily basis. Many offer a homestay option so that students will be immersed in the language outside the classroom.

Most courses operate on a weekly schedule, allowing students to enroll for as many weeks as they want. Some language institutes offer a broader curriculum involving courses on the country's history and culture, as well as recreational activities and excursions.

While language institutes generally welcome teenagers, you'll need to be fairly independent and have a relatively high level of maturity to get the most out of this type of program. Your teachers, classmates, and roommates are not likely to be from the United States, so you may not be able to slip back into English when you tire of using the language you're studying. It's good to keep in mind that most language institutes are privately owned operations and that many high schools and colleges will not readily give you academic credit for their courses. If you need academic credit, be sure to check with your school before enrolling in a language institute abroad.

AMERICAN ASSOCIATION OF OVERSEAS STUDIES (AAOS)

For information on AAOS and its French-language program, see its program listing in the Work/Volunteer section of this book, page 221.

AMERICAN INTERCULTURAL STUDENT EXCHANGE (AISE)

For information on AISE and its French- and Spanish-language programs, see its program listing in the Study Abroad section of this book, page 97.

ANGLO-GERMAN INSTITUTE (AGI)
Christophstrasse 4
D-7000 Stuttgart 1
Germany
Telephone: (49) 711–603858

The sponsor: The Anglo-German Institute is a nonprofit organization, established in 1972 as a branch of Pitman Training of London to teach English to Germans. In 1985, the German Language Centre began to offer German language instruction in Stuttgart.

The program: AGI offers German language courses throughout the year. Special summer courses (20 lessons plus extracurricular activities) are offered in July and August.

Supervision: There is one teacher to every 4 to 10 students.

Services for persons with disabilities: AGI will accept students with disabilities depending on the seriousness of the disability. At least eight weeks' advance notice is required.

Requirements: Students must be at least 16 years of age. There is no language requirement.

Living arrangements: Students live with local host families in their own room.

Finances: Summer courses cost 1,340 deutsche marks (approximately $900) for two weeks. Courses at other times of the year cost 1,950 deutsche marks (approximately $1,325) for four weeks. Program fee includes tuition, materials, accommodation with family, breakfast and evening meals, and full board at weekends. Summer course fees also include activities programs.

Deadline: No set deadline.

Contact: Mrs. Jutta Ross, Director (address above).

AQUITAINE SERVICE LINGUISTIQUE (ASL)

For information on ASL and its French-language study program, see its listing in the Homestays section of this book, page 277.

ATHENS CENTRE
48 Archimidous Street
11636 Athens
Greece
Telephone: (30) 1–701–2268
Fax: (30) 1–701–8603

The sponsor: Founded in 1969, the Centre is an educational organization which sponsors study and travel for foreigners in Greece as well as year-round language classes.

The program: Classes in all levels of modern Greek are available throughout the year at the Centre. Courses consist of 60 hours of instruction; class size varies from 8 to 15 students. All courses include information about films, plays, and lectures as a way of enhancing classroom language study. Each summer, the Centre sponsors three- and four-week travel programs entitled *Classical, Byzantine, and Modern Greece,* which include time in Athens and field trips to Santorini, Crete, Delphi, Olympia, Mycenae, Epidaurus, and Turkey. Lectures and workshops are incorporated into the programs.

Supervision: Bilingual instructors and counselors accompany the group on all field trips.

Requirements: Participants must be at least 16 years of age and entering their senior year in high school. Maturity, the ability to be on your own, and the ability to relate to adults as well as your peer group are necessary.

Living arrangements: Tour participants stay in hotels. Those who study at the Centre have access to a file of apartment sublets, hotels, and pensions nearby.

Finances: The language courses at the Centre cost approximately $260; fees for the tours range from $1,800 to $2,500, which includes accommodations, breakfast, field trips, and transportation within Greece.

Deadline: May 30.

Contact: Rosemary Donnelly, Program Director (address above).

BABEL
22 ter, rue de France
06000 Nice
France
Telephone: (33) 93–822744
Fax: (33) 93–882130

The sponsor: Founded in 1977, this is a school where French is taught with emphasis on the audiovisual method.

The program: Classes are taught at all levels and are arranged in two-week sessions from June through August. The school is located in the heart of Nice, one block from the beach. People enroll individually or in groups with their own leaders.

Supervision: The student-teacher ratio is 12 to 1.

Requirements: The minimum age is 16.

Living arrangements: The school arranges living accommodations and will help students find a place in a hotel, a family, or a university residence.

Finances: The 1992 fee for the two-week course is 2,250 French francs (approximately $450); the four-week course costs 4,500 French francs (approximately $900). This covers tuition and use of textbooks and equipment only. Side trips and accommodations can be arranged for an additional fee.

Deadline: Five weeks before the start of the course.

Contact: Monique Broch, Director of Studies (address above). To ensure a response, please include two international reply coupons with your letter.

BLYTH AND COMPANY

For information on Blyth and Company and its French- and Spanish-language study programs, see its listing in the Organized Tours section of this book, page 201.

CEI-CLUB DES 4 VENTS
1, rue Gozlin
75006 Paris
France
Telephone: (33) 1–43296020
Fax: (33) 1–43290621

The sponsor: This organization offers a variety of language programs and holiday camps for French-language students.

The program: French classes are offered in July and August. Semi-intensive courses provide 25 hours of classwork per week; intensive courses provide 40 hours per week. Courses are offered at several locations around France, and all include outings to nearby places of interest. Sports holidays, farmstays, and other holiday programs are also offered.

Supervision: For language classes, the student-teacher ratio is 10 to 1.

Requirements: Minimum age varies according to the program. Most programs require at least one year of previous French-language study.

Living arrangements: Language students have a choice of homestays or dormitory accommodations.

Finances: A two-week intensive French course costs 1,550 French francs (approximately $310); the four-week course costs 2,850 French francs (approximately $570). A Paris homestay with half-board costs 175 French francs per day (approximately $35) and dormitory accommodations in a double room costs 150 French francs per day (approximately $30). For other program costs, contact the organization.

CENTRAL AMERICAN INSTITUTE FOR INTERNATIONAL AFFAIRS (ICAI)
P.O. Box 10302–1000
San José
Costa Rica
Telephone: (506) 338571
Fax: (506) 215238

The sponsor: The Central American Institute for International Affairs (ICAI) has offered Spanish-language courses since 1984, in addition to other programs on Central American politics and culture.

The program: Language courses begin every Monday of the year. Students have four hours of instruction daily and live with Costa Rican families. Additional programs include tours of all seven states and principal cities.

Orientation: Students participate in a general orientation upon arrival.

Supervision: The student-teacher ratio is 10 to 1.

Requirements: The minimum age is 15.

Living arrangements: Students live with Costa Rican families.

Finances: A two-week program of only language study costs $560; the same program with cultural programs and tours to areas beyond San José costs $700. Fees include homestay with two meals per day and airport pickup. Scholarships are available.

Contact: Write to the address above or contact the U.S. office at the Language Studies Enrollment Center, P.O. Box 5095, Anaheim, CA 92814; (714) 527-2918.

CENTRE INTERNATIONAL D'ANTIBES
19 Reichert Circle
Westport, CT 06880
Telephone: (203) 226–0405

The sponsor: Since 1984, this organization has been offering a chance to "learn French under the Riviera sun" at a school a few minutes from the beach.

The program: Courses on all levels are offered year round, from two to eight weeks. Each class has a maximum of 14 students for regular classes and 6 students for intensive classes. For beginners, the sponsor claims that "in one day you'll be familiar with a number of common phrases; in a week you'll be able to manage by yourself in a store; in two weeks you'll know enough to explain your last weekend." Excursions are offered weekly to nearby destinations such as Nice, Monaco, the Lérins Islands, and St-Jean-Cap-Ferrat.

Supervision: Students staying with host families are supervised by the Centre during classes and excursions and by their host family in the remaining time.

Requirements: Minimum age is 14.

Living arrangements: Students may stay in a one- or two-room apartment in a high-standard resort complex, or they can live with a French family.

Finances: Tuition costs begin at $800, including homestay and meals.

Deadline: No set deadline.

Contact: Renée Chenette, Côte d'Azur Langues (address above).

CENTRE INTERNATIONAL D'ÉTUDES FRANCAISES DE TOURAINE
Château Bois Minhy
B.P.1
41700 Chemery
Loir et Cher
France
Telephone: (33) 54 790626
Fax: (33) 54790626

The sponsor: The Centre is a French-language school housed in a Renaissance-style castle built in the late 19th century. Located in the heart of the Loire Valley, the school is one and a half hours from Paris.

The program: Language lessons at all levels are offered for periods of 4, 8, and 16 weeks throughout the year. "Text and course outline follow the method developed and perfected by G. Mauger and endorsed by the Alliance Française."

Supervision: The student-teacher ratio is 12 to 1.

Requirements: The minimum age is 16. Students must take a placement test.

Living arrangements: Students live in single and double rooms in the château. Showers and toilets are located on each floor. There is also a swimming pool.

Finances: A four-week course costs 8,350 French francs (approximately $1,670), which includes room and board.

CENTRO DE ARTES Y LENGUAS (CALE)
Calle Nueva Tabachin 22-B
Cuernavaca 062170
Morelos
Mexico
Telephone: (52) 73–130603
Fax: (52) 73–184405

The sponsor: CALE is a Spanish-language institution in operation since 1969.

The program: CALE combines language learning with the study of Mexico's culture. Classroom learning is supplemented by outside social and cultural activities. Courses are offered at all levels, and instructors are native speakers. Classes last four hours daily, for a minimum of one week. Additional evening courses focusing on Mexican history and contemporary society are available at extra cost to groups at the Mexican Institute of Latin American Studies, with which CALE shares facilities. CALE also organizes additional cultural activities and excursions.

Supervision: There is a maximum of four students per instructor.

Requirements: Students must be at least 16 years of age.

Living arrangements: CALE has its own dormitory; if students prefer, the staff will help them find alternative accommodations. CALE particularly recommends living with a Mexican family, which can be arranged.

Finances: A one-time registration fee of $100 is required to reserve a space. This fee is not refundable, but is good for repeated visits. Tuition is $125 per week. For $260, students receive one week of classes, lodging with a local family, and meals. Transportation from the airport in Mexico City to the program site is provided free of charge.

Contact: Xavier Sotelo, President (address above).

CENTRO DE ESPAÑOL XELAJU
1022 St. Paul Avenue
St. Paul, MN 55116
Telephone: (612) 690–9471

The sponsor: Centro de Español Xelaju offers Spanish-language courses in Quezaltenango, Guatemala. Its Yum Kax division caters especially to the needs of high-school students.

The program: Students study Spanish while living with a Guatemalan family in Quezaltenango. Courses last five hours per day. Daily social and cultural activities, such as movies, lectures, and field trips, are also included. Cooking and weaving courses are offered at additional cost for materials.

Supervision: Students study one-on-one with an instructor.

Requirements: None, other than the desire to learn Spanish.

Living arrangements: Students stay with host families. Meals and laundry services are included.

Finances: The basic cost is $180 per week, which includes language classes, activities, homestay, in-country transportation, and health insurance.

Deadline: Four weeks before classes start.

Contact: Julio E. Batres, General Director (address above).

CENTRO DE ESTUDIOS DE CASTELLANO
Avenida Juan Sebastian Elcano, 120
29017 Malaga
Spain
Telephone and Fax: (34) 52–290551

The sponsor: This language school, founded in 1960, is located in a mansion in a quiet residential section of Malaga, "surrounded by gardens with tropical flowers and palm, orange, and banana trees." It is 70 meters from the beach and a 30-minute walk from the town center.

The program: Spanish courses at beginning and advanced levels start the first of each month. All teachers are Spanish, and classes are never larger than eight students. Lessons last from 9 A.M. to 1 P.M.; homework requires 10 to 15 hours per week. Three to four months is the suggested course length for beginners, but students may enroll for a stay of as short as one month.

Supervision: The student-teacher ratio is 8 to 1.

Requirements: The minimum age is 16.

Living arrangements: If they wish, students can be placed with Spanish families. If they prefer to stay in an apartment, the school will help with finding one.

Finances: One month's tuition costs 40,000 pesetas (approximately $425); room and full board in a family home costs 55,000 pesetas (approximately $580) per month.

Contact: F. Marín Fernández, Director (address above).

CENTRO DE IDIOMAS
Belisario Dominguez No. 1908
Mazatlán, Sinaloa
Mexico
Telephone: (52) 69–822053
Fax: (52) 69–855606

The sponsor: Founded in 1973, the centro offers Spanish conversation courses year-round for foreigners and also has a year-round enrollment of approximately 300 Mexicans who study English.

The program: Mazatlán, the site of the Centro, is located on the Pacific coast, across from the tip of the Baja Peninsula. It is a popular vacation spot because of its beaches and semitropical climate. Courses begin every Monday of the year except Easter and Christmas weeks. Courses are at all levels, and enrollment is limited to six students per class. Beginning students are advised to allow at least two months to achieve an intermediate level of competence.

Supervision: Students between the ages of 16 and 20 are placed with homestay families that have children of similar ages. Students under 16 may study in tutorial classes by special arrangement with an instructor from the Centro or with a family member during a homestay.

Living arrangements: Homestays with ''upper-middle-class families'' can be arranged; if the students prefer, they may stay in a hotel or an apartment. The Centro will provide information.

Finances: The fee for one month of study with four hours of classroom work per day, three activities per week (visits to local places of interest and so on), and room and board in a local home is $940.

Deadline: No set deadline, but if a homestay is desired, 30 days advance notice is necessary.

Contact: Dixie Davis, Director (address above).

CENTRO DE IDIOMAS DEL SURESTE (CIS)
Calle 66, No. 535 × 57 Edificio Alejandra
Mérida 97000 Yucatán
Mexico
Telephone: (52) 99–261155
Fax: (52) 99–269020

The sponsor: CIS is a Spanish-language school that has been in operation more than 10 years. It is accredited by the Dirección General de Educación Pública del Estado de Yucatán (Yucatán State Department of Education).

The program: CIS's Spanish-language program, which lasts a minimum of two weeks, starts every Monday year-round. Students are encouraged to speak only Spanish in their classes and in the homes of their host families. Classes are conducted three hours per day, five days per week. Beginner, intermediate, and advanced levels of study are offered. Students are placed in small groups averaging one to three students. Additional classroom study of two hours a day is available to students for an additional fee. Instructors are native speakers. The school is located in Mérida, the largest city on the Yucatán Peninsula and the gateway to the Mayan archaeological ruins. CIS also offers a one-week field trip around the peninsula, departing every week year-round. Participants visit the archaeological ruins of Uxmal, Kabah, and Chichén Itzá and also visit the beach at Progreso, major markets, and the Museum of Anthropology. An evening get-together with local students is included in the field trip.

Orientation: Prearrival information is sent to students by the National Registration Center for Study Abroad (NRCSA). Airport pickup is available. Upon arrival, a local orientation is given by school staff.

Supervision: Leaders are responsible for students' conduct at all times and are expected to accompany their group during activities.

Services for persons with disabilities: CIS accepts people with disabilities, but suggests people with severe disabilities be accompanied. Several classrooms are accessible to students in wheelchairs. Many public areas in Mérida, however, do not have facilities for disabled people.

Requirements: Participants must be at least 12 years old.

Living arrangements: For the language program, students are usually placed in local homes. Participants on the Yucatán field trip stay with local families (meals included) or in a student-class hotel (meals not included).

Finances: The two-week language program costs $315; each additional week costs $105. Two hours of extra daily study cost an additional $75 per week. Homestays, which include room and all meals, cost $105 per week. The fee for the Yucatán field trip is $340. NRCSA can make all travel arrangements, including out-of-town excursions.

Deadline: Applications and payment must be received 30 days prior to arrival.

Contact: Chloe Conaway (address above) or NRCSA (see page 173).

CENTRO DI CULTURA ITALIANA IN CASENTINO (CCIC)
Piazza Amerighi, 1
52104 Poppi (Arezzo)
Italy
Telephone: (39) 575–52774

The sponsor: CCIC is an Italian-language school for foreigners founded in 1980 in collaboration with the municipal administration of Poppi, a medieval town in northeast Tuscany.

The program: CCIC offers intensive courses two or four weeks long from April through October. All instruction is given in Italian, even at beginning levels. Language classes also include excursions and other extracurricular activities.

Supervision: The maximum student-teacher ratio is eight to one.

Services for persons with disabilities: Disabled or elderly persons will be given priority for ground-floor accommodations.

Living arrangements: Students live in double or single rooms in two-to four-room apartments which the school reserves in the historic center of town or in renovated cottages in the countryside. Accommodations have cooking facilities; however, at least a few nights a week students dine together in the school garden or a local restaurant.

Finances: The two-week course costs 440,000 lire (approximately $400); the four-week course costs 770,000 lire (approximately $700); each additional week costs 205,000 lire (approximately $180). Accommodations in a double room cost 300,000 lire (approximately $270) per week, and single rooms carry a 65,000 lire surcharge (approximately $60).

Deadline: One month before the course begins.

Contact: Stephen Casale, CCIC New York, 1 University Place, Apartment 17-R, New York, NY 10003; (212) 228-9273.

CENTRO LINGUISTICO CONVERSA
Apartado 17 Centro Colón
San José
Costa Rica
Telephone: (506) 217649

The sponsor: The Centro is a small language school founded in 1974 and located on a farm on a hilltop about 10 miles west of San José.

The program: Language courses at all levels usually last four weeks, but shorter periods can be arranged. Instruction is entirely in Spanish. Each week, a specific grammatical structure is presented. The methodology used at the Centro is "constant contact," which means that students develop a wide range of personal contacts with native Spanish speakers as a result of their daily routine. There is a maximum of four students per class.

Orientation: Airport pickup and return can be arranged. A first-day group orientation is given by the director.

Supervision: School staff reside in the lodge and act as supervisors during the evening.

Services for persons with disabilities: There are no specific policies regarding disabilities; however, the terrain may prove difficult for physically disabled participants.

Requirements: For the adult program, the minimum age is 14. For the children's program, the minimum age is seven.

Living arrangements: Students live with a Costa Rican family in the town of Santa Ana or stay at the Conversa's lodge.

Finances: A four-week course costs $1,545. Family plans are available. The fee includes all instruction, materials, daily transportation to and from the school, airport pickup, housing, laundry, and all meals. An additional fee of $600 is for optional housing at the lodge.

CENTRO LINGUISTICO ITALIANO DANTE ALIGHIERI
Via Dei Bardi, 12
Florence
Italy
Telephone: (39) 55–2342784

The sponsor: The Centro Linguistico Italiano Dante Alighieri is a school specializing in teaching the language and culture of Italy to foreigners. Founded in 1966, it is authorized by the Italian government and has headquarters in Florence with additional centers in Rome and Siena.

The program: Participants have a choice of group language courses (from 20 hours to 100 hours per month), cultural courses, and individual language courses. Classes run year-round, and it is possible to enroll from one to nine months. Each month, students take at least two guided tours in the city plus an outing to another famous city. The school also organizes meetings, dinners, and parties to encourage language learning in an out-of-the-classroom setting. Last year 1,200 people participated in the school's program.

Orientation: Beginning language students attend an orientation once they're in Italy.

Supervision: Arrangements can be made for full-time supervision of group. Single participants will be supervised by a host family.

Services for persons with disabilities: The Centro is able to accommodate most types of disabilities. Participants with disabilities are placed in small class groups in easily accessible classrooms.

Requirements: The minimum age is 15.

Living arrangements: Although room and board is not included in the fee, the school will help students find accommodations with a family, in a guesthouse, in a furnished room, in a residence, or in an apartment. Eight weeks' notice is required for these arrangements to be made.

Finances: The costs vary depending on the course or courses chosen. Some examples: a 16-hour cultural course costs $150; and 20-hour language course costs $185; a 100-hour language course costs $650; and 100 hours of individual language study costs $6,460. Half scholarships are available for all but the individual lessons. Students are responsible for their own travel arrangements. No insurance coverage is provided.

Deadline: One month before the course is scheduled to begin.

Contact: U.S. Student Programs, Institute of International Education, 809 U.N. Plaza, New York, NY 10017, or the address above.

CENTRO LINGUISTICO SPERIMENTALE
Via del Corso, 1
50122 Florence
Italy
Telephone: (39) 55–210592

The sponsor: The school, established in 1979, specializes in teaching Italian to people of all nationalities.

The program: Four-week courses operate throughout the year and include 20 days of four-hour classes. Classes have no more than 10 students. According to the sponsor, "In this relaxed atmosphere our students are able to immerse themselves in the language." Free afternoon and evening courses are offered on various aspects of Italian life, and every Saturday morning an art history teacher leads a group to a local church, museum, or palazzo. Once a month the school offers a day trip to a Tuscan city, and each week the teachers and students dine together at a restaurant or *trattoria*. Other course possibilities include art history, Italian history, literature, and cooking.

Requirements: Minimum age is 16.

Living arrangements: Students may stay with a family as a paying guest, in an apartment, or in a *pensione*.

Finances: The four-week course costs 595,000 lire (approximately $530). Accommodations are extra.

Deadline: One month before class begins.

Contact: M. Concetta Abruzzo, Director (address above).

CENTRO PONTEVECCHIO
Piazza del Mercato Nuovo 1
50123 Florence
Italy
Telephone: (39) 55–294511

The sponsor: This school has taught Italian language and culture since 1986.

The program: Language courses are offered in monthly sessions. Culture courses include Italian cooking, literature, politics, music, and art history. Students are given the chance to enjoy the cultural life of Florence.

Supervision: One teacher per 12 students.

Requirements: The minimum age is 16.

Living arrangements: The Centro arranges accommodations in single rooms in family homes, without board.

Finances: Fees range from 690,000 lire to 1,050,000 lire (approximately $620 to $940) per month depending on length of stay, type of course, and accommodations. Price includes fees, books, membership, tax, examinations, certificate, accommodations service, and some cultural and extrascholastic activities.

Deadline: One month ahead of time.

Contact: Simonetta de'Mari, Director of Studies (address above).

CIAL-CENTRO DE LINGUAS
Av. da Republica, 41-8°
1000 Lisbon
Portugal
Telephone: (351) 1–730231

The sponsor: The CIAL language school has offered courses in Portuguese language and culture since 1972.

The program: CIAL runs language programs for individuals and private groups year-round. Upon arrival, each student is tested and placed according to language proficiency. Students can enroll in programs that meet either three or six hours each day (it takes two to four weeks to complete each level). The program includes short excursions and other group activities. Students can also choose to enroll in optional courses such as Portuguese literature or art history.

Orientation: An orientation session is held upon arrival.

Supervision: The maximum number of students per teacher is six.

Services for persons with disabilities: CIAL attempts to integrate disabled persons in all programs.

Requirements: The minimum age is 16.

Living arrangements: CIAL will place students either with a Portuguese family in Lisbon or at a hotel, depending upon preference.

Finances: The six-hours-a-day course costs 61,000 escudos (approximately $480) for one week and 225,000 escudos (approximately $1,780) for four weeks. The three-hours-a-day course costs 34,000 escudos (approximately $270) for one week; 121,000 escudos (approximately $950) for four weeks. Groups receive discounted rates. Accommodations with a Portuguese family, including daily breakfast, cost 18,000 escudos (approximately $140) for one week and 55,000 escudos (approximately $430) for four weeks. Some scholarship aid is available.

Deadline: Students should apply at least two weeks before the course begins.

Contact: Renato Borges de Sousa, Director, or Orlando Couto, Director of Studies (address above).

COLLEGIUM PALATINUM
Château de Pourtales
161, rue Melanie
F-67000 Strasbourg
France
Telephone: (33) 88–310107
Fax: (33) 88–310814

The sponsor: The Collegium Palatinum is a commercial language institute founded in 1958 belonging to Schiller International University. Schiller is an independent university operating on the American system of higher education and accredited by the Association of Independent Colleges and Schools.

The program: Collegium Palatinum offers three different language programs: German in Heidelberg, Germany; French in Leysin, Switzerland; and Spanish in Madrid, Spain. Eight-week intensive courses are offered year-round. Four-week summer courses are offered during the months of July and August.

Supervision: The teacher-student ratio varies from program to program.

Requirements: The minimum age for the Spanish program is 16; for the French and German programs, 17.

Living arrangements: Students in Leysin live in single or double rooms in a student residence. In Heidelberg, they have a choice between a student residence and local host families. In Madrid, they stay with local host families, or in pensions and private apartments.

Finances: Course fees vary from program to program. Fees include intensive language instruction for 24 hours per week and activity programs. Room and board are extra.

Deadline: For Heidelberg and Leysin, four months in advance; for Madrid, one month.

Contact: Schiller International University, U.S. Information Office, 453 Edgewater Drive, Dunedin, FL 34698; (813) 736-5082.

CUAUHNAHUAC
Instituto Colectivo de Lengua y Cultura
Apartado. Postal 5-26
Cuernavaca 62051 Morelos
Mexico
Telephone: (52) 73–123673

The sponsor: The Instituto, founded in 1972, teaches Spanish to people from all over the world—students, teachers, professionals, and diplomats.

The program: New classes begin every Monday. Students may study for any length of time in classes of two to four students. The routine involves six hours of classroom work each day; a typical beginner can expect, after four weeks, to be able to survive in Spanish—to pronounce coherently and converse at a basic level.

Supervision: Host family mothers supervise the students. There may be curfew hours in the evenings for minors.

Services for persons with disabilities: Classes are given in rooms that are accessible to disabled persons.

Requirements: Minimum age is 14.

Living arrangements: Students live with a local family as a paying guest.

Finances: The four-week class costs $575. A double room is $14 per day, a single, $20. The registration fee is $70.

Contact: Contact the address above or the Cuauhnahuac U.S. representative, Marcia Snell, at 519 Park Drive, Kenilworth, IL 60043; (800) 245-9335.

DE FRANCE–SUMMER PROGRAM IN PARIS
P.O. Box 788
Wallingford, CT 06492
Telephone: (203) 269–8355

The sponsor: Established in 1957, De France's guiding principle is that the study of French should not be limited to language and literature, but also should include the experience of living in France.

The program: De France is based in Paris, where students live in private homes and attend three-hour daily courses (French Institutions, French Cinema and Theater, and History of French Art) taught entirely in French at Notre Dame de Sion, located near the Luxembourg Gardens. Although there is no formal instruction in grammar and literature, students are expected to use and develop the language skills they have learned before and during the program. The courses are offered at four levels of proficiency. The rest of the time is spent sight-seeing, attending plays, or taking day trips. The program lasts from June 25 to August 6;

four weeks in Paris are followed by a two-week holiday in the provinces with a vacationing French family.

Supervision: Students are supervised by De France teachers, staff, and the director during the day and on field trips, and by their host families in the evening.

Services for persons with disabilities: Each participant's case is handled individually. Activities often involve a lot of walking.

Requirements: The program is open to a maximum of 50 students. Students should be in 9th to 10th grades and have taken two years of French language.

Living arrangements: Students stay with host families throughout their stay.

Finances: The tuition for the summer session is $4,800, which includes airfare, classes, activities, room and board, and all other group expenses. Guidebooks, movies, laundry, dry cleaning, and pocket money are not included.

Contact: J. P. Cosnard des Closets, Director (above address).

DEUTSCH IN GRAZ (DIG)
Zinzendorfgasse 30
A-8010 Graz
Austria
Telephone: (43) 316–383747
Fax: (43) 316–383747

The sponsor: A nonprofit organization, DIG has offered courses in German as a foreign language since 1979.

The program: DIG has special language courses designed to suit the needs of young people. In addition to language training, the courses offer sports activities and an extensive leisure program. Courses last three weeks and take place in July and August. A special program for students ages 10 to 14 takes place in the village of Weiz, in the vicinity of Graz.

Supervision: There is a maximum of 12 students per teacher. The sponsors advise that ''students must comply with the Austrian law concerning the protection of children and young people. Children under 16 are allowed out, for example, without supervision until 10 P.M. If parents express the wish that their children should not remain unsupervised, there is a supervised evening program from Monday to Friday.''

Services for persons with disabilities: DIG will accommodate persons with disabilities.

Requirements: Two different programs require minimum ages of 10 and 15, respectively.

Living arrangements: There are various possibilities for accommodations in Graz. Students in Weiz can choose between a homestay or boarding school accommodations.

Finances: The three-week program for students 15 to 17 years old costs 6,900 Austrian shillings (approximately $660) including language courses, materials, outdoor activities, and evening supervision. Courses for students 10 to 14 years old cost 14,500 Austrian shillings (approximately $1,392).

Deadline: Four weeks before course begins.

DEUTSCH-INSTITUT TIROL (DIT)
Am Sandhügel 2
A-6370 Kitzbühel
Austria
Telephone: (43) 5356–71274
Fax: (43) 5356–72363

The sponsor: DIT is a commercial German-language school located in the Kitzbühel Alps. It is a member of the Federation Europeen des Ecoles (FEDE).

The program: This school, located in the small, picturesque town of Kitzbühel in the Tyrol, offers courses in German taught exclusively by native German speakers. Courses run throughout the year and may be as short as one week or as long as the student wishes. Language learning goes on in and out of the classroom at DIT; during after-class activities (in the company of at least one teacher), any language except German is taboo. Since Kitzbühel and its surroundings are world famous for skiing, DIT offers a combination plan that features German lessons in the morning and skiing in the afternoon.

Supervision: Students are supervised by the director, teachers, and the owner of their residence.

Requirements: Courses are geared to students ages 16 and over; however, arrangements can be made for students ages 12 to 15.

Living arrangements: Accommodations at DIT are in shared or single rooms with or without a shower. Breakfast and dinner can be arranged.

Finances: For 5,200 Austrian schillings per week (approximately $500), students receive instruction, a double room with shower, breakfast, and activities. Other options are available.

Contact: Hans Ebenhoh, Director (address above).

ECI

For information on ECI and its French-language program, see its listing in the Homestays section of this book, page 279.

ESCUELA INTERNACIONAL
Paseo de Carmelitas, 57
37002 Salamanca
Spain
Telephone: (34) 923–267334

The sponsor: Escuela Internacional is a private language academy created by "a team of young and enthusiastic teachers."

The program: Escuela Internacional offers four types of courses: monthly intensive Spanish classes offered year-round; beginning Spanish classes from October to the end of May; month-long summer courses; and three-month courses offered in fall, winter, and spring.

Requirements: For all programs, the minimum age is 16. Students must be in at least the 10th grade.

Living arrangements: Students live with local families, in shared apartments with other students, or in hotels.

Finances: Intensive courses cost 47,000 pesetas (approximately $500) for four weeks; beginners courses cost 365,000 pesetas (approximately $3,870); summer courses cost 59,000 pesetas (approximately $625);

and the three-month courses cost 132,000 pesetas (approximately $1,400). Homestays cost an extra 65,000 pesetas per month (approximately $690).

Deadline: One month prior to starting dates.

EURO ACADEMY
77A George Street
Croydon CR0 1LD
England
Telephone: (44) 81–686–2363

The sponsor: This commercial agency has organized language courses and homestays throughout Europe since 1971.

The program: Euro Academy offers homestays and language courses year-round. Programs take place in Spain, France, Germany, Italy, and Portugal. The organization accommodates both individuals and groups and also sponsors youth music tours for orchestras and choirs.

Orientation: Students are given an assessment test upon arrival.

Supervision: Local coordinators are available to assist participants.

Requirements: The minimum age for most programs is 12.

Living arrangements: All participants live with local families.

Finances: Prices vary from program to program. For example: four weeks of study at a secondary school in Tours, France, costs 670 British pounds (approximately $1,270); three weeks of language study in Zamora, Spain, costs 530 British pounds (approximately $1,000). All fees include room and board with a local family, tuition, and activities. Insurance is also provided.

Deadline: Fourteen days before departure.

EUROCENTRES
Seestrasse 247
CH-8038 Zurich
Switzerland

The sponsor: Since 1960 the Foundation for European Language and Education Centres, a nonprofit organization, has conducted language classes in 27 centers on three continents.

The program: Eurocentres participants can study French in Paris, Amboise, or la Rochelle, France, or in Lausanne and Neuchâtel, Switzerland; Italian in Florence; Spanish in Madrid or Barcelona; German in Cologne or Weimar, Germany, or Lucerne, Switzerland; and Japanese in Kanazawa, Japan. Students live among the people who speak the language—"you get to know them, their ideas, opinions, attitudes, their way of life. You hear, read, write, speak the language of today, all day, every day. You put what you learn directly into practice in and out of class, working on your own program, with a group of fellow students or taking part in the everyday life of the country you're in," the sponsors say. Courses last from two weeks to twenty-one weeks, and some operate year-round. Choices include the *Intensive Courses,* which last one month and may be extended to nine months; the *Compact Intensive Courses,* which last two, three, four, or six weeks; *Holiday Courses,* which last three to twelve weeks; and *Teacher Refresher Courses.* The Holiday Courses combine language learning with leisure and sports activities in a vacation setting. All the schools, except for the holiday centers, have multimedia learning centers equipped with resources—books, worksheets, computers, language labs, and videos—to help the student learn.

Supervision: There is a maximum of 16 students per Eurocentre instructor. All teachers are native speakers with university degrees.

Services for persons with disabilities: Eurocentres will attempt to accommodate disabled students. Most of the buildings have wheelchair access. Disabled students should notify Eurocentres in advance if special provisions are needed.

Requirements: Applicants must be at least 16 years of age. Students at all levels of language ability, including beginners, are accepted.

Living arrangements: Most students live in private homes chosen and regularly visited by Eurocentre staff. Although the homestay is recommended as an integral part of the learning process, anyone who would rather not stay with a family may stay in a hotel or may get help from Eurocentre staff finding other kinds of accommodations.

Finances: Tuition ranges from $1,053 to $4,043 depending upon length of stay, accommodation arrangements, and so on. For example: the four-week Holiday Course in Paris costs $1,112 for tuition alone, $1,724 with accommodation with a family and half-board, and $1,672 with accommodation in a hotel with breakfast provided. Scholarship aid is available for courses longer than 10 weeks.

Deadline: Preferably one month before the beginning of the course.

Contact: Any Council Travel office (see page 8 for addresses) or Eurocentres, 101 North Union Street, Alexandria, VA 22314; (703) 684-1494.

EUROCOLLEGE
Moosstrasse 106
A-5020 Salzburg
Austria
Telephone: (43) 662–824617

The sponsor: Eurocollege, in operation since 1976, offers language courses in Europe. Eurocollege offers German courses in Salzburg, Austria; French courses in Cannes and Paris, France; Italian courses in Florence and Sienna, Italy; and Spanish courses in Barcelona, Spain. Courses at all levels last for 2 to 12 weeks throughout the year.

The program: Eurocollege programs combine intensive morning language classes with afternoon recreational or cultural activities, such as swimming, windsurfing, skiing, sailing, volleyball, and soccer, depending upon location and season. At all locations, participants have many opportunities to practice their language skills with native speakers.

Supervision: Most programs provide housing in dormitories supervised by full-time live-in counselors or offer family homestays, in which case families supervise the students.

Services for persons with disabilities: Eurocollege accepts students with slight disabilities, but none of the locations is suitable for wheelchairs.

Requirements: The minimum age for the Salzburg program is 13; for Cannes and Barcelona, 16; for Florence, Paris, and Siena, 17.

Living arrangements: Depending on location, students live in dormitories, campus accommodations, or with host families. Some programs offer accommodations in apartments.

Finances: Fees are approximately $300 to $400 per week, including tuition, room, and board.

EUROPA-SPRACHCLUB
Diezstrasse 4A
7000 Stuttgart 80
Germany
Telephone: (49) 711-741061
Fax: (49) 711-742073

The sponsor: Europa-Sprachclub, a commercial language institute, has organized German-language courses throughout Germany since 1959.

The program: Courses are offered year-round in Augsburg, Berlin, Cologne, Düsseldorf, Frieburg, Hanover, Heidelberg, Munich, Stuttgart, Todtmoos, and Tübingen. While most programs include homestays, special programs include *Individual Homestays* and *German at a Teacher's Home,* in which students stay in the homes of language teachers who tutor them individually.

Requirements: The minimum age for most programs is 15. For homestay programs, "a good grounding" in German is required.

Living arrangements: Family homestays or group student housing.

Finances: Prices vary from program to program. A one-week "standard course" in Berlin with homestay and half-board costs 870 deutsche marks (approximately $580). A two-week individual homestay costs 980 deutsche marks (approximately $650). German at a Teacher's Home with fifteen lessons costs 1,500 deutsche marks per week (approximately $1,000).

EUROVACANCES

For information on Eurovacances and its German-language program, see its listing on the Study Abroad section of this book, page 106.

FERIENKURS DER STADT WINTERTHUR
Bacheggliweg 22
Ch-8405 Winterthur
Switzerland
Telephone: (41) 52-282902

The sponsor: This organization has offered summer German courses since 1935.

The program: From July 17 through August 5, German courses are held at the Winterthur State College. Three-week courses are offered at the beginner, intermediate, and advanced levels for three hours per day. Grammar, dictation, translation, composition, reading, and conversation are included at each level. Weekly excursions are offered to destinations in eastern or central Switzerland.

Orientation: An orientation session takes place one day before the course formally begins.

Requirements: The minimum age for participants is 14.

Living arrangements: Students live with local families who are selected by a school official.

Finances: Tuition, excursions, and room and board for the three-week course cost approximately 2,350 Swiss francs (approximately $1,000).

Deadline: June 28.

Contact: Vanda Hasenfratz, Director (address above).

FORMATION INTERNATIONALE VOYAGES ETUDES (FIVE)

For information about FIVE and its French-language program, see its listing in the Homestays section of this book, page 280.

FRENCH AMERICAN STUDY CENTER (FASC)
Boite Postale 176
14104 Lisieux
France
Telephone: (33) 1–31312201

The sponsor: For more than 16 years this language school, located in a small town in Normandy (one and a half hours from Paris and 15 minutes from Deauville) has specialized in teaching French to English speakers.

The program: In the *Intensive Program,* lasting 1 to 10 weeks, partic-

ipants live with a local family and "take a pledge to speak in French."
In the three-week *Vacation Learning,* program participants live at the
school. FASC also offers a winter program at Menton on the French
Riviera and special individual or group programs, which can be set up
at any time during the year.

Orientation: Students receive orientation materials in the mail.

Supervision: The student-teacher ratio is 10 to 1. Special supervision is
given to teenagers.

Requirements: French is offered at all levels. Participants must be age
14 or older. Interested students must send an application along with two
letters of recommendation.

Living arrangements: FASC offers homestays or accommodations in
its 23-room residence.

Finances: Fees range from $400 to $500 per week, including tuition,
room, and board. Groups can receive discounts of 25 to 35 percent.

Deadline: Two months before the program begins.

Contact: Ph. C. Almeras, Director (address above).

GRAN CANARIA SCHOOL OF LANGUAGES
Ruiz de Alda 12-3
E-35007 Las Palmas
Spain
Telephone: (34) 28–267971
Fax: (34) 28–278980

The sponsor: Since 1964 students from all over the world have come to
study Spanish at one of the three schools operated by this organization,
two in Las Palmas and one in Playa del Inglés. The schools are on the
island of Gran Canaria, one of the Canary Islands, located in the Atlantic
Ocean off the coast of Morocco.

The program: Classes begin every Monday of the year; however, classes
for total beginners start the first Monday of every month. A complete
course usually lasts 12 weeks, but students can enroll for as little as 2
weeks. Classes are held 20 hours per week, leaving time to enjoy the
Canary Islands.

Requirements: Minimum age is 14.

Living arrangements: Students have three choices: local homes, a three-story chalet with windows facing a garden, or a two-story house next to the beach.

Finances: Tuition for one week plus excursions, theater trips, and social activities is $98 for classes of 6 to 13 students. Private lessons (20 hours per week) are $495. Lodging costs $168 per week for a single room and half-board.

INDIANA UNIVERSITY HONORS PROGRAM IN FOREIGN LANGUAGES FOR HIGH SCHOOL STUDENTS
111 South Jordan
Bloomington, IN 47405
Telephone: (812) 855–5241

The sponsor: Since 1960, Indiana University has offered summer study programs in France, Germany, and Mexico for high-school juniors from Indiana. The school is a member of CIEE.

The program: Students can study in St-Brieuc (Brittany) in France, Krefeld (near Düsseldorf) in Germany, or San Luis Potosí (north of Mexico City) in Mexico. Programs last for seven weeks and include a homestay, five hours of language instruction per day, and field trips.

Orientation: Prior to departure, Indiana University offers a day of orientation.

Supervision: There is one instructor per 10 students. Host family supervises students in the evening.

Services for persons with disabilities: Indiana University accepts students with disabilities that do not hinder the student's participation in all activities of the program.

Requirements: Students must be a junior in high school in Indiana and have at least three years of language instruction.

Living arrangements: Students stay with host families.

Finances: Tuition is $3,500, including airfare. Scholarship grants of up to one-half the tuition are available.

Deadline: October 15.

Contact: Public and private high schools in Indiana.

INSTITUTE OF CHINA STUDIES
7341 North Kolmar
Lincolnwood, IL 60646
Telephone: (708) 677–0982

The sponsor: The Institute is a nonprofit organization registered in Illinois since 1979. It began recruiting U.S. students for Fudan University's Summer Study program in 1981.

The program: Fudan University's *Summer Study* program consists of four- to six-week courses beginning in early July. Chinese language courses taught by English-speaking teachers are at beginning to advanced levels; special courses can be arranged. Extracurricular activities include visits to local theaters, hospitals, factories, historical attractions, communes, and other cities. Fudan University is located in Shanghai, China.

Supervision: The coordinator of the summer program at Fudan University serves as supervisor for around 500 students.

Requirements: Participants must be at least 15.

Living arrangements: Participants stay in guest rooms at the university, two persons to a room.

Finances: The six-week program costs $2,500. This includes tuition, room and board, and international flights (West Coast departure and return).

Deadline: April 1.

Contact: Harry Kiang, Director (address above).

INSTITUTE OF SPANISH STUDIES
1315 Monterey Boulevard
San Francisco, CA 94127
Telephone: (415) 586–0180

The sponsor: The Institute is located in Valencia, Spain, and has been operating since 1950. Its U.S. office is in San Francisco.

The program: The Institute offers two five- to six-week *Summer Sessions,* which are available to both high-school and college students. Its participants can choose from three programs: independent study combined with poststudy travel; study followed by 11 days of travel; or the study session only. Courses include language study, the history of Spain, and Spanish art. Approximately 200 students participate each year.

Requirements: Participants must be at least 15 years old unless they are accompanied by an adult or are part of an escorted group. No previous knowledge of Spanish is required.

Living arrangements: Students live in private homes or a residence hall.

Finances: The costs vary depending on the plan chosen, ranging from $650 to $3,990, depending on whether the post-study tour and transatlantic airfare are included.

Deadline: Six weeks before start of the program.

Contact: Vilma Bellone, Registrar (address above).

INSTITUTO ALLENDE

For information on the Instituto Allende and its Spanish-language program, see its listing in the Creative Arts section of this book, page 188.

INSTITUTO IDEAL
Apartado Postal 22-B
Cuernavaca 62190 Morelos
Mexico
Telephone: (52) 73–170455
Fax: (52) 73–175710

The sponsor: IDEAL is a nonprofit educational organization.

The program: IDEAL offers a total immersion program for learning the Spanish language that puts equal emphasis on language and culture. Students can begin on any Monday throughout the year.

Orientation: A brief orientation is held on the first day of class in Cuernavaca.

Supervision: The student-teacher ratio is five to one (maximum).

Requirements: Unaccompanied students must be at least 16 years old. Classes are offered at all levels; no previous language ability is required.

Living arrangements: It is recommended that students board with Mexican families, paying $22 per day for private room and board or $15 for shared room and board.

Finances: A $100 registration fee plus $130 per week of study is required. Fee includes five hours of instruction daily, a coffee break, some parties, movies, and activities. Costs for optional cultural excursions range from $10 to $40. Groups of 10 from organizations or schools receive a scholarship.

Deadline: No set deadline, but since mail service is slow, write two months before you wish to begin.

Contact: Edmundo Sandoval, Director (address above).

INSTITUTO DE FILOLOGÍA HISPÁNICA
Apartado 144
Saltillo 25000 Coahuila
Mexico
Telephone: (52) 841–21511

The sponsor: The Instituto de Filología Hispánica is located in Saltillo, a city 200 miles south of the Texas border. It has offered Spanish-language courses for foreigners since 1968. The Instituto is a private institution of higher learning that also has an M.A. program in Spanish language and literature.

The program: Students can enroll in 3-, 6-, or 12-week sessions of total-immersion Spanish courses. There are 15 to 20 hours of instruction per week, depending upon the class schedule the student selects. Special extracurricular activities are offered to acquaint students with Mexico.

Supervision: The student-teacher ratio is four to one.

Requirements: Participants must be at least freshmen in high school.

Living arrangements: Homestays with Mexican families are encouraged and arranged by the Instituto. Students over the age of 18 may live in hotels if they prefer. The Instituto keeps a list of recommended hotels.

Finances: The 3-week session costs $500; the 6-week, $900; and the 12-week, $1,600. Room and board with a Mexican family costs $96 per week.

Deadline: Thirty days prior to the beginning of the session.

Contact: Ms. Teresa Valdes (address above).

INTERLOCKEN

For information on Interlocken and its language-study programs, see its listing in the Organized Tours section of this book, page 208.

INTERNATIONAL SUMMER CAMP VERBIER

For information on International Summer Camp Verbier and its language-study program, see its listing in the Outdoor Activities section of this book, page 257.

INTERNATIONALE FERIENKURSE FÜR DEUTSCHE SPRACHE UND GERMANISTIK (IFK)
Franz-Josef-Strasse 19/2
A-5020 Salzburg
Austria
Telephone: (43) 662–8765950
Fax: (43) 662–87659575

The sponsor: IFK is a language school which offers three-week courses as well as intensive ten-week courses in Salzburg. It has been in operation since 1948 and serves approximately 600 students per year.

The program: IFK offers two choices: 3-week summer courses or 10-week intensive courses beginning in October, January, or April.

Requirements: The minimum age for participation is 16.

Living arrangements: In Salzburg, rooms are available in private homes (during the whole year) or in student residences (only in summer).

Finances: The summer courses in Salzburg vary from 12,650 to 15,950 Austrian schillings (approximately $1,200 to $1,530), including German instruction, accommodations, breakfast, cultural and social activities. The 10-week courses in Salzburg cost 14,600 Austrian schillings (approximately $1,400), including German instruction, cultural and social activities.

Deadline: Two weeks before the beginning of the course.

Contact: Secretary (address above).

INTER SÉJOURS
179, rue de Courcelles
75017 Paris
France
Telephone: (33) 1–47630681
Fax: (33) 1–40548941

The sponsor: Inter Séjours is a nonprofit organization, founded in 1901, that sponsors language-learning holidays throughout Europe for French students, and also sponsors programs in France for non-French speakers.

The program: Participants study languages and live with local families in Perpignan and the Pyrénnées Orientales. Programs are offered year-round at all levels.

Orientation: Students attend a local orientation.

Supervision: The student-teacher ratio is 10 to 1. Students are supervised by their host families.

Requirements: Students must be 13 to 18.

Living arrangements: Students live with host families.

Finances: A two-week homestay with full board costs 3,500 French francs (approximately $700). Language classes cost 100 French francs per hour (approximately $20).

Contact: Marie-Hélène Pierrot, Director (address above).

ISOK
Jan-Tooropstraat 4
2225 XT Katwijk aan zee
The Netherlands
Telephone: (31) 1718–13533

The sponsor: ISOK, founded in 1969, places people who want to learn Dutch with Dutch families as paying guests.

The program: ISOK combines a stay with a Dutch family with language lessons—either in a group or privately. Host families take their guests on local excursions as well, to give them a chance to practice their language. Group lessons are given in a school in Katwijk; private lessons are given in the home of ISOK's principal, J. F. H. de Zeeuw. The program operates year-round.

Supervision: The program participants are under the supervision of the principal, who does the teaching and makes the homestay placements and visits. "We place advertisements, visit would-be host families, inspect rooms and homes and surroundings, and ask for references from vicars, priests, burgomasters, and so on."

Services for persons with disabilities: Participants with minor disabilities are accepted.

Requirements: There is no age limit. The only prerequisite is "a willingness to learn the Dutch language."

Living arrangements: The students live with a family in Katwijk and surrounding villages and towns, a region of the Netherlands where the purest Dutch is said to be spoken.

Finances: Room and board in a host family costs 280 guilders (approximately $170) a week. Group lessons for two hours per day are 15 guilders (approximately $10); private lessons are 25 guilders (approximately $15) per hour. Participants must arrange their own insurance and their own transportation.

Deadline: Registration should be completed three weeks before arrival.

Contact: J. F. H. de Zeeuw, Principal (address above).

K.I.S.S. DANISH LANGUAGE SCHOOL
Norregade 20
1165 Copenhagen K
Denmark
Telephone: (45) 33–114477

The sponsor: K.I.S.S. stands for Københavns Intensive Sprog Skole, a language school that has been in operation since 1973. It is subsidized by the state and the municipality of Copenhagen.

The program: According to K.I.S.S., its system of language learning is "hard and intensive"; it is mainly a speaking course in which pronunciation is key. "You are almost constantly speaking in class, speaking in chorus, in groups, reading aloud, repeating, and being corrected. We want to get you to speak like a Dane." Beginner classes start every month. The whole program runs for seven and a half months and is divided into 11 levels; the first 10 are approximately two and a half weeks long. Students may take as many levels as they wish.

Supervision: There are usually 8 to 14 students in a group.

Services for persons with disabilities: K.I.S.S. has accommodated minor physical disabilities in the past. There is no elevator for wheelchairs.

Requirements: Applicants must be at least 16 years old.

Living arrangements: Students make their own accommodation arrangements.

Finances: The hourly instruction fee is 11 Danish kroner (approximately $2) with a minimum enrollment of 21 hours.

Deadline: No set deadline, but there is a waiting list of usually two to three months.

Contact: Steen A. Christensen, Director (address above).

LANGUAGE STUDIES CANADA (LSC)
Greater Montreal Language School
1450, rue City Councillors, Suite 300
Montreal, Quebec H3A 2E6
Canada
Telephone: (514) 499–9911

The sponsor: Language Studies Canada is a commercial language institute. Its Greater Montreal Language School has taught French to foreign students since 1962.

The program: The *Summer Language Adventure* is held in two three-week sessions in July and August. Instruction is offered at elementary to advanced levels. The Montreal Language School is situated on the main Metro (subway) line in the heart of downtown Montreal. Students live with French-speaking families.

Orientation: Orientation is given on the opening day.

Supervision: The average student-teacher ratio is 10 to 1.

Requirements: The minimum age is 15; maximum is 17.

Living arrangements: Students have single rooms in family homes.

Finances: The three-week course costs 1,470 Canadian dollars (approximately $1,230), including tuition, books, and homestay.

Deadline: Twenty-one days prior to beginning of course.

LESSING-KOLLEG FÜR SPRACHEN UND KULTUR
Marbacher Weg 18
D 3550 Marburg 1
Germany
Telephone: (49) 6421–64091
Fax: (49) 6421–62362

The sponsor: Lessing-Kolleg, located 60 miles north of Frankfurt, is a language school that specializes in German for foreigners. It was founded in 1968.

The program: The school offers courses in German as a foreign language year-round. The month-long courses begin the first Monday of each month, and instruction is offered at all levels.

Supervision: Group leaders are qualified language teachers; there is one instructor per 12 students.

Services for persons with disabilities: The school admits disabled persons, but wheelchairs cannot be transported to the classrooms due to lack of an elevator.

Requirements: The minimum age is 15 and minimum grade level is 10th. Applicants should be motivated and interested in German culture and civilization.

Living arrangements: Students are encouraged to live with German families but may stay in student dormitories if they prefer.

Finances: One month of language instruction and family homestay including breakfast costs 1,650 deutsche marks (approximately $1,100). One month of instruction alone costs $1,225 deutsche marks (approximately $820).

Deadline: Ten days before the course begins.

Contact: Hermann Reidt, Director (address above).

MICHIGAN STATE UNIVERSITY
High School Honors Program
Office of Overseas Study
Room 108, International Center
East Lansing, MI 48824-1035
Telephone: (517) 353–8920

The sponsor: MSU sponsors more than 70 overseas study programs in 24 countries, primarily for college undergraduates and graduate students. The French program in Quebec, however, is specifically designed for high-school students. Michigan State University is a member of CIEE.

The program: The *Honors Program* in French lasts one month (late June to late July) and is held at the Collège de Rivière du Loup, 120 miles east of Quebec City on the south bank of the lower St. Lawrence River in the heart of a completely French-speaking region. Students attend classes five mornings a week, focusing on reading, writing, speaking, and understanding French. Afternoons are spent in activities in the surrounding villages, where the host families are located. During the stay, there are several full-day excursions: two to Quebec City, a boat trip on the St. Lawrence River, and one to the nearby lakeside resort of Pohenegamook. It is recommended that students who successfully complete this honors course of study be considered by their high schools as eligible for one-half unit of high-school credit. (Final decisions on credit rest with the students' schools.) In addition, students obtaining a grade of B+ or higher may have the option of receiving, upon payment of the appropriate fees, credit at Michigan State University.

Orientation: There are two sessions, one on MSU's campus and another when the students arrive at Rivière du Loup.

Supervision: The director of the program and program assistant are with the group for the duration of the program, and a program administrator is on call at all times. All excursions and outings are closely supervised.

Services for persons with disabilities: Arrangements can and will be made for participation by students with special needs.

Requirements: High-school students at least 15 years old who have completed two years of French with a B+ average are eligible.

Living arrangements: Students live with families in villages near the college. On weekends, activities will be divided between events at the college and family activities. "Materially, life in the Province of Quebec is comparable to that of the U.S. Rather than 'culture shock,' students can look forward to an experience combining a European outlook with the comfort and convenience of American life."

Finances: The fee of $1,998 includes room and board, tuition, administrative fees, and excursions. Transportation to Rivière du Loup is not included. Some scholarship aid is available.

Deadline: April 24.

Contact: Nona Anderson, Associate Director, Office of Overseas Study (address above).

**MINNESOTA-NANKAI SUMMER INTENSIVE CHINESE
    LANGUAGE INSTITUTE**
University of Minnesota
113 Folwell Hall
9 Pleasant Street
Minneapolis, MN 55455
Telephone: (612) 624–0386

The sponsor: The Minnesota-Nankai Summer Intensive Chinese Language Institute is affiliated with the University of Minnesota, a member of CIEE.

The program: The summer institute is an intensive Chinese-language program that offers nine weeks of classes supplemented by trips and activities, and an optional seven-day tour. The program takes place in the city of Tianjin in the People's Republic of China.

Orientation: Orientation sessions take place at the University of Minnesota, Minneapolis campus. Students are introduced to the program, to aspects of Chinese culture, and to the process of intercultural communication.

Supervision: The ratio of students to teachers is 10 to 1. Staff members supervise students and ensure that classroom instruction, housing, and travel are satisfactory.

Services for persons with disabilities: The program does not discriminate against disabled participants; however, there are no special services for participants with disabilities.

Requirements: The minimum age is 16, and students should be in 10th grade or above. At least one year of college-level Chinese is required.

Living arrangements: Students share rooms in the foreign students' dormitory at Nankai University. Meals are served in a dining hall.

Finances: The program costs $3,000 to $3,500, which covers room and board, tuition (at University of Minnesota), and fees and local travel in China. The program designates a travel agency that makes arrangements for participants. Students must travel to China together, but can return on their own. Travel to China is estimated to cost $1,429. The optional tour costs $480 for seven days.

Deadline: February 28.

NACEL CULTURAL EXCHANGES

For information on Nacel Cultural Exchanges and its language-study programs, see its listing in the Homestays section of this book, page 287.

NATIONAL REGISTRATION CENTER FOR STUDY ABROAD (NRCSA)
823 North Second Street
P.O. Box 1393
Milwaukee, WI 53201
Telephone: (414) 278–0631

The sponsor: NRCSA is an information and registration office for a consortium of 88 language schools in 17 countries. Approximately 20 of these schools accept students under the age of 18 individually or in groups for short-term (one week to three months) foreign-language courses. Member schools have affiliations with more than 300 U.S. universities.

The program: NRCSA offers four types of programs:

- *Mexico Discovery:* There are four to six programs each summer, each lasting from 10 to 20 days. Students tour Mexico with U.S. teachers and stay with Mexican families. All meals are included in the cost of the program.
- *Total Immersion—Spanish:* Participants study the Spanish language for a week while staying with a host family in Mexico or Spain.
- *Total Immersion—French:* Participants study the French language for a week while living with a host family in St-Malo, la Rochelle, or Dinan; or for three to six weeks in the summer, living in a student residence in Cap d'Ail.
- *Total Immersion—German:* Participants study the German language for 2 to 12 weeks while living in a school residence in Salzburg, Austria.

Orientation: Orientation materials are mailed to participants.

Supervision: Group leaders, host families, and host-school faculty supervise the students, with the exception of the Total Immersion programs in Spain, Mexico, and France, which do not have group leaders or direct supervision of participants.

Services for persons with disabilities: Each case is handled on an individual basis.

Requirements: Students should be at least 14 for the *Mexico Discovery* program. The *Total Immersion* programs require participants to be at least 16 years old in Spain, 15 years old in Mexico and France, and 14 years old in Austria. The Spanish and French programs require students to be at the intermediate level of the language.

Living arrangements: Homestay for the *Mexico Discovery* and the *Total Immersion* programs in Mexico, Spain, and France. School residence for the *Total Immersion* programs in Salzburg and Cap d'Ail.

Finances: The fees for the *Mexico Discovery* program range from $800 to $1,400, including airfare. Fees range from $250 to $950 for the *Total*

Immersion programs, depending on destination, and airfare is additional.

Deadline: Sixty days prior to start of program.

NORTHFIELD MOUNT HERMON SCHOOL

For information on Northfield Mount Hermon School's Chinese-, French-, and Spanish-language programs, see its listing in the Study Abroad section of this book, page 120.

OIDEAS GAEL
Gleann Cholm Gille
County Donegal
Ireland
Telephone: (353) 1–213566

The sponsor: Oideas Gael is a nonprofit organization founded in 1981 that offers Irish language courses and cultural activity holidays. Oideas Gael has centers in the Gaeltacht area of southwest Donegal in the Slieve League Peninsula, famous for its scenery, as well as Glenfin, located on the fringe of the Cruacha Gorma (Blue Stack Mountains) in the heart of the Donegal highlands.

The program: Options are available through spring and summer. Oideas Gael offers a variety of language courses directed toward spoken Irish, aiming at correct pronunciation, proper idiom, and development of vocabulary particularly relating to contemporary life. Courses are also offered in archaeology, painting, weaving and design, dancing, and hill-walking.

Supervision: There is a 15-to-1 ratio of students to teachers, who are also responsible for social supervision.

Services for persons with disabilities: Oideas Gael's newly built facilities have easy wheelchair access, and the organization has accommodated persons with disabilities in past years.

Requirements: Participants must be 16 to 21 years of age.

Living arrangements: Bed and breakfast, hostel, homestays (booking must be made directly—ask sponsor for details), or self-catering homes (in which participants cook for themselves).

Finances: Seventy-five Irish pounds (approximately 135 dollars) as course fee, which covers classes, lectures, recreational and cultural events, plus 95 Irish pounds (approximately $170) per week per person sharing a room if staying in specially approved homes with bed, breakfast, and evening dinner; or 35 Irish pounds (approximately $60) per week per person sharing a self-catering, modern, fully equipped house. Airfare and ground transportation to and from site is not included.

Deadline: None.

Contact: Liam ó Cuinneagaín, Director

OPEN DOOR STUDENT EXCHANGE

For information on Open Door Student Exchange and its language-study programs, see its listing in the Study Abroad section of this book, page 122.

RAMAPO COLLEGE OF NEW JERSEY

For information on Ramapo College of New Jersey and its language-study programs, see its listing in the Study Abroad section of this book, page 123.

SAB SPANISH CENTER AND TRAVEL AGENCY
P.O. Box 187
1ª calle 12-35 zona 1
Quezaltenango
Guatemala
Telephone: (502) 9–612042

The sponsor: SAB Spanish Center is a commercial Spanish-language school.

The program: While living in the Guatemalan city of Quezaltenango, participants can choose to study beginning to advanced Spanish on a one-to-one basis with an instructor or with a group.

Orientation: There is an orientation session on the first day of the program.

Supervision: Instructors supervise activities outside of the school.

Services for persons with disabilities: Arrangements can be made to accommodate participants with minor disabilities.

Requirements: Students should be older than 12. No previous knowledge of the Spanish language is required.

Living arrangements: Students live with Guatemalan families who "provide communication, food, and laundry services and give love and care to them."

Finances: Plan A, seven hours of instruction per day, costs $200 a week. Plan B, five hours daily, costs $150. Plan C, four weeks of lessons for four hours daily, costs $400. All homestays cost an additional $75 a week. Weekend tours to areas of interest in Guatemala are available at extra cost.

ST. GEORGE'S SUMMER SESSION IN FRANCE
St. George's School
Newport, RI 02840
Telephone: (401) 847–7565

The sponsor: For more than 15 years, St. George's has offered a summer language study program for high-school students that includes immersional living experience and excursions in Normandy.

The program: St. George's program in language and living in northern France lasts from the end of June to the end of July. During the four weeks of study, students live with a French family and visit cultural and historic sites, while their fluency in French is nurtured in tutorial sessions by native teachers. Tutorial sessions meet for two and one-half hours each weekday morning. Students with sufficient fluency in French can be placed in local businesses for speaking experience. Excursions and optional trips are arranged, and the last two days are spent in Paris.

Orientation: A two-day intensive language and cultural orientation takes place at St. George's in Newport before the students depart.

Supervision: A local native director in Caen oversees the program and is available in case of emergency. American group leaders (1 to every 15 students) are selected on the basis of their French-language ability and experience with young students. They are responsible for daily supervision and organizing excursions.

Services for persons with disabilities: St. George's accepts participants with disabilities who are independently mobile.

Requirements: The programs are open to students 14 to 18 years old. Language requirements vary from one to three years of secondary-school classwork.

Living arrangements: Students live with French families selected by the local program director. "Every effort is made to place participants with peers, but every student is placed in a home where the parents are well informed and well connected with the community."

Finances: The four-week study-homestay program costs $2,975, including tuition, room, and board, but not airfare.

Deadline: May 15.

Contact: Timothy Richards, Director (address above).

SCUOLA LEONARDO DA VINCI
Via Brunelleschi 4
50123 Florence
Italy
Telephone: (39) 55–294247

The sponsor: This school, founded in 1977, offers foreign students a variety of courses in the language and culture of Italy.

The program: The Scuola offers a great variety of courses. Language courses operate on a four-week basis at all levels, and meet 20 hours per week. Classroom study is combined with guided tours of Florence and its museums. Language courses can also be arranged on a one-to-one-basis. The Scuola also offers courses in the history of art, Italian cooking, Italian wines, Italian literature, Italian cinema, ceramics, photography, restoration of paintings, and so on.

Supervision: The school staff is in charge of day-to-day details; on excursions, teachers accompany the group.

Living arrangements: Students can choose to live in an apartment, with a family, or in a pension. The Scuola will help students find a place to stay.

Finances: The fee for the four-week language course is approximately $555, not including room and board.

Deadline: One month in advance of registration.

Contact: Gianni Mannu, Director (address above).

SÉJOURS INTERNATIONAUX LINGUISTIQUES ET CULTURELS

For information on Séjours Internationaux Linguistiques et Culturels and its French-language program, see its listing in the Homestays section of this book, page 292.

SPRACHSCHULE LERCH
Interschool A.G.
Kohlstattgasse 3
A-6020 Innsbruck
Austria
Telephone: (43) 512–588957

The sponsor: Since 1959, Sprachschule Lerch has offered German-language instruction at all levels in Innsbruck, the Tyrolean capital.

The program: Students attend intensive language courses in practical German each morning, Monday through Friday. The courses involve conversation, reading, vocabulary exercises, grammar, and phonetics. Each student is tested and placed in a course according to his or her language ability. During free time in the afternoons, evenings, and on weekends, students participate in activities and excursions arranged by the school, such as theater performances, Tyrolean evenings, dances, and concerts. Students also have time to take advantage of the many recreational activities available in Innsbruck, including horseback riding, swimming, and skiing. Sprachschule Lerch offers month-long courses between June and September. Some language and skiing courses are available during the academic year and during Christmas and Easter holidays.

Supervision: The courses are taught by qualified German instructors. An instructor accompanies students on all excursions arranged by the school.

Requirements: The minimum age is 14.

Living arrangements: Each student lives with a host family and shares a room with a young person from a different country. If a course is particularly crowded, students might be housed in student pensions.

Finances: One-week course fees are 5,500 Austrian schillings (approximately $530) for tuition, accommodation with a host family, and breakfast, or 6,100 Austrian schillings (approximately $580) for tuition, host family accommodation, and full board. There is a nonrefundable application fee of 500 Austrian schillings (approximately $50). Scholarships may be available to groups.

Contact: Helmut Lerch, director (address above).

TORRE DI BABELE
Via Bixio, 74
00185 Rome
Italy
Telephone: (39) 6–7008434

The sponsor: This language school, founded in 1984, is accredited by the Italian Language Schools Association. The school is located in the Esquilino district, near Rome's main train station and a few minutes from the Colosseum and the basilica of San Giovanni.

The program: Torree di Babele offers two programs:

- *Italian in Rome* offers two-week language courses year-round in the school's four-story building. Courses are available at beginning to advanced levels. Students choose from four hours of group instruction daily, four hours of group instruction plus two of individual instruction, or nonintensive courses which give two hours of instruction twice a week.
- *Italian at the Seaside* takes place from July to September in Pisciotta, in the province of Salerno. Classes are given for periods of two or four weeks. Courses are held in the town center, Pisciotta-paese, which is situated among olive groves on a hill 170 meters above sea level.

Orientation: There is an orientation at the beginning of each course.

Services for persons with disabilities: Persons with disabilities are welcome.

Requirements: The minimum age is 16. Beginners are welcome.

Living arrangements: Students share apartments with cooking facilities. Homestays are available in Rome.

Finances: A two-week "group intensive" course in Rome costs 370,000 lire (approximately $330). Two-week courses in Pisciotta cost 380,000 lire. Room and board are extra.

UNISCO
37, rue Cardinet
75017 Paris
Telephone: (33) 1–46221613
Fax: (33) 1–40539629

The sponsor: UNISCO stands for Organisation de Voyages Universitaires et Scolaires. It is a commercial organization that has organized language-study programs in France since 1956.

The program: Programs run throughout the year, but primarily from June through September. Participants study in the cities of Paris, Montargis, Gien, Chamousseau, Nantes, Angers, and Forges-les-Eaux. Language study is provided along with scheduled sports and activities.

Supervision: Group leaders are responsible for the daily supervision of students. There is one group leader for every 12 students, and a maximum of 15 students per teacher.

Requirements: The minimum age for most programs is 14, although some accept students 12 or older.

Living arrangements: Students live in college dormitories or with local families.

Finances: Costs vary from program to program. For example: a four-week program with homestay in Giens and excursions to Paris and Bourges costs 7,650 French francs (approximately $1,530); a two-week program in Paris with residence in a dormitory and excursions to Versailles and Normandy costs 4,650 French francs (approximately $930).

Contact: Dominique Auger, Managing Director (address above).

UNIVERSITY OF KANSAS
Department of Slavic Languages and Literature
Lawrence, KS 66065
Telephone: (913) 864–3313
Fax: (913) 864–4555 (Slavic Department)

The sponsor: The University of Kansas cooperates with Hrvatska matica Iseljenika (The Croatian Homeland Foundation) in presenting the Summer Croatian Language and Folk-Culture School in Zagreb, Croatia. The University of Kansas is a member of CIEE.

The program: From the end of June to the beginning of August, participants study the language and culture of the Croats, a South Slavic nation formerly a part of Yugoslavia. The program consists of language instruction at the beginner, intermediate, and advanced levels and a folklore program consisting of the study of national costumes, architecture, music, dance, and customs. Extracurricular events, such as weekend excursions and visits to village festivals, are included.

Supervision: Supervision is provided by the program director and teaching assistant.

Requirements: Applicants must be between the ages of 17 and 35. Although most participants are undergraduate college students, high-school seniors are also accepted. The summer school primarily attracts young adults of Croatian descent, but the program is open to non-Croatian students ''who demonstrate their desire and scholastic ability to participate in this intensive course.''

Living arrangements: Accommodations are dormitory style.

Finances: Contact the sponsor for up-to-date information.

Deadline: April 1.

Contact: Director, Croatian Summer Program (address above).

VIENNA INTERNATIONAL UNIVERSITY COURSES
Universität
A-1010 Vienna
Austria
Telephone: (43) 222–421254

The sponsor: This school has been in existence since 1922, teaching German to foreign students from beginning level to a "perfectionist course."

The program: The school offers courses during the year, special four-week courses during July and August, and three-week courses in September. Summer courses are offered at six levels, from a beginner's course to a course for teachers of German. Tours of Vienna and the surrounding area, trips on the Danube, excursions to the alpine and lake districts of Austria and to the Neusiedler See are offered during each summer session.

Supervision: The student-teacher ratio is 20 to 1. There is no special supervision.

Requirements: Minimum age is 16,

Living arrangements: During the summer session, students make their own arrangements or stay in a single or double room in one of seven student hostels. They are responsible for making their own meal arrangements.

Finances: The cost of a summer course and accommodation is 9,700 Austrian schillings (approximately $930). Excursions cost extra.

CREATIVE ARTS

*I*n this section you will find programs that focus on all types of creative arts, including the visual arts, the performing arts, and creative writing. Painting, creating video productions, acting, dancing, singing, and writing are only a few of the options available.

Most of the programs involve a short-term stay, from two weeks to a month, and include instruction at various levels, from beginning to advanced. Usually, students stay in dormitories or housing arranged by the sponsoring organization. The program participants often represent the host country and a number of other countries; however, a few of the programs described in this section accept only American participants.

AMERICAN ASSOCIATION OF OVERSEAS STUDIES

For information on the American Association of Overseas Studies and its film internship program, see its listing in the Work/Volunteer section of this book, page 221.

ANGLO AMERICAN MEDIA WORKSHOPS
12 East 86th Street, Suite 408
New York, NY 10028
Telephone: (212) 737–1559

The sponsor: Anglo American Media Workshops is a nonprofit organization that provides training for screenplay writing and video production techniques.

The Program: Master Video in London gives teenagers the opportunity to write and direct an original video program in London with members of the BBC and the Royal Academy of Dramatic Arts. *Television Jour-*

nalism in Israel, which takes place in Jerusalem and Tel Aviv, draws on the resources of the BBC, ABC, CBS, CNN, NBC, and Israeli Television to help students learn the tools of the trade. Both programs last the month of July.

Orientation: The director and staff meet with applicants prior to beginning of program in London or New York.

Supervision: Staff members supervise participants; there is one staff member for every 10 students.

Services for persons with disabilities: Minor disabilities can be accommodated.

Requirements: Participants should be at least 16 years old and in the 10th grade.

Living arrangements: Students live in student residences at Imperial College, London, and the University of Tel Aviv.

Finances: Tuition for both programs is $3,000, including room and board, video equipment, and materials, but not airfare. Scholarships are available.

Deadline: May 5.

ARVON FOUNDATION
Totleigh Barton
Sheepwash
Devon EX21 5NS
England

The sponsor: Founded in 1968, the Arvon Foundation is a nonprofit organization that receives financial support from the Arts Council of Great Britain. It operates a residential center dedicated to the study of creative writing.

The program: Arvon, according to its literature, "has one simple aim—to provide the opportunity to live and work informally with professional writers." To do this, the Foundation operates two residences. Lumb Bank, in West Yorkshire, is an 18th-century mill owner's house; Totleigh Barton is an 11th-century thatched manor house situated in the Devon countryside. Each course lasts five days. During that time, stu-

dents explore and practice imaginative writing along with two professional writers. There are 14 to 16 students per course.

Orientation: Part of the first day the focus is on creativity. Each day
time is set aside to talk with the tutors about individual work; the
evenings often include workshops and readings from tutors and students.

Supervision: There is no organized supervision. Students supervise
themselves and each other.

Services for persons with disabilities: Ground-floor accommodations
have ramps for wheelchairs. The Arvon Foundation has accommodated
students with various physical disabilities in the past.

Requirements: Most of the students are 16 or over, but "we welcome
any student who has an active interest in writing and is prepared to be
part of a conviviality, sharing in the cooking and simple running of the
houses." The Arvon courses are available to groups as well as individuals.

Living arrangements: Life at Totleigh Barton and Lumb Bank is communal. Students share in the daily work of the house.

Finances: The fee of 200 British pounds (approximately $380) includes
board and tuition for the five-day stay.

Deadline: There is no formal deadline. Brochures for the coming year
are available in January, and courses run from March through October.

Contact: Julia Wheadon, Senior Administrator (address above).

DORA STRATOU DANCE THEATRE
8 Scholiou Street
10558 Athens, Plaka
Greece
Telephone (30) 1–3244395

The sponsor: The Dora Stratou Dance Theatre has dedicated itself,
since its founding in 1953, to preserving Greece's "heritage of traditional dance, together with the country's music, song, costumes, and
instruments for the Greeks themselves and the world at large." It is a

nonprofit, government-funded organization with its own 1000-seat theater in Athens that hosts performances daily.

The program: Daily classes in Greek folk dance and folk culture and ancient Greek dance for young people and adults take place in the theater, on Philopappou Hill, opposite the Acropolis. Courses are conducted in English.

Supervision: The student-teacher ratio is 10 to 1. No supervision is provided outside of class and organized activities.

Requirements: The minimum age is 16.

Living arrangements: The school will help to arrange hotel accommodations in Athens for participants. There is a youth hostel nearby.

Finances: For students, programs cost 20,000 drachmas (approximately $100 per week).

Contact: Professor Alkis Raftis, President (address above).

FRIENDSHIP AMBASSADORS FOUNDATION
273 Upper Mountain Avenue
Upper Montclair, NJ 07043
Telephone: (201) 744–0410

The sponsor: The Foundation's motto is "Music is the medium, friendship the message." The group arranges tours for performance groups from the United States to Austria, Bulgaria, China, Czechoslovakia, Finland, France, Great Britain, Greece, Hungary, Ireland, Poland, Portugal, Romania, Spain, Sweden, countries of the former Soviet Union, and Yugoslavia. Begun in 1971 with a tour of 120 students to Czechoslovakia, Friendship Ambassadors has since programmed trips for more than 35,000 Americans from virtually every state in the United States.

The program: Friendship Ambassadors designs two- to four-week programs throughout the year, balancing performances and people-to-people contact. A typical itinerary includes three performances per week, interaction with the audience, and educational sight-seeing. Performance sites range from concert halls to community centers, school auditoriums, churches, hospitals, and amphitheaters.

Orientation: The staff of Friendship Ambassadors publishes orientation handbooks for each country listed above and meets with the participants, parents, and teachers before departure.

Requirements: There are no age requirements, but groups must submit a performance tape.

Living arrangements: Participants generally stay in hotels or guesthouses. In some countries, homestays are arranged.

Finances: Costs range from $900 to $2,500 per person and include airfare, concert arrangements, room and board, guides, local transportation, and entrance fees. Most groups who perform and travel with Friendship Ambassadors do their own fundraising.

Deadline: No official deadlines, but groups are encouraged to begin planning more than a year in advance.

Contact: Jonathan Mills, Executive Director (address above).

INSTITUTO ALLENDE
Ancha de San Antonio 20
San Miguel de Allende
37700 Guanajuato
Mexico
Telephone: (52) 465–20190

The sponsor: This well-known school of arts and crafts and Spanish language was founded in 1938. It is incorporated with the University of Guanajuato but operates as an autonomous unit. The Instituto is a fully accredited member of the Asociación Nacional de Universidades e Institutos de Enseñanza Superior.

The program: The Instituto is an international college for English-speaking students that emphasizes arts, crafts, and the study of Spanish. Both credit and noncredit courses are offered year-round. The courses include painting, drawing, printmaking, sculpture, silverwork, batik, enameling, ceramics, and weaving. Four-week language courses include conversational Spanish, intensive Spanish, and something called "total impact" Spanish, which involves instruction on a one-to-one basis for three to six hours daily. Not far from San Miguel are archaeological sites, historic towns, and craft centers, which participants visit in connection with many of the classes. Life at San Miguel is lively; there are

English-language films, regularly scheduled concerts, ballets and symphonies, dances, parties, gallery openings, poetry readings, tennis, golf, and horseback riding.

Requirements: Applicants must be at least 16 years old and in 10th grade. Although its credit programs attract students who wish to earn undergraduate and graduate transfer credit or a master of fine arts degree, the school welcomes serious noncredit students for short-term enrollment.

Living arrangements: Students make their own accommodation arrangements. San Miguel offers a wide choice of accommodations, and students may choose from a list provided by the Instituto.

Finances: Costs for classes range from $170 for a four-week fine arts and crafts course to $218 for the four-week *Aspects of Mexico* course. Four weeks of *Total Impact* Spanish costs $490 for three hours per day to $860 for six hours per day. There's an additional $10 registration fee.

Contact: Nell Fernández, President (address above).

INTERLOCKEN

For information on Interlocken and its drama program, see its listing in the Organized Tours section of this book, page 208.

INTERNATIONAL SUMMER ACADEMY OF FINE ARTS
Kaigasse 2
P.O. Box 18
A-5010 Salzburg
Austria

The sponsor: This art school, set up in 1953, is supported by the town and county of Salzburg and by the Ministry of Education of Austria.

The program: From the middle of July to the middle of August—five weeks in all—participants draw and paint alongside well-known artists. Sculpture, architecture, stage design, goldsmithing, photography, video, stone sculpture, graphic arts, and modeling are also taught. "Participants must be willing to work seriously and intensively. Professors expect students to be able to work at least somewhat independently." The Summer Academy is not for complete beginners who have never worked with a brush or pencil.

Requirements: The minimum age is 17; some knowledge of German is helpful but not absolutely necessary. Skill in the fine arts is required.

Living arrangements: The school helps students find a place to stay either in fellow students' homes or with private families in Salzburg who are chosen by the Salzburg Tourist Office.

Finances: Tuition is 8,000 Austrian schillings (approximately $760) for the five-week session. Students must pay for their own transportation, room and board, and insurance.

Deadline: June 15.

Contact: Dr. Barbara Wally, Manager (address above).

IRISH SCHOOL OF LANDSCAPE PAINTING
The Blue Door Studio
16 Prince of Wales Terrace
Ballsbridge, Dublin 4
Ireland
Telephone: (353) 1–685548

The sponsor: Founded in 1957 by painter Kenneth Webb, this is a "holiday painting school" staffed by professional painters.

The program: The school accepts advanced and amateur painters; its emphasis is on the individual student's standard of personal achievement. One-week courses held in Connemara begin at different times during the summer; a three-day course is held in Dublin during summer and winter months. Students can stay for several weeks if they prefer. Students paint outdoors from 10 A.M. to 6 P.M., five days a week.

Supervision: The school does not provide group leaders, but tutors are available to students in cases of emergency.

Services for persons with disabilities: The school welcomes many students with disabilities, but cannot accept wheelchair-bound participants.

Requirements: Participants must be at least 14 years of age.

Living arrangements: Students stay in hotel or guesthouses.

Finances: The cost for the Clifden, Connemara, course is 100 Irish pounds (approximately $180) per week. The three-day Dublin course costs 75 Irish pounds (approximately $130). Hotel rooms, including breakfast and dinner, are available to students and accompanying guests at special weekly rates.

Deadline: May 6.

Contact: Clare Cryan (address above).

LOWER ASTON HOUSE POTTERY AND PAINTING SUMMER SCHOOL
Aston Bank
Knighton-on-Teme
Tenbury Wells
Worcestershire WR15 8LW
England
Telephone: (44) 584–79404

The sponsor: Founded in 1981, the Lower Aston House Pottery and Painting Summer School is an institution for persons from all countries who are interested in the arts.

The program: The Lower Aston House offers courses in pottery and painting. Weekend courses are offered in May, June, October; weeklong courses take place in July and August. Programs are organized for maximum teacher-student interaction, with individual help and advice for students at all levels, from the beginner to the experienced amateur artist. In the pottery class, participants' best five pots will be fired and glazed at the end of the stay, with a small supplemental charge for postage and packaging. Participants can also take away their pots free of charge without firing them.

Supervision: All courses are taught by an experienced staff working with small groups to allow for personal attention in an informal setting. Student-teacher ratio is 9 to 1.

Services for persons with disabilities: Persons with disabilities are welcome, but the Lower Aston School has no special facilities.

Requirements: Participants must be over 14 years of age. For the pottery class, participants should bring a smock, a pair of jeans, and an old towel. For the painting class, participants must provide most of their own painting supplies. Contact sponsor for details.

Living arrangements: Individual rooms in a family house, including "all comforts and home cooking."

Finances: For the weekend stay, the cost is 107 British pounds (approximately 200 dollars) for the weeklong stay, 255 British pounds (approximately 480 dollars). This includes full room and board and instruction. There is an additional charge of 8 British pounds for the weekend and 25 British pounds for the week for a single room.

Deadline: One week prior to course.

Contact: Tina Homer, Organizer (address above).

NSTS–STUDENT AND YOUTH TRAVEL

For information on NSTS and its painting program, see its listing in the Organized Tours section of this book, page 213.

OIDEAS GAEL

For information on Oideas Gael and its creative arts programs, see its listing in the Language Study section of this book, page 175.

THE OXFORD SCHOOL OF DRAMA
Sansomes Farm Studios
Woodstock
Oxford OX7 1ER
England
Telephone: (44) 993–812883

The sponsor: The Oxford School of Drama has offered teenagers the opportunity to study and perform since 1981.

The program: Located in the center of Oxford, the school conducts two-week acting courses at the introductory to advanced levels. Courses run from July to the end of August.

Supervision: The live-in staff supervises participants. There is one staff member for every 10 students.

Requirements: Participants should be 14 to 18 years old.

Living arrangements: Students live in student accommodations with live-in housekeepers. The school contains communal dining and recreation areas.

Finances: The tuition is 500 British pounds (approximately $950) for two weeks and 1,000 British pounds for four weeks, which includes accommodations, breakfast, dinner, travel during the courses, and theater tickets.

Deadline: April 30.

PERFORMING ARTS ABROAD
P.O. Box 844
Kalamazoo, MI 49005
Telephone: (616) 629–4901

The sponsor: This commerical tour operator has specialized in tours for nonprofessional musicians since 1962.

The program: PAA assembles student music ensembles for summer performance tours of Europe (England, France, Switzerland, Italy, Austria, Germany, and Holland) or the South Pacific (Hawaii, Australia, and New Zealand). Individual students in band, orchestra, or choir can hone their skills during the summer months under the direction of a highly skilled conductor, while gaining cultural insights and travel experience.

Orientation: Prior to departure, students are supplied with complete tour background information and music for rehearsal. Groups assemble for rehearsals and orientation at the first destination on the itinerary.

Supervision: One or more PAA staff members escort the group, with a ratio of one escort to 10 students. The conductor of the ensemble shares this responsibility.

Services for persons with disabilities: Disabilities are handled on an individual basis. PAA has accommodated students in wheelchairs and with other physical disabilities in the past.

Requirements: Acceptance is based upon a positive recommendation from the individual student's music teacher or school music director. A recommendation form is sent to the teacher by PAA upon receipt of the student's application for the program.

Living arrangements: Accommodations range from hotels and universities to homestays, depending upon the itinerary.

Finances: The 21-day European concert tour costs $2,200 per person, including round-trip airfare from New York City. The 16-day concert tour of the South Pacific costs $2,300, including round-trip airfare from Los Angeles or San Francisco. Tour prices include complete coordination of concert and rehearsal arrangements; all transfers as required by the itinerary; breakfast and dinner daily; sight-seeing arrangements; all taxes and tips for hotel and restaurant services; and historical, geographical, and cultural information on each destination.

Deadline: May 1.

Contact: Ted Tilbury, President (address above).

PORTUGUESE YOUTH HOSTEL ASSOCIATION

For information on the Portuguese Youth Hostel Association and its creative arts programs, see its listing in the Organized Tours section of this book, page 215.

SILVERBIRCH SPINNING AND WEAVING WORKSHOP
Whiting Bay
Isle of Arran KA27 8QR
Scotland

The sponsor: The Silverbirch Workshop was set up in 1975 to explore the possibilities of producing textiles on the Isle of Arran using preindustrial hand methods.

The program: Week-long sessions during the summer focus on handspinning, weaving, and natural dye production.

Supervision: There is a supervisor at the workshop.

Services for persons with disabilities: Students with physical and mental disabilities are accepted and accommodated. Past participants have included blind and wheelchair-bound students.

Requirements: Minimum age is 16.

Living arrangements: Participants sleep and eat at local guesthouses, just a few minutes walk from the workshop.

Finances: The cost of the workshop with room and board is 225 British pounds (approximately $430).

Deadline: April 1.

Contact: Lynn Ross, Director (address above).

STUDIO ART CENTERS INTERNATIONAL (SACI)
Via San Gallo, 30
50129 Florence
Italy
Telephone: (39) 55–486164

The sponsor: This American-based school was founded in 1975 to provide "excellence in studio art courses and art history utilizing the resources of Florence."

The program: Summer programs begin in May and run through mid-August; academic-year programs are available as well. Classes are taught in English.

Orientation: An orientation period is offered at the beginning of the program, during which the dean and program director answer questions the students may have.

Supervision: Resident dean and program director act as supervisors.

Services for persons with disabilities: Some facilities can accommodate physically disabled students.

Requirements: Minimum age is 17; students should be in their senior year of high school and have "a sincere interest in visual arts." Two teacher recommendations and transcripts are required.

Living arrangements: Students live in apartments.

Finances: A six-week late-spring course costs $3,000, which includes tuition, field trips, library use, and evening lectures and seminars. Four-week summer courses are $2,100. The academic-year program is $6,000.

Deadline: Six weeks before the beginning of the course.

Contact: Jules Maidoff, Director (address above).

SUMMER MUSIC SUMMER SCHOOL
22 Gresley Road
London N19 3JZ
England
Telephone: (44) 71–2725664

The sponsor: This music school, operating since 1967, is at Wellington College, Crowthorne, Berkshire, about 25 miles southwest of London. The college was built by Queen Victoria in 1853 in honor of the duke of Wellington.

The program: The program takes place in August and offers classes in string quartets, chamber music, symphony orchestras, wind ensembles, choirs, opera, song recital, conducting, composing, contemporary music, Renaissance dance, music theater, and a workshop in writing fiction. During the evenings, there are many concerts and a barn dance.

Supervision: Staff supervises participants.

Services for persons with disabilities: Participants with minor disabilities will be accommodated (does not include wheelchairs).

Requirements: Minimum age is 14; beginners are welcome.

Living arrangements: Participants usually live at the school in single or double rooms. Some nearby bed-and-breakfast accommodations are available for anyone preferring to live off-campus. All meals are provided for on-campus residents; all except breakfast for those staying off-campus.

Finances: The fee of 190 British pounds (approximately $360) for students living at the school includes room and board and classes.

Deadline: One week before program begins.

Contact: Murray Gordon, Organizer (address above).

TOTNES SCHOOL OF GUITARMAKING
Collins Road
Totnes
Devon TQ9 5PJ
England
Telephone: (44) 803–865255

The sponsor: The Totnes School of Guitarmaking was established in 1981 by guitar maker Norman Reed. It is located in a small pre-Norman town in the rural southwest of England, three and a half hours by train from London.

The program: Courses last 12 weeks, during which time students use seasoned hardwoods to build the guitar (or related instrument) of their choosing. The finished instrument belongs to the student at the end of the course. "For many, this is the first guitar they have built. For some, their first woodwork ever. Yet 95 percent leave with a finished, playing instrument." The school is located in a building dating from about 1700, which also houses a professional guitar workshop and retail shop. Advice on organizing one's own workshop is part of the course. Sessions are held from September 21 to December 11, January 11 to April 2, and May 3 to July 23.

Orientation: "After dealing with formalities, the first day is devoted to selecting timber, reading from drawings, and the sharpening, care, and use of tools."

Supervision: Group tuition alternates with individual attention.

Requirements: "The only qualification for entry to the course is wanting to build an instrument."

Living arrangements: Students usually take lodgings with families in the town.

Finances: The fee is 2,295 British pounds (approximately $4,360) including tuition and materials.

Contact: Norman Reed (address above).

ORGANIZED TOURS

*O*ften arranged by commercial tour organizers, the travel programs in this section offer participants a variety of sight-seeing and touring options. Some focus on popular tourist spots while others go to less-visited areas. Some include lectures or discussions on specific topics, such as the art history or natural environment of a particular country. Generally, participants stay in campgrounds, hotels, pensions, and hostels, while some include short-term homestays at some of the places visited. Groups may travel by bus, minivan, or train.

AMERICAN COUNCIL FOR INTERNATIONAL STUDIES (ACIS)
19 Bay Street Road
Boston, MA 02215
Telephone: (800) 888–ACIS or (800) 666–ACIS

The sponsor: ACIS is the educational travel division of American Institute for Foreign Study (AIFS), a commercial agency. It has offices in Atlanta, Boston, Chicago, and Los Angeles. In 1992, about 22,000 people went abroad through ACIS.

The program: ACIS offers four types of programs to teenagers:

- *Miniprograms:* There are more than 30 of these in all; they cover Canada, Europe, Mexico, the former Soviet Union, and the United Kingdom. The trips, which last 8 to 12 days, are scheduled at Christmas time, in the spring, and during the summer. ACIS describes these trips as "intensive, escorted sight-seeing excursions with educational guide-lecturers."
- *Summer Homestay Programs:* Participants spend from four to

six weeks living with families in France or Spain. Some itineraries include travel as well, and all include language instruction.

- *Summer Campus Programs:* There are nine different programs, all of which run during the summer and last from four to five weeks each. Participants travel to Britain, France, Russia, Spain, and Switzerland and stay in college residences or with families. Each program has a theme, such as language study, music, or culture and politics.
- *Summer Traveling Programs:* These are designed to give "a broad view of European, Pacific, and Asian cultures." There are more than 20 itineraries, ranging in length from two to six weeks. Each with a different theme, such as art, culture, history, or politics.

Supervision: The Mini, Campus, and Summer Traveling programs are led by American teachers or administrators. For every 6 to 15 participants, there is one group leader, who supervises the group and attends staff meetings. In the homestay program, the student is supervised by the family and a local ACIS resident director.

Requirements: Most ACIS programs are open to·high-school students 14 to 19 years old.

Living arrangements: These can include homestays, centrally located hotels, student residences, or university campuses.

Finances: Programs range from $979 (for the Miniprograms) to $3,349. Fees include round-trip airfare, hotels, meals (breakfast and dinner), and day trips to museums and other points of interest. Some of the programs offer scholarships.

Deadline: Sixty days before the start of the program. Late enrollments are accepted if space permits, subject to a late fee of $75.

AMERICAN YOUTH HOSTELS

For information on American Youth Hostels and its travel programs, see its listing in the Outdoor Activities section of this book, page 245.

AMERICAN ZIONIST YOUTH FOUNDATION (AZYF)
110 East 59th Street
New York, NY 10022
Telephone: (212) 339–6002

The sponsor: Founded in 1963, the American Zionist Youth Foundation is a nonprofit organization sponsoring educational programs for Jewish American youth with the purpose of bringing them closer to Israel and Judaism.

The program: AZYF sponsors its own programs for high-school students and also publishes *The Complete Guide to Israel Programs,* which lists programs of other organizations. Among its own programs are a six-week winter sight-seeing program in Israel and a two-week spring tour of Poland in remembrance of the Holocaust.

Supervision: Students are accompanied by group leaders.

Requirements: The minimum age for most programs is 15.

Living arrangements: Participants live in dormitories, on kibbutzim, or in hotels, depending on the program.

Finances: Costs vary according to the program.

Contact: Israel Program Center (address above).

ANGLO-CONTINENTAL HOLIDAYS
200 Pinehurst Avenue
New York, NY 10033
Telephone: (212) 568–0270

The sponsor: Anglo-Continental Holidays is a commercial tour company based in Great Britain that has sponsored tours for U.S. teenagers for 20 years.

The program: The *Live with a British Family* tour program lasts from four to six weeks during the summer. Participants explore London, taking excursions every day. For those who stay for five weeks, there's a three-day holiday in Edinburgh. The six-week program includes five days in Paris. The guides in London are local university students; two American teachers—a husband-and-wife team—accompany the group on the flight.

Supervision: Anglo-Continental staff or British university students are in charge of daily supervision of program participants. The host families act as surrogate parents.

Requirements: The minimum age is 13, maximum is 19.

Living arrangements: In London, participants stay in local homes; on the excursions to Scotland and Paris, lodging is in hotels.

Finances: The basic four-week tour is $2,375, not including airfare.

Deadline: Early reservations are recommended.

Contact: Melvin I. Goldfarb, U.S. Representative (address above).

AQUA VIVA

For information on Aqua Viva and its travel program, see its listing in the Outdoor Activities section of this book, page 246.

ATHENS CENTRE

For information on Athens Centre and its travel programs, see its listing in the Language Study section of this book, page 136.

THE BIKING EXPEDITION

For information on the Biking Expedition and its travel programs, see its listing in the Outdoor Activities section of this book, page 247.

BLYTH AND COMPANY
68 Scollard Street
Toronto, Ontario M5R 1G2
Canada
Telephone: (416) 964–2569

The sponsor: Operating since 1977, this commercial travel agency specializes in educational programs for students, including language immersion, environmental studies, grand tours, and sports programs.

The program: Blyth and Company offers the following programs:

- "enrichment" programs in Oxford, England
- language immersion programs in St-Jean-Cap-Ferrat, France, and Marbella, Spain
- environmental studies in Costa Rica, Grand Cayman Island, and the Galapagos Islands
- bicycle tours in Europe

Most programs last for a month during the summer.

Supervision: There is an average of one supervisor per eight participants.

Requirements: Participants should be between the ages 14 and 19 and in the 9th through the 12th grades. Language experience is needed for some of the language immersion programs.

Living arrangements: Depending on the program, students stay in hotels, homestays, or on campuses.

Finances: Fees range from $2,995 to $3,995, not including airfare. Scholarships are available.

BUTTERFIELD AND ROBINSON
70 Bond Street, Suite 300
Toronto, Ontario M5B 1X3
Canada
Telephone: (800) 678–1147

The sponsor: This commercial travel agency specializes in organizing programs designed to "promote active discovery and involvement in a foreign environment," and has been doing so since 1966.

The program: Butterfield and Robinson offers two programs:

- The *Student Biking Tour of Europe* travels from Paris to Berlin. Students bike through France, Switzerland, Austria, and Germany. There are transfers by train and ferry.
- The *Student European Adventure* begins in Munich and ends in Paris. Students bike, hike, canoe, climb, and travel by train.

Supervision: The participant-leader ratio is 10 to 1.

Services for persons with disabilities: Butterfield and Robinson is willing to accommodate certain cases.

Requirements: For the *Student Biking Tour*, students must be 17 to 21; for the *European Adventure*, students must be 14 to 16.

Living arrangements: On the bicycle tour of Europe, students stay in family-owned inns, chalets, and *Gasthöfe* (guest houses) in the countryside, and small hotels in the cities.

Finances: $3,560 for the Student Biking Tour; $3,475 for the European Adventure. Fees do not include airfare, but Butterfield and Robinson is able to arrange transportation on group flights for participants.

Deadline: No official deadline, but programs tend to fill up by March.

Contact: Denise Girard, Director of Student Programs (address above).

CAMP NORWAY

For information on Camp Norway and its Norwegian travel program, see its listing in the Outdoor Activities section of this book, page 250.

CET
110 Washington Street
Boston, MA 02124
Telephone: (617) 296–0270

The sponsor: CET is a commercial organization specializing in academic programs and educational tours of China for students of all ages. It was founded in 1979.

The program: China in Perspective is an introduction to Chinese civilization, including history, culture, language, geography, and political and economic organization. The curriculum consists of four parts: lectures on specific topics, activities and field trips designed to complement the lectures, daily ''survival Chinese'' classes, and a weekly seminar summarizing the lessons of each week. The program is based on the Beijing Foreign Language Normal College in west central Beijing. Faculty are drawn from China and the United States. The program lasts from July 8 to August 8.

Orientation: Participants receive predeparture materials. There is an orientation upon arrival in Beijing.

Supervision: The student-teacher ratio is 10 to 1. Each group is accompanied by a U.S. director fluent in Chinese and with an M.A. in a related field.

Services for persons with disabilities: Persons with disabilities are welcome to participate.

Requirements: The minimum age is 13. There is no language requirement.

Living arrangements: Students are housed in dormitory suites of two to three rooms with hot showers.

Finances: The $3,100 fee includes room, board, tuition, texts, visa fees, departure taxes, activities, and round-trip international airfare from New York. (With departure from Los Angeles, the fee is $2,900.)

Deadline: May 1.

CITIZEN EXCHANGE COUNCIL (CEC)
12 West 31st Street, 4th Floor
New York, NY 10001
Telephone: (212) 643–1985

The sponsor: CEC is a nonprofit educational organization devoted to person-to-person exchanges between citizens of the United States and Canada and countries of the former Soviet Union.

The program: CEC's *High School Conferences in Russia* bring teacher-student groups from U.S. and Canadian high schools to meet their counterparts in Russia. Each conference features a full week stay in a medium-sized Russian city, during which participants join with English-speaking students in discussions and informal activities. Visits to Moscow and St. Petersburg at the beginning and end of the program provide introductions to Russian history and culture. The program takes place in March and April.

Orientation: A predeparture orientation takes place on the date of departure.

Supervision: Student groups are accompanied by teachers from their high school. CEC group leaders are fluent in Russian and have prior study or work experience in Russia.

Services for persons with disabilities: "CEC does not discourage participation by disabled persons, but accommodating them in Russia has been problematic."

Requirements: The minimum age is 14. No language ability is required. U.S. high schools make group reservations with CEC; selection of students, teachers, and other accompanying adults is handled within each school.

Living arrangements: Hotels in Moscow and St. Petersburg; hotels and homestays in cities where the conferences take place.

Finances: The cost per person is approximately $2,295, including airfare, hotels, meals, and conference materials. A deposit of $300 is required to reserve a place for your group.

Deadline: January 16.

CULTURAL EXCHANGE TRAVEL
755 Boylston Street, Suite 703
Boston, MA 02116
Telephone: (617) 236–1565

The sponsor: Cultural Exchange Travel is a commercial company that organizes international trips for students and faculty groups.

The program: Sight-seeing trips lasting one to two weeks travel to the countries of eastern Europe, the former Soviet Union, and China. More extensive language courses and homestay programs are also available. Special itineraries for school groups with specific interests can be arranged.

Orientation: Students receive information packets about the countries to be visited before departure.

Supervision: Student-faculty groups are accompanied by group leaders with language fluency and previous experience in the country.

Requirements: None.

Living arrangements: Hotels, homestays, and some dormitories on language programs.

Finances: Fees vary according to program and city of departure. For example, a 17-day trip to China, departing from New York, costs $3,059; a 16-day trip through Russia and the Ukraine, departing from Chicago, costs $2,639. Teachers receive discounts, a free trip, or stipends, depending on how many students they enroll.

THE EXPERIMENT IN INTERNATIONAL LIVING

For information on The Experiment in International Living and its travel programs, see the listing for World Learning Inc. in the Homestays section of this book, page 294.

FORMATION INTERNATIONALE VOYAGES ETUDES (FIVE)

For information on FIVE and its travel programs, see its listing in the Homestays section of this book, page 280.

FORUM TRAVEL INTERNATIONAL
91 Gregory Lane, Suite 21
Pleasant Hill, CA 94523
Telephone: (510) 671–2900

The sponsor: A nonprofit organization, Forum International was founded in 1956 with the purpose of "creating a worldwide forum for education, research, and action on a transdisciplinary, supranational, and ecosystemic basis." Forum Travel International is its travel subsidiary.

The program: Forum International has more than 1,300 travel programs geared toward "exploring nature, culture, and people . . . with special emphasis on environmental integrity, social responsibility, human health and fitness in their widest sense, and the ecosystemic interrelation among these various factors." Programs take place year-round in 135 different countries.

Orientation: Orientations vary according to the program.

Supervision: There are 4 to 15 participants per group leader.

Services for persons with disabilities: Persons with disabilities are accepted on special trips.

Requirements: The minimum age is 10.

Living arrangements: Participants stay in private homes, inns, and lodges, or camp on outdoor adventures.

Finances: Program costs range upwards from $35 per day, including room and board in most cases.

Deadline: Sixty days ahead of time.

FRIENDSHIP AMBASSADORS FOUNDATION

For information on Friendship Ambassadors Foundation and its travel programs, see its listing in the Creative Arts section of this book, page 187.

GENCTUR TOURISM AND TRAVEL AGENCY

For information on Genctur and its Turkish travel programs, see its listing in the Work/Volunteer section of this book, page 232.

GIRL SCOUTS OF THE USA
830 Third Avenue
New York, NY 10022
Telephone: (212) 940–7500

The sponsor: The Girl Scouts needs no introduction. It is the largest voluntary organization for girls in the world, open to all girls from 5 to 17 who subscribe to its ideals as stated in the Girl Scout Promise and Law. Girl Scouts of the USA has operated international projects for more than 50 years. As a member of the World Association of Girl Guides and Girl Scouts (WAGGGS), it is part of a worldwide family of youth and adults in 118 countries.

The program: Each member organization of WAGGGS is an independent entity, and many of the members conduct international projects, inviting other member organizations to send representatives. The inviting organization is responsible for the conduct of the project within its national boundaries. In the recent past, there have been international opportunities in Australia, Austria, Egypt, Finland, Iceland, India, Ireland, Italy, Jamaica, New Zealand, Portugal, Singapore, Sri Lanka, Thailand, and Zambia. The types of projects vary; there are national encampments, community service projects, home visits, and world center sessions.

Supervision: All international projects have one or more adult leaders— someone 21 or over who has experience working with high-school-age girls, previous travel experience, and "experience and love for Girl Scouting," among other qualifications.

Requirements: Applicants must be active in Girl Scouting and between the ages of 14 and 18. Individual councils nominate candidates; the final selection is made by a National Selections Task Group.

Finances: Fees vary between $600 and $900. Scholarships are available from the Juliette Low World Fellowship Fund.

Deadline: Varies with the program.

Contact: Your local Girl Scout Council.

GREEN TOURS

For information on Green Tours, and its outdoor tour programs, see its listing in the Outdoor Activities section of this book, page 254.

INSTITUTE OF SPANISH STUDIES

For information on the Institute of Spanish Studies and its travel programs in Spain, see its listing in the Language Study section of this book, page 163.

INTERLOCKEN
RD2, Box 165
Hillsboro Upper Village, NH 03244
Telephone (603) 478–3166

The sponsor: A nonprofit organization, Interlocken has offered summer programs for teenagers since 1961. Both travel and residential programs stress the group experience; students ''enjoy the camaraderie and strength of group living as they make new friends and grow as individuals.''

The program: Interlocken's *Crossroads Student Travel* programs emphasize experiential learning, cross-cultural experiences, and group living. The *Drama Britain* program offers young people the opportunity to develop the skills and knowledge of theater and dance while traveling in the British Isles. Cycling programs tour Canada and Europe. There are also language programs in Canada, France, Mexico, and Spain, and a wilderness adventure program in New Zealand.

Interlocken's *World Friendship Exchange* programs focus on people-to-people interaction, offering teenagers from North America the opportunity to live, travel, work, and play with their peers in the host country. Friendship Exchange programs are available in the Caribbean, East Africa, Egypt and Israel, and Russia.

In cooperation with Global Roots Community Service, a California-based nonprofit organization, Interlocken also sponsors community service projects in Africa, Asia, and Latin America.

Supervision: ''Leaders are adult professionals selected for their maturity, enthusiasm, stability, good judgment, warmth, and ability to relate closely and sensitively with teenagers.'' Groups vary in size depending on the character and goals of the program; most programs have 12 to 25 students with two to four adult leaders.

Services for persons with disabilities: Interlocken will accept individuals with disabilities if they are able to engage in the program as designed.

Living arrangements: Crossroads Travel programs usually include camping and homestays with local families. *Friendship Exchange* programs often include homestays and living with young people from the host country in residential youth camps.

Requirements: For most international programs offered by Interlocken, participants should be in the 9th through 12th grades. However, some programs accept seventh and eighth graders.

Finances: International programs range in cost from $2,585 to $3,595, not including airfare. Some scholarship aid is available.

Deadline: Applications are accepted on a rolling basis.

INTERNATIONAL BICYCLE FUND

For information on International Bicycle Fund and its travel programs in Africa, see its listing in the Outdoor Activities section of this book, page 255.

INTERNATIONAL SUMMER INSTITUTE

For information on International Summer Institute and its travel programs, see its listing in the Study Abroad section of this book, page 115.

IRISH AMERICAN CULTURAL INSTITUTE

For information on the Irish American Cultural Institute and its travel programs in Ireland, see its listing in the Study Abroad section of this book, page 116.

ISRAEL YOUTH HOSTELS ASSOCIATION (IYHA)
Youth Travel Bureau
3, Dorot Rishonim Street
P.O. Box 1075
Jerusalem 91009
Israel
Telephone: (972) 2–252706
Fax: (972) 2–250676

The sponsor: The Israel Youth Hostels Association offers affordable accommodations and special programs for youth visiting Israel.

The program: IYHA offers one- to four-week travel programs including desert safaris in the Sinai and the Negev, Eilat–Red Sea Holidays, nature tours, and a trip to Egypt.

Requirements: Programs are offered for all ages.

Living arrangements: Students stay in youth hostels.

Finances: Contact the organization for current costs.

Deadline: No set deadline.

JUGI TOURS

For information on Jugi tours and its travel programs in Switzerland, see its listing in the Outdoor Activities section of this book, page 258.

MUSIKER STUDENT TOURS
1326 Old Northern Boulevard
Roslyn, NY 11576
Telephone: (516) 621–0718, or (800) 645–6611 outside New York

The sponsor: Musiker Student Tours is a family-owned company established in 1966.

The program: Musiker Tours offers a range of programs that emphasize sight-seeing and recreational and cultural activities. Programs include a five-week *Action Europe* tour that visits Italy, Switzerland, France, Belgium, and England. All tours include visits to museums and historic sites, plus such activities as cruises, skiing, whitewater rafting, tennis, and going to the theater.

In cooperation with UCLA Extension, Musiker sponsors *Summer Discovery at Cambridge University*, an academic program that offers college credit in such subjects as acting, literature, communications, political science, and history. Courses are taught by Cambridge University faculty.

Supervision: Most staff members are tour alumni who have trained for five years. The student-leader ratio is eight to one. Leaders are on duty at all times and responsible for everything.

Services for persons with disabilities: Students with disabilities are invited to inquire. Students in wheelchairs may have a difficult time traveling.

Requirements: Students should be between 14 and 18 years old and entering their sophomore year of high school to freshman year in college.

Living arrangements: On the *Action Europe* tour, students stay in hotels. Participants in the *Summer Discovery* program are housed in Cambridge University's New Hall College.

Finances: The *Action Europe* tour costs $4,900, including three meals daily, all activities, excursions, admissions, and recreational activities. *Summer Discovery* costs $3,695, including room, academic programs, breakfast and dinner daily, and activities. Airfare is extra.

Deadline: Applicants accepted on a rolling admissions basis.

NATIONAL REGISTRATION CENTER FOR STUDY ABROAD (NRCSA)

For information on NRCSA and its travel program, see its listing in the Language Study section of this book, page 173.

NORTH AMERICAN FEDERATION OF TEMPLE YOUTH (NFTY)
Union of American Hebrew Congregations—Youth Division
NFTY in Israel Office
P.O. Box 443, Bowen Road
Warwick, NY 10990
Telephone: (914) 987–6300

The sponsor: NFTY is the youth division of the Union of American Hebrew Congregations, the national reform movement in Judaism. For more than 20 years, NFTY has sponsored long- and short-term programs in Israel for high-school and college students.

The program: NFTY offers three summer programs and one semester program:

- *Israel Academy* is primarily a travel program that explores ancient and modern Israel and includes a camping trip in the desert. Living and working in a kibbutz for two weeks is one of the features of the five-and-a-half-week tour.
- *Israel Safari* is similar to the Academy tour, but instead of the kibbutz experience, participants spend time at an Israeli field

school exploring the geology, geography, flora, and fauna of the country.

- *Archaeological Dig* combines a tour with work on an excavation.
- *The Eisendrath International Exchange Program* is an academic semester. The program provides an in-depth look at historic and contemporary Israel while enabling students to continue their normal high-school curriculum with full credit. Students spend part of the semester living with an Israeli family, and part of the time working on a kibbutz.

Recent high-school graduates might also consider other NFTY programs, some of which are suitable to the year between high school and college. Ask for details on the College Israel Academy and College and Kibbutz academic-year programs.

Orientation: A brief orientation takes place at the airport before departure.

Supervision: Group leaders have prior experience working with young people and are responsible for daily supervision, including general counseling and leading group discussions.

Services for persons with disabilities: Persons with disabilities are welcome; however, wheelchair-bound students might have great difficulty participating.

Requirements: The Eisendrath Exchange Program requires participants to have completed 10th grade. Other programs require participants to have completed ninth grade. There is no language requirement.

Living arrangements: These vary with the program. Participants stay in hotels, hostels, and/or kibbutzim. Participants in the semester-long program stay with families who live in a city, development town, youth village, or kibbutz.

Finances: Costs for the summer programs range from $3,995 to $4,095; the semester program costs $5,850. Fee includes round-trip airfare from New York, room and board, and all touring costs. While the participant is in Israel, insurance is provided through that country's national health network; information on other insurance is provided.

Deadline: May 1.

Contact: Paul Reichenbach, Director, Israel Programs (address above).

NSTS—STUDENT AND YOUTH TRAVEL
220 St. Paul Street
Valletta VLT 07
Malta
Telephone: (356) 944983

The sponsor: NSTS is the student/youth travel organization of Malta, a country of islands in the Mediterranean, south of Italy. NSTS promotes educational and cultural development through travel by providing low-cost accommodation, transportation, entertainment, and a variety of special programs to young people. NSTS is a member of the International Student Travel Confederation (see page 61).

The program: Besides offering a full range of travel services and historical cultural day excursions in Malta, NSTS organizes a number of special programs:

- *An Appreciation of Baroque Art:* This two-week course is designed to give students an appreciation of Baroque painting and architecture through a series of lectures and visits to places of interest throughout Malta.
- *Archaeology in Malta:* Participants spend two weeks attending lectures on methodology, Maltese history, the megalithic temples, and historical archaeology; taking trips to places of historical and archaeological interest and doing survey work, clearance work, or actual excavations.
- *Sports Encounters:* This program allows amateur sports clubs and school teams to meet their Maltese counterparts in specially organized tournaments. Sports range from basketball to tennis and waterpolo. Cultural programs can be combined with the basic sports programs and programs that are custom-designed.
- *Painting:* A practical holiday course that offers participants the opportunity to paint Maltese landscapes while receiving instruction on techniques of watercolor, oil painting, and sketching. Materials for the course are provided.

Supervision: Participants in all programs are attended by trained personnel.

Services for persons with disabilities: NSTS will try to make the necessary arrangements for participants with disabilities.

Requirements: The minimum age is 14.

Living arrangements: These vary from student residences to family homestays.

Finances: Fees vary with the program.

Deadline: Six weeks prior to beginning of program.

PERFORMING ARTS ABROAD

For information on Performing Arts Abroad and its travel program, see its listing in the Creative Arts section of this book, page 193.

PHENIX INTERNATIONAL CAMPUSES
7651 North Carolyn Drive
Castle Rock, CO 80104
Telephone: (303) 688–9397

The sponsor: Phenix International, a commercial agency founded in 1970, offers student travel-study programs that combine homestays, language assistance, cultural classes, and sight-seeing.

The program: Phenix offers spring and summer travel programs. Spring programs include homestays in Paris and Munich with travel to surrounding areas and a sight-seeing trip to Mexico. Summer programs include the following:

- *Germany, North to South:* A four-week journey beginning in Berlin and including a homestay in Bavaria with excursions to Nuremberg, Regensburg, and Amberg. The last week is spent in Munich and in Salzburg, Austria.
- *España es su Casa:* A four-week sight-seeing tour beginning in Madrid. A homestay in Pamplona includes family activities, local excursions, and the famous Festival of San Fermín (featuring "*la corrida de toros*"—"the running of the bulls"). The last week is spent in Barcelona.
- *Adventures in France:* A three-week tour including four days in Paris and a homestay on the Riviera.
- *Treasures of France:* A four-week tour including five days in Paris, travel to Normandy and the Riviera, plus a homestay in Bourges.
- *Modern and Historic Mexico:* A 17-day tour that includes Mexico City and Teotihuacán, plus a homestay in Puebla.

- *Russia Today:* Three weeks of travel to St. Petersburg and Moscow, plus a homestay in the Black Sea resort of Sochi. Meetings with local young people and language lessons are also available.

Orientation: Orientations are held monthly between January and June for students living in the Denver area and include cultural simulations, language practice, and general preparation. Students from outside Colorado receive orientation materials by mail.

Supervision: For every eight students, there is one teacher-chaperone and one "American coordinator," an educator with overseas and study-travel program experience who acts as the link to the various overseas representatives.

Services for persons with disabilities: Phenix will make individual arrangements to the extent possible, as long as the best interests of the group can be served.

Requirements: Participants must be 13 to 19 years old. One year of language study is required for language programs. Applicants must have references from a teacher and a school counselor.

Living arrangements: These include homestays, hotels, and youth hostels.

Finances: Program fees range from $959 to $2,820, depending on the destination and the length of the trip. The fee includes round-trip airfare from Denver or the gateway city nearest you, all travel, sight-seeing, room and full board.

Deadline: There is no set deadline, but early application is recommended.

Contact: Nellie B. Jackson, Manager (address above).

PORTUGUESE YOUTH HOSTEL ASSOCIATION
(Associação de Utentes das Pousadas de Juventude)
Tourism Department
Rua Andrade Corvo 46
P-1000 Lisbon
Portugal
Telephone: (351) 1–571054

The sponsor: The Portuguese Youth Hostel Association operates 16 youth hostels in various parts of Portugal. It also sponsors a variety of tours for young people.

The program: There are a variety of tours for individuals or groups, most of which last about a week and focus on a particular region of Portugal. An 18-day trip through all of Portugal is also offered. Other program options emphasize particular activities, such as canoeing, mountaineering, windsurfing, and diving, or arts and crafts, including instruction in tapestry, basket-weaving, and pottery.

Supervision: Youth hostel wardens are responsible for the well-being of the hostel and hostelers staying there. There are tour guides for the day-stops throughout the tour programs.

Requirements: Most of the outdoor activities and arts and crafts programs have minimum ages—16 years old for canoeing, mountaineering, and tapestry, and 18 years old for the others.

Living arrangements: Accommodations are in Portuguese youth hostels.

Finances: Consult the organization for current costs.

PUTNEY STUDENT TRAVEL (PST)
International Road
Putney, VT 05346
Telephone: (802) 387–5885

The sponsor: PST, a commercial agency, has been organizing "non-touristy" educational travel programs since 1952.

The program: Most PST programs last five to six weeks. They include trips to Australia, Canada, China, the Caribbean, Costa Rica, Ecuador, England, France, Holland, Hungary, New Zealand, Scandinavia, Spain, countries of the former Soviet Union, and the United States. According to the sponsor, "Our travel plans are special. They emphasize doing—having fun, getting off the beaten track, making friends, and being involved with people—rather than just touring or sight-seeing." The emphasis is on the active: participants might sail with Breton fishermen, explore the steppes of Russia, or hike through Denmark. Special language-learning trips to Spain and France emphasize speaking the languages in natural, everyday living situations.

Supervision: Leaders must be college graduates completely fluent in the language, with experience living abroad and working with teenagers. There is one leader for every eight students.

Services for persons with disabilities: While its programs tend to be physically demanding, PST is able to accommodate people with limited disabilities (for example, visual and hearing impairments, learning disabilities, minor physical disabilities).

Requirements: Students 13 to 18, 8th through 12th grade, are eligible. Groups are formed according to age of participants. "Students should recognize that participation in PST is challenging, that they are expected to make a positive contribution to the success of the program and the morale of the group, and to maintain high standards of personal behavior."

Living arrangements: Participants stay in small inns, chalets, student centers, and hostels—places where they have a chance to meet people from other countries.

Finances: Fees, which are all-inclusive, range from $2,990 to $5,880.

Deadline: No set deadline, but programs usually fill up by early spring.

Contact: Jeffrey Shumlin, Director (address above).

SCOTTISH YOUTH HOSTELS ASSOCIATION (SYHA)
7 Glebe Crescent
Stirling FK8 2JA
Scotland
Telephone: (44) 786–51181

The sponsor: SYHA, founded in 1931, is an organization that offers young people budget accommodations at more than 80 locations throughout Scotland.

The program: The organization offers a number of all-inclusive *Breakaway Holiday* packages, which offer a choice of hill-walking, canoeing, sailing, windsurfing, pony trekking, and golfing vacations. Other programs give participants the freedom to explore Scotland at their own pace. The *Scottish Wayfarer* and *Explore Scotland* passes give 7 or 14 days unlimited travel within the pass area by coach, rail, and boat.

Overnight accommodation vouchers, an SYHA handbook, timetables, and a touring map are included.

Supervision: Supervision is provided by qualified instructors on the *Breakaway Holiday* packages, and hostels are staffed by wardens at all times.

Services for persons with disabilities: SYHA has no specific programs, but most of the wardens are willing to help disabled individuals or groups that visit. Some hostels cannot accommodate wheelchairs.

Requirements: Persons must be at least five years old to use Scottish youth hostels. On *Breakaway Holidays*, participants must be 14 years old (12 years old for pony trekking).

Living arrangements: Participants stay in youth hostels.

Finances: Breakaway Holiday costs begin at 48 British pounds (approximately $90) for a week. Included in the costs are activity fees, accommodations, and in some cases, meals.

Deadline: Full payment is required six weeks prior to holiday dates.

STUDENT HOSTELING PROGRAM

For information on Student Hosteling Program and its international bicycle tours, see its listing in the Outdoors Activities section of this book, page 268.

STUDENTS ABROAD
42 Edgewood Avenue
Mount Vernon, NY 10552
Telephone: (914) 699–8335

The sponsor: Students Abroad has been operating tour programs for teenagers since 1958.

The program: Students Abroad offers travel programs to countries in western Europe and the South Pacific, international resident camps in Austria and Switzerland, and summer ski and tennis camps in Europe and the South Pacific.

Supervision: The ratio of participants to leaders is four to one. All leaders are at least 25 years old.

Services for persons with disabilities: Students Abroad is working with the Vail Association to incorporate a ski program for blind students in the summer camp.

Requirements: Programs are open to students of all ages.

Living arrangements: Depending on the program, accommodations vary from pensions and student centers to inns and first-class hotels.

Finances: Fees range from $3,400 to $5,800. All travel is included.

Deadline: No set deadline. Trips depart last week in June.

Contact: Edward Finn, Director (address above).

WEISSMAN TEEN TOURS
517 Almena Avenue
Ardsley, NY 10502
Telephone: (914) 693–4289, or (800) 942–8005 outside New York

The sponsor: Weissman Teen Tours has offered a five-week package tour of Europe since 1974.

The program: On the 35-day summer program, participants travel through Belgium, England, France, Holland, Italy, and Switzerland by plane, bus, railroad, and hydrofoil. Activities include a full range of guided sight-seeing programs, London theater performances, a medieval banquet, a moonlight gondola ride in Venice, a cruise on the river Seine, skiing in Zermatt, tennis, swimming, and more.

Supervision: Ronee and Eugene Weissman, the founders and operators of Weissman Teen Tours, accompany each group. There is also one group leader for every eight students. Group leaders must have foreign language ability, experience working with teenagers, and prior experience. Their responsibilities involve daily supervision, including nightly curfew checks and acting as "a friend and adviser" to tour members.

Requirements: Participants must be from 15 to 18 years old. Students entering their junior and senior year in high school or their first year of college are eligible.

Living arrangements: Accommodations are in hotels.

Finances: The 1992 tour cost $5,895, including full room and board, and all activities, but not airfare.

Deadline: Varies.

Contact: Ronee Weissman, Vice President (address above).

WESTCOAST CONNECTION TRAVEL CAMP
217 Wolseley North
Montreal West, Quebec H4X 1W1
Canada
Telephone: (514) 488–8920, or (800) 767–0227 in the United
  States

The sponsor: Westcoast Connection Travel Camp is a teen travel program "that combines the excitement and fascination of discovering and exploring Europe with the fun and camaraderie of summer camp." It was founded in 1982.

The program: The *European Discovery* program takes participants on a month-long tour of France, Italy, Switzerland, Belgium, Holland, England, and Spain. *Cycling Adventure—France* takes cyclists through the Loire Valley, the Riviera, the Alps, Paris, Versailles, and Geneva. Both programs take place during July and August.

Supervision: There is one leader for every five to six students on *European Discovery* and one for every four on the cycling tour.

Services for persons with disabilities: Each case is handled individually.

Requirements: Campers should be from 14 to 18 years old and in 9th through 12th grades.

Living arrangements: Both programs combine private campsites with two- and three-star hotels.

Finances: The *European Discovery* program costs $4,395; *Cycling Adventure—France* costs $3,395. Fees include accommodations, ground transportation, three meals and two snacks a day, and all activities and admissions. Airfare is not included.

Deadline: No set deadline, but early registration is encouraged.

WORK/VOLUNTEER

*A*t first, work may not sound like the most alluring thing to do on a trip abroad. However, some of the most exciting opportunities for teens abroad include working as a volunteer or a trainee. Working with scientists to study volcanoes in Iceland, participating in an archaeological dig in Israel, working as an intern for a law firm in England, or helping with immunization in Ecuador are only a few of the possibilities that the organizations in this section offer. Another option is to join a workcamp, which involves voluntary service with an international group of young people. Most overseas work programs open to teenagers are short-term, lasting from a few weeks to a few months.

AFS INTERCULTURAL PROGRAMS

For information on AFS and its work/volunteer programs, see its listing in the Study Abroad section of this book, page 91.

AMERICAN ASSOCIATION OF OVERSEAS STUDIES (AAOS)
158 West 81st Street, Box 112
New York, NY 10024
Telephone: (212) 724–0804, or (800) EDU–BRIT outside New York

The sponsor: The American Association of Overseas Studies (AAOS), a division of Janet Kollek and Associates, is a commercial agency established in 1984.

The program: AAOS provides academic study and internship opportunities in Paris and London that give young people hands-on experience in film, law, business, government, journalism, and medicine. AAOS also offers a French-language immersion program in Montpellier. Programs take place during the summer.

Supervision: Group leaders supervise internships, lead tours, and are available for discussions. There is one leader for every five participants.

Requirements: The minimum age is 14. Participants in the Paris internship program must speak "passable French."

Living arrangements: Participants live in school dormitories.

Finances: The London and Paris academic study-internship programs cost $4,872 for four weeks, including tuition, room and board, excursions, and activities. Film projects cost $5,072. Internships only (without academic study) cost $2,295. The Montpellier French immersion program costs $4,195 for four weeks.

Deadline: Rolling admissions.

Contact: Janet Kollek Evans, Director (address above).

AMERICAN FARM SCHOOL
Office of Trustees
1133 Broadway, Suite 1625
New York, NY 10010
Telephone: (212) 463–8434

The sponsor: For almost 90 years, the American Farm School has trained young men and women in Greece to become master farmers and village leaders. More than 225 participants enroll each year to learn the latest applicable farming techniques on the school's 375-acre campus farm.

The program: The *Greek Summer* program offers American high-school students the opportunity to live in a rural Greek village with a family and work on a volunteer farm project while getting to know Greek culture. *Greek Summer* runs from mid-June to the end of July. Students spend six weeks in a Greek village and at the Farm School. The projects usually involve construction of a road or sidewalk in a village, building a playground, raising pigs and chickens, and tending vegetable gardens. The program includes a nine-day excursion through Greece and ends with a hike up Mount Olympus.

Supervision: There are five counselors and one director for 44 students at the work sites. Homestay families supervise the students in the evening.

Requirements: Participants must be high-school students ages 15 to 18 in 10th through 12th grades.

Living arrangements: Students live with a Greek family in the village an hour or two from the Farm School.

Finances: The tuition is $1,950. A $500 tax-deductible contribution to the school accompanies the application and is refunded if the applicant is not accepted. Airfare is additional. Scholarships are available.

Deadline: No set deadline.

Contact: Patricia Mulhern, Program Coordinator (address above).

AMERICAN FRIENDS OF THE COLLÈGE LYCÉE CÉVENOL INTERNATIONAL

For information on American Friends of the Collège Lycée Cévenol International and its work/volunteer program, see its listing in the Study Abroad section of this book, page 95.

AMIGOS DE LAS AMÉRICAS
5618 Star Lane
Houston, TX 77057
Telephone: (800) 231–7796

The sponsor: Amigos de las Américas is a nonprofit voluntary service organization that works on public health projects in Mexico, the Caribbean, and Central and South America. Since its founding in 1965, more than 14,000 volunteers have served. The head office of Amigos is in Houston, where the projects and the 20 local training chapters are coordinated.

The program: Young people spend from four to eight weeks in a village of Central America or the Caribbean, helping to implement a variety of health programs. Some of the specific projects have included dental hygiene instruction in Costa Rica, community sanitation and latrine construction in Mexico, and yellow-fever immunization and eyeglass distribution in Ecuador. The long-term goal of every Amigos program is threefold: "leadership development opportunities for North American youth, improved community health in Latin America, and better cross-cultural understanding on both continents."

Orientation: The orientation and training is extensive. Consisting of approximately 124 hours of training over a three- to six-month period, it focuses on public health issues. Latin American history and culture, Spanish language, and human relations. Some high schools and colleges will give academic credit for the Amigos training and experience.

Supervision: There are 8 to 10 volunteers per field staff member. Volunteer teams are visited by field staff "to ensure that the volunteers are happy, healthy, and working well with the community."

Requirements: Participants must be at least 16 years old and have a basic knowledge of Spanish. Amigos requires that all participants undergo a lengthy training period before beginning their assignment. For those who live near a local chapter, this training is done locally. Those who are too far from a chapter to make this practical are called "correspondent volunteers" and are trained through correspondence with the Houston office.

Living arrangements: Volunteers live either with families in the host villages or in a public building—a clinic, hospital, or school.

Finances: In 1992 total costs were as follows: Mexico, $2,325; Central America and the Caribbean, $2,425; South America, $2,535; and Brazil, 2,585. These fees include international airfare, training materials, supplies, and room and board. Individual Amigos chapters help with fundraising. Correspondent volunteers are given a fund-raising kit. Some scholarship aid is available.

Deadline: March 1.

Contact: The address above or your local chapter (call the toll-free number above to see whether there's a chapter near you).

BANGLADESH WORK CAMPS ASSOCIATION (BWCA)
289/2, Work Camps Road
North Shajahanpur
Dhaka 1217
Bangladesh
Telephone: (880) 2–403479

The sponsor: BWCA is a nonprofit youth voluntary service organization founded in 1958 to promote leadership development and self-help. BWCA operates a number of projects throughout Bangladesh, such as health education courses; a school for the poor; reforestation projects; construction of roads, bridges, and homes in impoverished areas; and income-generating projects for unemployed youths.

The program: BWCA's *Study Bangladesh* program is designed for foreign visitors. Activities include participating in BWCA workcamps, visiting various project sites, meeting volunteers, and discussing issues related to world peace and development. The actual nature and itinerary of the program varies from person to person: "In fact, it is an individual project which is designed on the basis of the foreign volunteer's interest and desire." BWCA also sponsors a homestay program, in which visitors are invited to stay with the families of local workcamp participants. The project is open year-round, but participation between the months of November and April is preferable.

Orientation: Every program has a welcome and orientation function before the participant begins work.

Supervision: There is one leader for every 10 workcampers. Leaders have command of English.

Requirements: The minimum age is 15; maximum is 30.

Living arrangements: Volunteers live in schools, hostels, tents, sponsors' homes, and low-cost hotels. "The accommodations of a workcamp cannot be described as luxurious, but it does provide for basic needs and permits the group to live on its own, prepare its own meals, and develop its own way of living together."

Finances: A $25 fee must accompany the application form. Upon arrival, participants pay $125 per week or $20 per day. BWCA charges a $100 fee for homestays. These costs include all meals, accommodations, ground transportation, and minor medical expenses. Airfare is not included.

Deadline: Three months before start of program.

Contact: Abdur Rahman, Organizing Secretary (address above). Enclose two international postal reply coupons.

CHANTIERS D'ÉTUDES MÉDIÉVALES
4, rue du Tonnelet Rouge
67000 Strasbourg
France
Telephone: (33) 88–371720

The sponsor: Since 1964, the association has organized workcamps for young people interested in the study and restoration of monuments and sites dating back to the Middle Ages.

The program: Groups work on excavation sites with archaeologists, historians, architects, and ceramics experts from the Center of Medieval Archaeology in Strasbourg. Participants sign up for 15-day sessions during the summer in Ottrott or Petit-Koenigsbourg.

Requirements: The minimum age is 16 and some knowledge of French is required. Participants under 18 need to have parents' approval.

Living arrangements: Volunteers stay in barracks, houses, or schools.

Finances: Fees are 525 French francs (approximately $100) for participants under 18 and 430 French francs (approximately $80) for participants above the age of 18.

Deadline: June 15.

CHRISTIAN WELFARE AND SOCIAL RELIEF (CWASRO)
39 Soldier Street
P.O. Box 981
Freetown
Sierra Leone
Telephone: (232) 224096

The sponsor: Founded in 1980, CWASRO is a nonprofit relief organization engaged in educational and vocational activities and youth exchange.

The program: CWASRO offers workcamps throughout rural areas in Sierra Leone. Volunteers serve from three weeks to three months during the summer and fall. Services include construction, education, and social work.

Orientation: The volunteer's first week is spent in orientation.

Supervision: Group leaders speak English and make sure that volunteers have clean clothes, food, and lodgings.

Requirements: CWASRO accepts volunteers from 11 to 45 years old.

Living arrangements: Volunteers live in camps, hostels, or local homes.

Finances: The fee is $500 plus $50 for orientation, including room and board.

Deadline: Applications must be received by the end of June.

Contact: Rudolph David Hill, Director (address above).

CLUB DU VIEUX MANOIR
10, rue de la Cossonnerie
75001 Paris
France
Telephone: (33) 1–45088040

The sponsor: The Club is involved in the restoration of historical sites—gardens, fortresses, and churches—throughout France. Founded in 1953, it offers volunteers a chance to work and learn restoration techniques at the same time.

The program: Volunteers participate in restoration projects that usually take place during spring vacation or during the summer. "The volunteer with an inquisitive mind learns something new every day and gains manual experience as he or she receives instruction in archaeology, architecture, handicrafts, and history." Although it is possible to participate for as few as five days, a stay of 15 to 30 days on a site is necessary to gain any kind of familiarity with the kind of work that is being done.

Supervision: Group leaders are responsible for the supervision of the volunteers. Those under the age of 18 may leave the site during their stay only when accompanied by a group leader.

Services for persons with disabilities: The Club requires a certificate of good health and an aptitude for workcamp activities.

Requirements: The minimum age is 13. Applicants must be in good health.

Living arrangements: Accommodations are rustic—shelter is provided during the winter, but when the weather is warm, camps are set up in the open air. Running water is not always available. Participants must bring a sleeping bag and blanket. Meals are prepared by the participants.

Finances: Room and board costs 60 French francs (approximately $12) per day and all travel costs are the responsibility of the participant. Insurance, required upon registration, costs 70 French francs (approximately $14).

Deadline: Fifteen to thirty days before you want to begin.

Contact: Rosalind Guillemin, site director (address above). Enclose a self-addressed envelope and international postal reply coupon.

CIEE INTERNATIONAL WORKCAMPS
205 East 42nd Street
New York, NY 10017
Telephone: (212) 661–1414

The sponsor: CIEE is a member of UNESCO's Coordinating Committee on International Voluntary Service (CCIVS), whose purpose is to promote international cooperation through the exchange of volunteers. As a U.S. cooperator in this international exchange, CIEE coordinates the applications and placements of American youth on projects sponsored by CCIVS members throughout Europe and in several African and Latin American countries.

The program: Workcamps last from two to four weeks and generally involve working on a community service project alongside young people from other parts of the world. While working, volunteers have a chance to learn something about the native culture, practice the language of the country, and interact with their counterparts from other countries. Actual projects vary from country to country. Here are a few examples of some that took place recently: in the French Alps, participants created a nature path in the outskirts of a small village; in Klingber, Germany, a small town on the Baltic Sea, volunteers built a playground for small children; and in Hiddenhausen, Germany, young people collected and repaired tools to send to self-help projects in the Third World.

Supervision: Each workcamp has one or more group leaders who are past participants of workcamps. Group leaders facilitate work and living arrangements; they are not meant to act as chaperones or guardians.

Services for persons with disabilities: Participants with disabilities are placed in workcamps according to their disability and the nature of workcamp's project.

Requirements: Volunteers must be mature and responsible. Age requirements vary depending on the country, but the minimum age is usually 18. Some camps in Germany accept individuals 16 years or older; however, prospective participants should be aware that most individuals will be between 20 and 30 years of age, with some participants over 30. The atmosphere of the camp is one of self-government in which all participants are expected to be responsible for themselves and also to contribute to group life. Volunteers on workcamps in France and Spain should have a working knowledge of the language.

Living arrangements: Accommodations vary, from tents and hostels, to schools and churches.

Finances: There is a $135 application fee. Room and board are provided for the duration of the project. Volunteers are responsible for their own transportation to and from the project site.

Deadline: There is no deadline, but participants are encouraged to apply by the end of April for summer workcamps.

Contact: CIEE, International Voluntary Service Department (address above).

EARTHWATCH
680 Mount Auburn Street
Box 403N
Watertown, MA 02272
Telephone: (800) 776–0188

The sponsor: Earthwatch, a nonprofit organization founded in 1971, recruits members of the public to join research scientists in archaeology, marine biology, animal behavior, ecology, and anthropology projects all over the world. With headquarters in Massachusetts, Earthwatch has field offices in Los Angeles, Oxford, and Melbourne, and volunteer field representatives in 50 cities. In 1992 the organization sponsored 140 expeditions in 50 countries and 27 states.

The program: Two- to three-week expeditions take place year-round—there are more than 400 departure dates. Some samples: in Costa Rica Earthwatch groups conduct continuing research on bottlenose dolphins; in New Zealand participants explore and measure the inner workings of a dormant volcano; in Zimbabwe groups count and observe endangered black rhinos.

Orientation: Participants receive a 60- to 70-page briefing book with background reading, plus field training on site.

Supervision: The supervising scientist and staff work closely with participants; usually there is one staff member for every five participants. "The Principal Investigator is responsible for all aspects of running the expedition team. Students are, however, treated as peers by adults, and respond wonderfully to this experience." Many students participate on Earthwatch expeditions.

Services for persons with disabilities: Earthwatch welcomes disabled applicants and will place them in appropriate projects.

Requirements: The minimum age is 16; if a parent goes along, 14 or 15 years old is acceptable. No special skills are necessary.

Living arrangements: Depending on the program, accommodations might include university dorms, small rented cottages, tents, research stations, or old castles.

Finances: The costs range from $800 to $2,200, with the average about $1,400. This tax-deductible donation to the expedition covers room and board, ground transportation, and equipment. Airfare to the site is not included.

Deadline: No set deadline, but application at least 90 days in advance is recommended.

THE EXPERIMENT IN INTERNATIONAL LIVING

For information on The Experiment in International Living and its work/volunteer program, see the listing for World Learning Inc. in the Homestays section of this book, page 294.

FOUNDATION FOR FIELD RESEARCH (FFR)
P.O. Box 2010
Alpine, CA 91903
Telephone: (619) 445–9264
Fax: (619) 445–1893

The sponsor: Founded in 1982, this nonprofit organization sponsors research expeditions by finding volunteers to assist scientists in the field. The Foundation supports expeditions that need and can make use of nonspecialists' help. Citizens subsidize research expeditions by volunteering their help and labor to a scientist in the field, and by contributing a tax-deductible share of the project's cost.

The program: Four times a year the Foundation publishes *Explorer News,* which describes the projects that need volunteers. Some of the recent projects included *Primate Census in Liberia,* a two-week expedition involving the observation of monkeys in a tropical rain forest in Africa; *Prehistoric People of Pearls* in Grenada, a two-month expedition to excavate a 2,000-year-old prehistoric site; *Quetzal Quest,* a 10-day project to search for nests of the quetzal in Chiapas, Mexico; and *Saving the Caguama,* a one-week project to patrol sea turtle nesting beaches in the Sea of Cortez off Baja California in Mexico. The staff of FFR wants to be sure that participants understand what is involved: "Joining a Foundation expedition is an educational and exciting experience, but we are not a tour company. Once in the field, be prepared to work. If you have always dreamed of being an archaeologist, marine biologist, or naturalist, then this is your big chance. When you join an archaeological excavation, you will actually dig and screen; when you join a marine biological expedition, you will actually dive and collect specimens; when you join the study of an endangered animal, you will actually search for and observe that animal."

Supervision: Each group is headed by a scientist whose research design has been approved by the Foundation. A field manager also accompanies each expedition. The ratio of participants to leaders is between 5 and 15 to 1.

Requirements: Participants must be at least 14 years old. "Volunteers generally have not had previous experience but join to learn by doing, to meet new friends, and to have an adventure."

Living arrangements: These vary with the project. Groups often camp; at times, they stay in dormitories or local pensions.

Finances: Each volunteer is asked to make a tax-deductible contribution as a share of the project's cost. Programs include lodging, meals prepared by a cook, ground transportation, field gear, research equipment, and a preparatory booklet. Some samples: the *Primate Census in Liberia* cost $1,485, and includes bearers who carry your equipment; *Saving the Caguama* costs $725, and includes van transportation from San Diego, California. Some scholarship help is available.

Contact: Tom Banks or Annie Cody (address above).

GENCTUR TOURISM AND TRAVEL AGENCY
Yerebatan Cad. 15/3
Sultanahmet
Istanbul 34410
Turkey

The sponsor: Genctur is a commercial agency founded in 1979 that organizes workcamps, study tours, homestays, group travel, exchanges, and language courses in Turkey.

The program: Genctur sponsors a *Teenage Voluntary Workcamp*. The 1992 program took place in Milas, a small town in the south of Turkey, though destinations vary each year. This program is for ages 15 through 17 and is offered for two weeks in summer. In 1992, work included cleaning the surroundings of a castle, making paths, carrying branches, and collecting stones. The program includes a sight-seeing tour in return for voluntary work. Also offered is *Junior Camp—Active Holiday*, which takes place for two weeks during June and July; in 1992 the site was Erdek, by the Marmara Sea. This program is for ages 11 through 15. The program is much like an American summer camp with language courses (Turkish, French, and German) as well as special activities. Participants also take a one-day excursion-picnic to the national park.

Supervision: Most of the staff are professional teachers, although Genctur also employs sports specialists and activity instructors. There is a ratio of 10 participants to every staff member. Two teachers are native English speakers.

Services for persons with disabilities: Campsites are not always accessible for persons with disabilities.

Requirements: For the voluntary workcamp, participants must be able to do four to five hours of light work per day.

Living arrangements: Participants in the workcamp program stay in boarding-school dormitories. In the junior camp, participants sleep in wooden huts with an average of two to three persons per room.

Finances: A $90 fee for the *Voluntary Workcamp* includes room and full board plus the sight-seeing tour, but does not include airfare to Turkey or ground transportation to the camp. A $310 fee for the *Junior Camp* includes full board, transport once at the camp, activities, and a sight-seeing tour. It does not include airfare to Turkey or ground transportation to the camp.

Deadline: Deadline for the 1992 *Voluntary Workcamp* program was July 1. Contact Genctur for future deadlines. The deadline for the *Junior Camp* program is two weeks before the camp starts.

Contact: Zafer Yilmaz, Workcamps Coordinator.

GIRL SCOUTS OF THE USA

For information on Girl Scouts of the USA and its work/volunteer programs, see its listing in the Organized Tours section of this book, page 207.

INTERLOCKEN

For information on Interlocken and its work/volunteer programs, see its listing in the Organized Tours section of this book, page 208.

INTERNATIONAL EXCHANGE CENTER (IEC)
2 Republic Square
226168 Riga
Latvia
Telephone: (7) 0132–327216

The sponsor: IEC is a nonprofit organization that promotes personal contact between people of Latvia and other countries.

The program: IEC offers two summer programs from June through August: workcamps and children's summer camps. Workcamps take place for the most part on Latvian farms where Latvian high-school students volunteer as part of their curriculum. Children's summer camps, mostly on the Baltic Sea, invite older teenagers to serve as counselors.

Orientation: Orientations are held at the campsite before program begins.

Supervision: There is approximately one group leader for every five to seven participants.

Requirements: The minimum age for workcamps is 15; for camp counselor positions, 17. A basic knowledge of Latvian or Russian is desirable.

Living arrangements: Participants live in cabins or dormitories.

Finances: Camp counselors and workcamp participants pay $95, which includes room and board, as well as pocket money in the local currency.

Deadline: Two months before program starts.

Contact: Edward Geller, Chairman (address above).

ISRAEL ANTIQUITIES AUTHORITY
P.O. Box 586
Jerusalem 91000
Israel
Telephone: (972) 2–292607
Fax: (972) 2–292628

The sponsor: Founded shortly after the establishment of the state of Israel, this government agency oversees all archaeological digs in that country.

The program: Volunteers are needed for archaeological digs throughout Israel. At times they are needed in the Authority's Jerusalem office. The department does not place volunteers; instead, it distributes a listing of possibilities each January. Archaeological excavations take place in Israel throughout the year, but the main season begins in June and continues through September. "Most archaeologists enlist volunteer help on their digs, as volunteers tend to be highly motivated to work, learn, and gain rich experience, although the work itself is usually difficult and tedious." Some recent examples include a month-long dig at Tel Gerisa, a large harbor city on the Yarkon River from the Bronze and Iron Age; Akhziv, a Phoenician cemetery on the coast; and Tel Nizzana, the remains of a large town in the Negev dating from the Hellenistic, Roman, Byzantine, and early Arab period. In addition to the work involved on the digs, most expeditions include the opportunity to attend informal lectures and discussions about the site. The Authority also sponsors day-long digs and guided archaeological tours, which include several days of excavation.

Requirements: Most digs require volunteers to be 18 years old, but some will accept 17-year-olds. "Volunteers should be in good physical condition and able to work long hours in very hot and dry weather." The work includes digging, shoveling, hauling baskets, cleaning pottery shards, and more. The minimum period of participation is one to two weeks.

Living arrangements: Accommodations range from sleeping bags in a field to rooms in a hostel or kibbutz near the site. A fee for room and board is often, but not always, required. Excavations conducted in a city often require the volunteer to find his or her own accommodation.

Finances: Each excavation has its own fee. At times, room and board are provided; some digs provide pocket money, while others require the volunteers to pay their own way. Day-long digs cost $20 per person in groups of 15 people or fewer. Two-week guided archaeological tours cost $450 to $580.

Contact: Applicants should write to the address listed above for the department's listings. Once they have found a site that interests them, they must contact the director of the project itself.

MALTA YOUTH HOSTELS ASSOCIATION (MYHA)
17, Triq Tal-Borg
Pawla PLA 06
Malta
Telephone: (356) 239361

The sponsor: The Malta Youth Hostels Association is a member of Hostelling International.

The program: MYHA runs a workcamp program in which volunteers administer, maintain, and repair youth hostels or work on hostel-related projects throughout Malta. Volunteers work three hours a day, seven days a week.

Requirements: The minimum age is 16.

Living arrangements: Volunteers live in youth hostels.

Finances: Volunteers receive free accommodations and daily breakfast.

Deadline: Three months before the desired starting date. Sessions begin on the 1st and 15th of each month.

Contact: The W.S. Organizer (enclose three international postal reply coupons).

MOBILITY INTERNATIONAL USA (MIUSA)
P.O. Box 3551
Eugene, OR 97403
Telephone: (503) 343-1284 (voice and TDD)

The sponsor: MIUSA is the U.S. branch of Mobility International, a nonprofit organization founded in London in 1973 in order to integrate people with disabilities into international educational exchange programs and travel. Mobility International now has offices in more than 30 countries. (For more detailed information on MIUSA and its publications, see page 28.)

The program: MIUSA's programs include organizing international educational exchange programs, which include disabled and nondisabled people working together in the United States and overseas. MIUSA programs have taken place in Italy, England, Germany, Costa Rica, China, Mexico, and the former Soviet Union. Themes of the exchange vary, but the goals are to increase international understanding through people-to-people contact, and to improve the lives of disabled people around the world by sharing information and strategies for independent living. The exchange experiences last three to four weeks, and usually include a community service component and a stay with a family in the host country. MIUSA also offers an international leadership program.

Supervision: The participant-leader ratio is usually five to one.

Services for persons with disabilities: Persons with and without disabilities are encouraged to apply for all programs. Students who need language interpretation are also accommodated.

Requirements: Applicants should have an interest in disability rights, independent living, and international understanding. Specific requirements vary depending on the program.

Living arrangements: Accommodations vary according to the program, but might include youth hostels, homestay families, tents, or hotels.

Finances: Fees for participation vary according to the program. Some scholarships for persons needing to use attendants or sign language interpreters may be available.

Deadline: Varies depending on the project.

Contact: Susan Sygall, Director.

NORTH AMERICAN FEDERATION OF TEMPLE YOUTH (NFTY)

For information on NFTY and its work/volunteer programs, see its listing in the Organized Tours section of this book, page 211.

NOTHELFERGEMEINSCHAFT DER FREUNDE
Auf der Kornerwiese 5
6000 Frankfurt/Main 1
Germany
Telephone: (49) 69–599557

The sponsor: The name of this organization means "Emergency Volunteers of the Community of Friends." It organizes workcamps in Germany and abroad to promote better understanding among all peoples.

The program: Workcamps are held at Easter and during the summer for three or four weeks. Volunteers from all over the world work in regions hit by catastrophes or in distressed areas. They might help construct a building for the handicapped, the elderly, or other people in need, or counsel people involved in a disaster.

Supervision: Workcamp volunteers are supervised by group leaders, who are former workcamp volunteers and have attended workcamp leader seminars.

Requirements: Minimum age is 16 for junior camps.

Living arrangements: Volunteers live in houses; boys and girls are separated.

Finances: The fee is 70 deutsche marks (approximately $45). Room and board are included.

Deadline: April 30.

Contact: Paul Krahe, President.

NSTS—STUDENT AND YOUTH TRAVEL

For information on NSTS and its work/volunteer programs, see its listing in the Organized Tours section of this book, page 213.

OPERATION CROSSROADS AFRICA
475 Riverside Drive, Suite 242
New York, NY 10115
Telephone: (212) 870–2106

The sponsor: A nonprofit organization, Operation Crossroads Africa has been involved in educational and cultural exchanges in Africa,

North America, and the Caribbean for more than 30 years. Its activities are based on the conviction that "communication between persons of different nationalities, races, religions, and cultures is both necessary and desirable."

The program: Crossroads programs in Africa are limited to individuals age 18 and over; the *Caribbean Workcamp* program is designed for 14- to 18-year-olds. Participants spend six weeks during the summer working alongside their peers on community-defined projects in select Caribbean and Central American countries. The type of work varies from project to project, but usually consists of helping local residents build schools and community centers, or participating in arts and crafts or athletic programs.

Orientation: A one- or two-day orientation held in the New York area just prior to departure covers issues of group dynamics, health, regional history, and culture.

Supervision: There is one leader for every group of 10 students. Leaders are carefully screened adults who have extensive experience working with young people, and are responsible for the safety and welfare of each participant. They manage group funds, coordinate the work project with the local sponsor, and arrange weekend and end-of-summer outings.

Requirements: Participants may be high-school freshmen, sophomores, juniors, or seniors, and they must be 18 or over for the Africa program. No special skills are required other than enthusiasm for Crossroads and its philosophy of cross-cultural learning. Appropriate language ability is helpful for those desiring placement in a French- or Spanish-speaking country.

Living arrangements: The group lives together with the leader in a facility donated by the local community, such as a house, school, or community center.

Finances: The fee of $2,500 covers round-trip airfare from New York, housing, food, orientation, medical insurance, and incidental expenses related to the trip. It does not include personal spending money. Many former participants have raised their fees through fund-raising in their school, religious, or work community. Crossroads will provide prospective participants with fund-raising assistance. Some scholarship aid is available.

Deadline: March 1.

Contact: Director, Africa and Caribbean Overseas Program (address above).

OUTWARD BOUND CITY CHALLENGE
Roscoe House
62 Roscoe Street
Liverpool LI 9DW
England
Telephone: (44) 51–707–0202

The sponsor: This program is part of Outward Bound Trust, a group providing personal development opportunities for young people. It has been operating since 1970.

The program: This is the urban equivalent of Outward Bound. Its purpose is to "give participants a real sense of their own potential, both as an individual through greater awareness of their strengths and weaknesses, and as a member of a group through an increased understanding of other people." To do this, participants work with disadvantaged people in inner-city communities. Each day's work is followed by a review session where "the need to give and receive information at an open and honest level grows as the course progresses." Courses are two weeks long and take place in July and August in Coventry and Liverpool, England.

Requirements: The minimum age is 17.

Living arrangements: Participants stay in small dormitories and help with the preparation of meals.

Finances: The fee ranges from 305 to 564 British pounds (approximately $580 to $1,070), including room and board, special clothing and equipment, insurance, information packets, and transport to and from the nearest British Rail station.

Deadline: One month before course begins.

RAMAPO COLLEGE OF NEW JERSEY

For information on Ramapo College's archaeological dig in Israel, see its listing in the Study Abroad section of this book, page 123.

R.E.M.P. ART.
1, rue des Guillemites
75004 Paris
France
Telephone: (33) 1–42719655
Fax: (33) 1–42717300

The sponsor: The name stands for the Union des Associations de Chantiers de Sauvegarde et d'Animation pour le Réhabilitation et l'Entretien des Monuments et du Patrimoine Artistique (the Union of Skilled Workers for the Restoration and Preservation of Historical Monuments). Its 150 member associations are dedicated to restoring old buildings and monuments all over France.

The program: R.E.M.P. ART. publishes a catalog each year of its members' projects—workcamps that last a weekend, a month, or longer. Projects all involve the restoration of historic buildings, including churches, castles, abbeys, and chapels.

Supervision: Each workcamp has its own leader at the site.

Requirements: For some workcamps, 14- to 17-year-olds are eligible; others require applicants to be 18 or over.

Living arrangements: These vary, but camping is common.

Finances: Applicants pay a fee of approximately $40. The charge for room and board is about $6 to $8 a day.

STUDENT CONSERVATION ASSOCIATION
P.O. Box 550
Charlestown, NH 03603
Telephone: (603) 826–4301

The sponsor: The Student Conservation Association is a national nonprofit organization founded in 1957 that fosters environmental stewardship through volunteer service at national parks and public lands, working to manage and conserve natural resources.

The program: SCA offers a seven-week summer exchange program with the Russian Republic for five American youths. The group travels to Russia and, together with five Russian youths, works for four weeks on service projects in Valdai National Park. Included in this time are opportunities to visit various cultural sites. Then the entire group returns to the United States to work for three weeks in North Cascades National Park in Washington state with the opportunity, upon completion of the projects there, to backpack in the park and travel in the area.

Also offered is the *Conservation Leadership Exchange Program*, designed for U.S. and Mexican youths between the ages of 16 and 18. Under the direction of two adult supervisors, conservation crews of four Mexican and four U.S. participants work together for four weeks to help protect public lands while learning the basics of natural resource management. The program takes place in national parks or forest areas in Mexico and the United States.

Supervision: One or two U.S. supervisors and at least one supervisor from the other country accompany the group. Leaders have language ability, experience working with youth, and experience in the work to be done.

Services for persons with disabilities: "Anyone who can perform the work planned can apply."

Requirements: Participants must be between the ages of 16 and 18, in high school or a recent graduate, with some knowledge of Russian or Spanish preferred. Also, applicants must submit three references: two personal or employment references and one school reference.

Living arrangements: Volunteers usually live in tent camps and prepare their own meals.

Finances: The application fee is $5. Room and board are provided. Participants are responsible for paying for travel to and from the program site and providing personal clothing and equipment. SCA arranges travel to and from Russia and assists with travel to and from Mexico. Financial aid is available to help with in-U.S. travel costs.

Deadline: March 1.

Contact: Wallace Elton, Public Relations Director (address above).

VOLUNTEERS FOR PEACE (VFP)
43 Tiffany Road
Belmont, VT 05730
Telephone: (802) 259–2759

The sponsor: VFP, founded in 1981, coordinates volunteer placement in international workcamps throughout the United States, Europe, North Africa, Central America, and countries of the former Soviet Union.

The program: In its *International Workcamp Directory*, which is available for $10 (deductible from the placement fee), VFP lists workcamps that include reconstructing an open-air museum in Czechoslovakia, enlarging a park in Denmark, and restoring a three-masted ship in Finland. Workcamps take place from July to September, usually for two to three weeks at a time. Write or call for a free copy of VFP's newsletter.

Supervision: All workcamps have leaders who supervise participants. The ratio is usually 12 participants to one leader.

Services for persons with disabilities: VFP places volunteers with disabilities throughout western Europe. Each camp has its own policy regarding acceptance of the disabled.

Requirements: The minimum age for placement is 16.

Living arrangements: Volunteers live together in a variety of communal settings—tents, dorms, houses, and so on.

Finances: The placement fee is $125, which includes room and board for a two- to three-week program.

Deadline: No set deadline, but it is best to apply before May 20 to get first choice of workcamp.

Contact: Peter Coldwell, Director (address above).

WORLD HORIZONS INTERNATIONAL
P.O. Box 662
Bethlehem, CT 06751
Telephone: (203) 266–5874

The sponsor: Founded in 1987, World Horizons is a nonprofit community service organization that sends high-school students to locations throughout the Caribbean, Central America, rural Alaska, Maine, Hawaii, and Western Samoa.

The program: Coed groups of about 10 young people from the United States live and work together with teenagers from the host country from

June through August. This intercultural program combines group projects with student-initiated individual internships in areas of the participant's interests. Group interactions might include a light construction project, such as refurbishing a school, medical clinic, or day-care center, or establishing a day camp for local children. "With each project, whether it be group or individual, the student will engage in an experience of intercultural work, learning, and living that will last well beyond the summer."

Orientation: A one-day orientation is held prior to departure.

Supervision: Group leaders are responsible for the well-being of the students at all times. The ratio of students to leaders is 10 to 1.

Living arrangements: Students live together in a house, dorm, or community building provided by the local host organization.

Requirements: Participants must be 15 to 18 years old and in 9th through 12th grades. Knowledge of Spanish is required for service in Spanish-speaking countries.

Finances: The 1992 fee was $3,150, including airfare from New York, room and board, and all incidental expenses.

Contact: Judy Manning, Executive Director (address above).

OUTDOOR ACTIVITIES

*C*anoe trips in the Canadian wilderness, summer camps in Europe, biking tours in Africa, and scuba diving in the Caribbean are a few of the programs offered by the organizations described in this section. All of the programs are short-term, lasting from a week to an entire summer. Some programs combine an outdoor activity with sight-seeing, leadership training, or language instruction.

ACTIONSAIL/ACTIONDIVE
P.O. Box 5507
Sarasota, FL 34277
Telephone: (813) 924–6789
Fax: (813) 924–6075

The sponsor: Actionsail/Actiondive is a nonprofit organization that has operated sailing and diving adventure programs for teenagers since 1970.

The program: Accredited by American Sailing Association and the Professional Association of Diving Instructors, Actionsail offers sail training aboard 50-foot sailing yachts in the Caribbean and the Mediterranean seas. Courses are offered from mid-June through mid-August.

Supervision: Leaders are certified instructors in sailing and diving, and supervise full-time on yachts. The ratio of students to leaders is four to one.

Requirements: Participants should be between 13 and 18 years old. No experience is necessary.

Living arrangements: Participants live aboard the sailing yachts.

Finances: Program costs vary from $2,240 to $2,760, not including airfare.

Deadline: No set deadline; however, the program usually fills early in May.

Contact: James Stoll, Director (address above).

AMERICAN FRIENDS OF THE COLLÈGE LYCÉE CÉVENOL INTERNATIONAL

For information on American Friends of the Collège Lycée Cévenol International and its outdoor activities programs, see its listing in the Study Abroad section of this book, page 95.

AMERICAN INTERCULTURAL STUDENT EXCHANGE (AISE)

For information on AISE and its outdoor adventure program in Australia, see its listing in the Study Abroad section of this book, page 97.

AMERICAN YOUTH HOSTELS (AYH)
P.O. Box 37613
Department 837
Washington, DC 20013-7613
Telephone: (202) 783–6161

The sponsor: AYH was founded in 1934 and now has more than 100,000 members and 40 local councils throughout the United States. Its purpose is to encourage low-cost travel for young people and adults through a worldwide network of hostels—more than 6,000 in 70 countries, with more than 200 in the United States. This nonprofit organization is a member of CIEE.

The program: AYH sponsors a number of international tours, including some in Europe. Although most people think "bicycle" when they think of AYH, the organization also sponsors hiking, motor, and other trips in addition to bike tours. Possibilities include the *Heart of Europe*, one of AYH's oldest and most popular tours, which involves biking from London to Salzburg to Amsterdam—a total of six countries in 43 days; and *European Spotlight*, which explores central Europe by public transportation, from the countryside to the cities. Trips take place in the summer.

Supervision: There are usually nine tour members to each trip leader. Trip leaders, who have successfully completed AYH's leadership training course, are responsible for the health and well-being of the group, and for making sure the group gets to its nightly accommodations.

Requirements: Trips are offered for all ages, with many designed for youth ages 15 to 18. All trips, even motor trips, are geared to people in good physical condition. AYH membership is required ($10 for ages 17 and younger; $25 for ages 18 to 54).

Living arrangements: Accommodations are usually in Hostelling International hostels. Hostels have separate bed and bath facilities for men and women. Most have kitchens where groups prepare their own meals. A few hostels have cafeterias; all have rooms for relaxing and socializing. Overnight guests are expected to perform a small domestic chore at the hostel. "No two hostels are alike—from a castle in Germany to a sailing ship in Sweden."

Finances: Trips abroad cost from $400 to $3,450. The fee includes overnight accommodations, group-prepared meals, money for a group activities budget, and administration and leadership costs. International airfare is not included. Insurance is the responsibility of the participants, and an additional $50 refundable "emergency" deposit is required.

Deadline: All applications must be accompanied by a $400 deposit, and any balance must be paid 60 days before the trip departure.

Contact: AYH Travel Department (address above). A free catalog describing all trips offered in the United States and abroad will be sent to anyone who requests it.

AQUA VIVA
Carsac
24200 Sarlat
France
Telephone: (33) 53 592109

The sponsor: Aqua Viva is a commercial outdoor adventure club founded in 1969.

The program: Aqua Viva specializes in canoe excursions. Canoers travel down the river Dordogne, "a calm (grade 1) river with occasional small rapids." There is also a *Fantasy Week*, which combines several activities, such as hiking, biking, and canoeing. Both programs involve camping and visiting sites of interest en route.

Orientation: A one-day orientation covers basic canoeing skills.

Supervision: Group leaders are certified canoeing instructors and are required to know at least three languages.

Requirements: Participants must be at least 16 years old and good swimmers. There is no upper age limit.

Living arrangements: Participants sleep at campsites where Aqua Viva has permanent cooking facilities.

Finances: Programs cost between 1,500 and 1,750 French francs (approximately $300 to $350).

THE BIKING EXPEDITION
10 Maple Street
P.O. Box 547
Henniker, NH 03242
Telephone: (603) 428–7500

The sponsor: The Biking Expedition is a commercial organization that has planned summer bicycle trips for young people since 1973.

The program: The Biking Expedition offers trips to Canada, England, France, Germany, Switzerland, and Scotland from the middle of June until the end of August. Each trip is open to two and occasionally three school-year levels to maintain a high level of group compatibility. Trips are also rated according to skill level: introductory, moderate, and challenging.

Orientation: Participants spend two days in Henniker checking out equipment, learning safety fundamentals, packing gear, and reviewing the itinerary.

Supervision: Leaders travel with the group and are responsible for everything along the way, including supervising the students in buying and preparing meals and making travel plans. The ratio of participants to leaders is usually six to one.

Requirements: Applicants must be 13 to 18 years of age. They must be "capable of keeping up physically and being a contributing member of a small group."

Living arrangements: Accommodations are a combination of camping and hosteling.

Finances: Fees range from $2,455 to $4,526, including food, lodging, airfare, and all program features.

Deadline: April 30.

BLYTH AND COMPANY

For information on Blyth and Company and its outdoor activities programs, see its listing in the Organized Tours section of this book, page 201.

BRITISH SCHOOLS EXPLORING SOCIETY
Royal Geographical Society
1 Kensington Gore
London SW7 2AR
England
Telephone: (44) 71–584–0710
Fax: (44) 71–581–9918

The sponsor: The British Schools Exploring Society is an educational charity that provides students with the opportunity to take part in expeditions to "remote and harsh environments." The Society was founded in 1932 by the late Surgeon Commander G. Murray Levick, a member of Scott's 1910 Antarctic expedition.

The program: The Society offers two basic programs; a six-week expedition during summer vacation and a three- to four-month "gap" program designed for those who plan to take time off between secondary school and the next step in their education. Expeditions travel to arctic and subarctic regions of Greenland, Iceland, Norway, North America, and Russia. Past expeditions have also traveled to Africa, India, and the South Pacific. Participants contribute to scientific fieldwork, such as studying glacial and volcanic activity. While these programs are designed for UK school students, limited numbers of overseas "guests" are accepted.

Orientation: Participants receive a handbook and have a two-day residential briefing in the United Kingdom.

Supervision: Expeditions are led by outdoors skills experts and scientists. There are usually six participants to each leader.

Services for persons with disabilities: Persons with disabilities are welcome as long as they have full walking mobility.

Requirements: The minimum age is 16 and the maximum is 20. Applicants must be enrolled in a full-time educational program. An interview is a required part of the application process. Some knowledge of camping and hill-walking is important. Also important are enthusiasm, determination, common sense, the ability to work as a member of a team, physical fitness, and a sense of humor. "As all expeditions need a broad cross section of abilities among their members, there will be places for the academically inclined and the artistic as well as those with an adventurous and enquiring nature."

Living arrangements: Participants live in three-person tents.

Finances: Participants are expected to raise funds as a contribution to the expedition, and the Society provides assistance in this effort. Contributions range from 1,550 British pounds to 2,950 British pounds (approximately $2,950 to $5,600), depending on the program. Because the society is a charitable organization, the contribution is less than the real cost of each expedition. Assistance is given to those who cannot meet the suggested contribution: "No one who has shown the appropriate commitment and effort to raise the contribution, but were unable to meet it in full, has been denied a place." The contribution covers insurance, travel (from the United Kingdom), food and group equipment, but not personal clothing and equipment.

Deadline: For standard expeditions, October 31; for "gap year" programs, one year before departure date.

Contact: Peter F. Steer, Executive Director (address above).

BUTTERFIELD AND ROBINSON

For information on Butterfield and Robinson and its outdoor activities programs, see its listing in the Organized Tours section of this book, page 202.

CAMP AROWHON
72 Lyndhurst Avenue
Toronto, Ontario M5R 227
Canada
Telephone: (416) 975–9060

The sponsor: This coed camp has been operating for more than 50 years; it is accredited by the American Camping Association and the Ontario Camping Association.

The program: The camp is located in Algonquin Park in Ontario. The season runs from June 29 to August 23; campers sign up for four to eight weeks. Up to 100 boys and 100 girls attend the camp each session. Campers come from the United States, Canada, and Europe. "We have strived to build an atmosphere of holiday fun on a foundation of mutual respect and to foster a desire to achieve skills in camp activities. We believe that personal accomplishment—a striving for excellence—brings a feeling of self-worth that is the root value of a summer camp experience." Camp Arowhon also has a Counsellor in Training (CIT) program for campers 16 years old.

Supervision: There is one counselor for every three campers.

Requirements: Campers must be 7 to 16 years old.

Living arrangements: Campers live in cabins spread along the shore of Teepee Lake, with six campers and two counselors to a cabin. All cabins have bathrooms.

Finances: An eight-week session costs 3,450 Canadian dollars (approximately $2,900), one month is 2,200 Canadian dollars (approximately $1,850). CIT fees are 2,650 Canadian dollars and 2,090 Canadian dollars, respectively.

Deadline: No set deadline; however, the fees rise by 200 Canadian dollars for applications filed after March 15.

Contact: Joanne Kates, Director at winter address above.

CAMP NORWAY
Sons of Norway International
1455 West Lake Street
Minneapolis, MN 55408
Telephone: (612) 827–3611

The sponsor: Camp Norway is sponsored by Sons of Norway International, a nonprofit organization dedicated to preserving Norwegian heritage.

The program: Camp Norway offers a program of Norwegian language courses, discussions on cultural and social issues, field trips such as hiking or a picnic at a *seter* (mountain farm), and other sports and cultural activities. The camp takes place from June 30 to July 30 in Sandane with an optional Bergen-to-Oslo trip. Four semester credits are offered in conjunction with Augsburg College. High-school credit can also be earned.

Supervision: The ratio of students to teachers is seven to one.

Requirements: The minimum age for participants is 16. Students must have a B average or better.

Living arrangements: Students live in bungalows.

Finances: The fee for Sons of Norway members is $1,870; for non-members, $1,920. Fees include travel from Oslo to Sandane, one over-night stay en route, full room and board, instruction, all field trips, and activities. Scholarships are available through the Sons of Norway.

Deadline: Scholarship applications must be received by March 1; application to Camp Norway should be made prior to applying for scholarships. The application deadline is June 15.

CENTRALE DES AUBERGES DE JEUNESSE LUXEMBOURGEOISES
18, place d'Armes
Boite Postale 374
L-2013 Luxembourg
Telephone: (352) 225588
Fax: (352) 463987

The sponsor: This nonprofit organization is the youth hostel association of Luxembourg and is affiliated with the Hostelling International. It has been in operation since 1934 and is also a member of the International Student Travel Confederation (ISTC).

The program: The Luxembourg hostel association offers the following do-it-yourself tours:

- *Cycling Tour of Luxembourg:* This tour, which provides accommodations and full board in youth hostels for seven nights, a rented bicycle, a topographical map of the country, a handbook, and a tourist guidebook, starts any day of the week from March 1 to October 31.

- *Canoeing as You Please:* This program begins at the youth hostel in Lultzhausen, a village of five houses on the Lake of the Upper Sure, an artificial water basin 20 kilometers long in the heart of the Ardennes. All motorized boats are banned from the lake.
- *Individual Hiking Tour:* This tour begins in Luxembourg City and provides seven nights in a hostel, full board, a map, a handbook, and a guidebook. Hikers need sturdy shoes and all-weather clothes.
- *International Hiking Tour:* 15- to 30-kilometer walks from one youth hostel to another include visits to tourist and cultural attractions.

Requirements: All participants must have a youth hostel card and be at least 16 years old.

Living arrangements: All accommodations are in youth hostels.

Finances: Fees range from 5,350 Luxembourg francs (approximately $170) to 8,050 Luxembourg francs (approximately $260).

Deadline: Usually two weeks before program begins.

CHILDREN'S INTERNATIONAL SUMMER VILLAGES (CISV)
MEA House, Ellison Place
Newcastle-upon-Tyne NE1 8XS
England
Telephone: (44) 91–2324998

The sponsor: CISV is a nonprofit organization founded in 1946 by Dr. Doris Allen, a psychologist at the University of Cincinnati who believed that youths from different nations could use the experience of living together to help create a peaceful world. In 1951 CISV had 55 participants from 9 countries; by 1991 it had involved 88,882 participants from 93 countries.

The program: CISV offers four program possibilities:

- *The Village Program* is a four-week international summer camp in which delegations of two boys and two girls (all 11 years old) from 12 countries participate with adult leaders and six junior counsellors in a multilanguage camp that combines traditional camp activities with cross-cultural communication and cooperative living.

- *The Interchange Program* is a family-centered exchange between two CISV chapters. A delegation of five boys and girls plus an adult reciprocally host partners from another country for two to four weeks; a short multinational camp stay is usually included.
- *Seminar Camps* are three-week programs conducted for 30 young people 17 to 18 years of age by an international staff of five adults, with a focus on fostering peace, international relations, and cooperative living.
- *Associated Organization Exchanges* involve the reciprocal exchange of delegations with Eastern European Associated Organizations for youth 12 to 15 years old (plus adult leaders).

Supervision: Adults traveling with student delegations are responsible for supervision of participants en route to the CISV activity, during the program, and returning home. They are joined by CISV staff.

Services for persons with disabilities: CISV accepts candidates with disabilities and tries to locate barrier-free facilities; but this is difficult in many countries that have no legal obligation to upgrade facilities to accommodate the disabled.

Requirements: The Village Program is for 11-year-olds; the Interchange and Associated Exchanges are for students 12 to 15 years old; and the Seminar is for 17- and 18-year-olds. Tolerance and a genuine interest in peace and global cooperation are important to CISV participation.

Living arrangements: The three camp programs involve communal living in a boarding school or camp setting. Interchange participants live with host families.

Finances: An administrative fee of approximately $190 is charged for the Village, Interchange, and Associated Organization Exchange Programs; a fee of 140 British pounds (approximately $266) for the Seminar Camp includes room and board.

Deadline: January 15.

Contact: CISV USA, c/o Sally Stein, Executive Director, 1202 Peters Avenue, Troy, OH 45373; (513) 335-4640.

GENCTUR TOURISM AND TRAVEL AGENCY

For information on Genctur and its outdoor activities programs, see its listing in the Work/Volunteer section of this book, page 232.

GORDONSTOUN INTERNATIONAL SUMMER SCHOOL

For information on Gordonstoun International Summer School and its outdoor activities programs, see its listing in the Study Abroad section of this book, page 111.

GREEN TOURS
DVL Rejser
Kultorvet 7
DK-1175 Copenhagen K
Denmark
Telephone: (45) 31–33132727

The sponsor: Green Tours is an independent nonprofit agency within the Dansk Vandrelaug, the Danish member of Hostelling International. Since 1972, Green Tours has specialized in outdoor adventure tours in the Nordic countries.

The program: Green Tours offers a range of activity holidays that include hut-based hiking holidays in Denmark, the Lapland mountains, and the Faeroe Islands; bicycling tours in Denmark, camping tours and mountain and glacier walking in Greenland; and canoeing tours among Greenland's seals and icebergs. Green Tours also arranges special tours for groups. Tours are offered June through September.

Supervision: Tours usually have a maximum of 16 persons.

Services for persons with disabilities: Persons with disabilities are welcome to participate.

Requirements: Each holiday is graded so that participants can choose the one most suited to their fitness level.

Living arrangements: Participants camp or stay in mountain huts, youth hostels, or hotels.

Finances: Contact the organization for current costs.

Deadline: Participants must book at least two months in advance.

INTERLOCKEN

For information on Interlocken and its outdoor activities programs, see its listing in the Organized Tours section of this book, page 208.

INTERNATIONAL BICYCLE FUND
4887 Columbia Drive South
Seattle, WA 98108-1919
Telephone: (206) 628–9314

The sponsor: The International Bicycle Fund, a nonprofit organization, was founded in 1984 by David Mozer, a former Peace Corps volunteer in Liberia. Mozer is an African studies specialist and an avid cyclist.

The program: Bicycle Africa offers the adventurous and curious a chance to experience the diverse cultures of Africa. Participants need not be experienced long-distance cyclists, since the cycling level is "moderate." Bicycle Africa has tours from 15 to 30 days in west, central, southern, and east Africa. Tours include the following:

- *West Africa People to People:* "The tropical zone of West Africa provides a lush setting for meeting a fascinating people: some are traditional, some are 'modern' and many seem to be caught in between." On this program, participants have the opportunity to meet traditional villagers, chiefs, government officials, and missionaries. Itineraries vary among Côte d'Ivoire, Ghana, Togo, Benin, Senegal, Gambia, Mali, and Burkina Faso.
- *East Africa—From Anthropology to Zoology:* "East Africa provides visitors with a rich mix of geological wonders, colorful indigenous tribes, renowned wildlife, tantalizing environmental diversity, motivated rural economic development, modern urban centers, and specimens of the oldest known human fossils." Participants bicycle across steppes and scenic plateaus past lakes, waterfalls, and snowcapped mountains; in the game parks, vans are used for transportation.
- *Cameroon—Country of Contrast:* "One of the world's best kept secrets is the diversity, beauty, and friendliness of the Cameroons." The program itinerary skirts the coast, passes the base of 14,000-foot Mount Cameroon, climbs through mountains and verdant highlands, crosses waterless plains, and ends amid the geological wonders and wildlife areas of the north.
- *Zimbabwe Sojourn.* In addition to its political history, Zimbabwe is noteworthy for its environmental awareness, land reform, ma-

terial and musical culture, and its 2,000-year-old wall paintings of the hunter-gatherer San people. The program takes participants to Victoria Falls, on raft trips on the Zambezi River, on bike rides among the kopjes, to rock art and stone sculptures, the Great Zimbabwe Ruins, wildlife, museums, and more.

Supervision: Each tour group (usually 10 people or fewer) is accompanied by a guide who must have extensive knowledge of the program country, firsthand knowledge of the route to be traveled, and bicycle and leadership skills. Participants should be mature and independent as they are responsible for themselves much of the time.

Services for persons with disabilities: Bicycle Africa provides motor transportation at the participant's expense. Participants should be able to travel independently.

Requirements: No minimum age. Applicants should be healthy and in good physical condition.

Living arrangements: Accommodations include hotels, guesthouses, hostels, and homestays.

Finances: The program fees range from $900 to $1,290 and include room and board (two meals a day). International airfare is not included.

Deadline: Rolling admissions.

Contact: David Mozer, Director (address above).

**INTERNATIONAL SUMMER CAMP MONTANA
   SWITZERLAND**
P.O. Box 218
Armonk, NY 10504
Telephone: (914) 273–5850

The sponsor: This organization is a summer camp for boys and girls of all nationalities that combines American-style camping with "European traditions in the development of physical and intellectual achievement." It has been in existence since 1961 and is located in the heart of the Alps, in the French-speaking part of Switzerland.

The program: Campers participate in water sports, riding, tennis, summer skiing, ice skating, trailcraft, basketball, and crafts, and also have the opportunity to study French or German. Excursions to a number of picturesque spots in Switzerland are included, along with day and overnight hikes to neighboring mountain areas.

Supervision: The ratio of campers to counselors is three to one.

Requirements: Minimum age is 8, maximum is 17.

Living arrangements: Campers live in an enormous stone building; many of the rooms have balconies.

Finances: An all-inclusive program that includes transportation from New York and a three-week stay at the camp costs $3,460.

Deadline: Early application is suggested.

Contact: R. F. Gilbert, Director (address above).

INTERNATIONAL SUMMER CAMP VERBIER
Incoming Travel Service
Case Postale 1102
1001 Lausanne
Switzerland
Telephone: (41) 21–265675
Fax: (41) 21–268414

The sponsor: This international summer camp is organized by Incoming Travel Service, a Swiss travel agency established in 1988.

The program: The summer camp is held in Verbier, a ski resort situated 130 kilometers from Geneva at an altitude of 1,500 meters. The camp is divided into two sections, one for 7- to 12-year-olds and another for 13- to 18-year-olds. Campers participate in scheduled activities such as sports, language classes, and excursions.

Supervision: There is one group leader for every five participants.

Services for persons with disabilities: Participants with minor disabilities are accepted.

Requirements: The minimum age is 7, maximum is 18.

Living arrangements: Younger participants live in a lodge house. Older participants live in nearby hotels, three to five per room.

Finances: A two-week session costs 2,200 Swiss francs (approximately $1,650), including room and board, sports, language courses, and all activities.

INTERNATIONAL SUMMER INSTITUTE

For information on International Summer Institute and its outdoor activities programs, see its listing in the Study Abroad section of this book, page 115.

JUGI TOURS
Neufeldstrasse 9
CH-3012 Berne
Switzerland

The sponsor: Jugi Tours is the travel division of the Swiss Youth Hostel Federation.

The program: From late June to mid-October, Jugi Tours offers a number of walking, mountaineering, and cycling tours in and around Swiss valleys and mountains. Participants spend one to two weeks with "an international group of young people in a friendly and relaxed atmosphere." The programs include the following:

- *Rambling Weeks:* The ramblers are based at a youth hostel with a picturesque setting, such as Zermatt or Grindelwald. Group leaders arrange half- and full-day walks according to the interests and physical condition of participants. According to the sponsor, "Zermatt offers a great variety of beautiful walking tours at the foot of the Matterhorn. Even today the village has kept its traditional character with its wooden chalets and romantic lanes."
- *Mountaineering Courses:* These courses are offered at beginning and advanced levels in several locations in the Swiss Alps. Experienced Swiss mountain guides introduce participants to rock climbing, ice and glacier techniques, and rope handling.
- *Cycling Tours:* A two-week bicycle tour through Central Switzerland and a weekly tour from Basel to Lausanne are designed for young people who prefer a more easygoing pace.

Supervision: Group leaders are selected by Jugi Tours staff and must be experienced hikers. Most speak three or more languages. There is approximately one group leader for every 20 participants. Leaders are not expected to chaperon the young people, but they lead the tours, accept the group's suggestions, and work to provide "an unforgettable vacation" for the participants.

Services for persons with disabilities: Jugi Tours can accommodate some disabilities.

Requirements: Minimum age is 16. Knowledge of German is helpful, since that is the "official" language of the tours; most leaders also speak English.

Living arrangements: Participants stay in youth hostels with dormitory-style rooms.

Finances: Most programs last for seven days and cost from 275 to 770 Swiss francs (approximately $200 to $575). Youth hostel accommodations, breakfast and dinner, and local transportation to program sites are included.

Deadline: No set deadline, but early booking is encouraged.

Contact: Ursula Muhlemann (address above).

LOCH INSH WATERSPORTS AND SKIING CENTRE
Insh Hall, Kincraig
Inverness-shire PH21 1NU
Scotland
Telephone: (44) 540–651–272
Fax: (44) 540–651–208

The sponsor: Loch Insh Watersports and Skiing Centre is a recreational holiday center in northern Scotland that has offered watersport and skiing programs since 1969.

The program: Visitors to this holiday center can participate in a number of summer sports programs including windsurfing, cycling, sailing, canoeing; during the winter, snow skiing is offered. Most programs run for two, five, or seven days and include instruction. For those who want to try their hand at a variety of different activities, the *Sport-a-Day* program offers five sports in one week. Evening activities at Insh Hall include barbecues, swimming, ski films, and Scottish dancing.

Supervision: Resident staff are available at the center in case of emergency. Sports programs are run under the supervision of instructors.

Services for persons with disabilities: The chalet is equipped for disabled residents.

Requirements: The minimum age is 12 for unaccompanied children.

Living arrangements: Participants share rooms in suites in Insh Hall, a 19th-century building that has been modernized for the holiday center. Facilities include a TV lounge, sauna, minigym, pool table, table tennis, and dart boards.

Finances: Course fees range from 85 to 222 British pounds (approximately $160 to $420). Meals are included.

Deadline: One month prior to course.

Contact: Clive Freshwater, Director (address above).

NATIONAL OUTDOOR LEADERSHIP SCHOOL (NOLS)
288 Main Street, Box AA
Lander, WY 82520
Telephone: (307) 332–6973

The sponsor: Founded in 1965, the National Outdoor Leadership School (NOLS) operates as a nonprofit licensed private school and offers college credit through the University of Utah.

The program: NOLS courses are educational wilderness expeditions that include up to 20 people and generally last from two to five weeks; a semester course includes a series of expeditions spanning as many as 14 weeks. "The NOLS program is designed to teach you to be safe, competent, and comfortable in the wilderness. Our objective is to give you the skills to enjoy and conserve the wilderness so that by the end of the course you can lead groups of family or friends on a rewarding and safe wilderness expedition." Many NOLS programs take place in the United States (Alaska, Washington, and Wyoming), but some are international—the *Semester in Kenya*, the *Semester in Patagonia*, short-term courses, and a spring and fall semester in Baja California, Mexico.

The 65-day *Semester in Kenya* includes a three-week mountaineering expedition on Mount Kenya, backpacking through the Nguruman Escarpment and the Loita Hills, exploration of the Great Rift Valley, safari, and sailing on the Indian Ocean. Passing through various ecological habitats, from the veldt and rock and snow to coral reefs, participants study biology, geology, and ecology. "This is a tough expedition. Your pack will weigh 60 pounds, sometimes 70. On Mount Kenya, it often rains or snows. While you're backpacking through Masai country, it may be 90 degrees in the shade, if you can find any. Vehicles tend to break down in remote places, and you may have to push them out of the mud."

The 75-day *Semester in Patagonia* combines mountaineering, kayaking, and hiking. The *Semester in Patagonia* sometimes includes rock-climbing or other activities as well. "Because this is NOLS's newest course, the exact format is being adjusted to include the widest variety of outdoor opportunities the time can allow. Flexibility in our schedule and in our activities gives us the best ability to explore and learn."

In Baja, the semester courses include kayaking, sailing, natural history, technical climbing, fishing, skin diving, and Mexican culture. The three-week courses involve sea kayaking and sailing expeditions along the Baja California coastline.

Supervision: NOLS instructors have completed an intensive five-week training course and either hold advanced first-aid cards or are registered emergency medical technicians. They are responsible for participants 24 hours a day, though students are taught how to take care of themselves.

Services for persons with disabilities: A disability may interfere with an individual's ability to take part in a particular program safely. Call the NOLS Admissions Office for further details.

Requirements: The minimum age is 17 for the semester courses and mountaineering courses, 16 for wilderness hiking courses. Final acceptance of all students is contingent upon NOLS approval of a medical review.

Living arrangements: NOLS participants camp, sometimes under difficult conditions. All courses are wilderness expeditions.

Finances: The semesters in Kenya and Patagonia cost $6,750; the Baja semester costs $6,300; the short-term Baja course costs $1,900. Tuition does not include equipment, optional college credit, or travel to and from the starting point of the course. Participants must make their own travel arrangements. Scholarships are available based on need.

Deadline: No specific deadline, but the semester courses often fill six months prior to the starting date, and summer courses can fill four months prior.

Contact: Admissions Office (address above).

OUTWARD BOUND
Chestnut Field
Regent Place
Rugby Warwickshire CV21 2PJ
England
Telephone: (44) 788–560423
Fax: (44) 788–541069

The sponsor: Since 1942, Outward Bound has conducted personal development courses for people of all ages. These provide an opportunity for people to "learn about their attitudes, their potential, and their relationships with each other." There are five Outward Bound schools in the United Kingdom.

The program: The goal of the Outward Bound movement is to offer participants an opportunity for personal growth and self-discovery through a series of courses offered year-round. The basic three-week course is given at all of the U.K. centers. In the first week, participants learn basic techniques of navigation, search and rescue, rock climbing, canoeing, and expedition planning. The climax of the course is an extended expedition of three to four days as a virtually self-sufficient unit. More extensive expeditions take place in Scotland, Wales, and the Lake District. Examples include trekking through the mountains of Snowdownia, canoeing through the Scottish lochs, and sailing around the islands off Scotland's coastline.

Supervision: According to Outward Bound, leaders are "possibly some of the most experienced mountaineers and sailors in the U.K." There is at least one leader for every 10 participants.

Services for persons with disabilities: Outward Bound accepts persons with disabilities (disabilities accommodated in the past include blindness, Down's syndrome, cerebral palsy, and Tourette's syndrome). Special programs for persons with disabilities are also available.

Requirements: Outward Bound programs are generally available to anyone age 14 and over. A special preliminary week-long program is held for 10- to 13-year-olds. There is no fitness standard—"all Outward Bound asks is that you are prepared to have a go."

Living arrangements: Participants stay in dorms, except when camping.

Finances: Course costs range from 199 to 525 British pounds (approximately $380 to $1,000), depending on location and length of program. The fee includes room and board, instruction, and equipment.

Deadline: No set deadline.

Contact: Contact the address above for a course catalog, then contact the appropriate center.

PORTUGUESE YOUTH HOSTEL ASSOCIATION

For information on the Portuguese Youth Hostel Association and its outdoor activities programs, see its listing in the Organized Tours section of this book, page 215.

PUTNEY STUDENT TRAVEL

For information on Putney Student Travel and its outdoor activities programs, see its listing in the Organized Tours section of this book, page 216.

RHIWIAU RIDING CENTRE
Llanfairfechan
Gwynedd LL330 EH
Wales
Telephone: (44) 248–680094

The sponsor: Rhiwiau is a family-owned horseback riding center where "we have a relaxed and informal atmosphere and try to make your holiday fun, exciting, and instructive."

The program: The Centre accommodates 25 people at a time. The program includes instruction in jumping, two- and three-hour rides through the woods, and training in stable management. Guests can expect to do 18 to 20 hours of riding per week. Minibus trips, swimming, or visits to the Anglesey Sea Zoo can be arranged for nonriding time. Programs begin every Saturday throughout the year.

Supervision: Family and staff members supervise guests. Students under 18 are not allowed out at night without supervision.

Services for persons with disabilities: Minor physical and mental disabilities can be accommodated. Facilities are not wheelchair-accessible.

Living arrangements: Accommodations are "motel-style." Mrs. Hill, the owner, prepares the meals.

Finances: The fee for young people under 16 is 185 British pounds ($350); over 16, 205 British pounds ($390). There is a 10-percent reduction for groups of 10 or more. Prices include room and board, riding, evening activities, and local field trips. Insurance is not included.

SAIL CARIBBEAN
79-B Church Street
Northport, NY 11768
Telephone: (516) 754–2202

The sponsor: Sail Caribbean, in operation since 1979, specializes in sailing programs for young people. As a training facility for the American Sailing Association, it also offers participants national certification in sailing.

The program: Sail Caribbean sails a fleet of chartered yachts through the Virgin and Leeward Islands for two to six weeks in the summer. The goal of the program is learning to sail, and instruction is given throughout the trip. The program is based on cooperative living in a coed environment. Each group, under the guidance of a skipper, is responsible for the operation of the yacht, its cleaning and maintenance, and the daily preparation of meals. Full scuba certification is also available, along with instruction in marine biology and oceanography.

- *Virgin Islands Program:* Participants sail around the more than 50 islands and cays of the U.S. Virgin Islands. Besides learning to sail, windsurf, snorkel, and waterski, crew members attend a Fourth of July celebration in St. John featuring steel bands and local foods, take a Land Rover trip along the mountain roads of Tortola, and visit Bluebeard's Castle overlooking the waterfront of St. Thomas. This program includes three to four hours of sailing per day and is appropriate for the novice sailor.

- *The Leeward Islands Programs:* These excursions focus on a more diverse group of larger islands. The emphasis is on ocean sailing and navigation. Participants certified in scuba diving are able to take scheduled trips to deeper waters.

Supervision: Group leaders must have extensive sailing and supervisory experience. They are responsible for the operation of the yacht, sailing instruction, and coordinating the activities and living arrangements of the crew. There is one instructor for every four participants.

Requirements: Participants must be between 13 and 19 years old, seventh graders through high-school seniors. No prior sailing experience is required.

Living arrangements: Participants live on 50-foot yachts, 10 per boat.

Finances: Program fees range from $1,500 to $5,500 and include accommodations, full board, equipment rentals, and instruction.

Deadline: Spring.

Contact: Michael Liese, Owner/Director (address above).

SCOTTISH YOUTH HOSTELS ASSOCIATION

For information on the Scottish Youth Hostels Association and its outdoor activities programs, see its listing in the Organized Tours section of this book, page 217.

SEA QUEST EXPEDITIONS/ZOETIC RESEARCH
P.O. Box 2424
Friday Harbor, WA 98250
Telephone: (206) 378–5767

The sponsor: Sea Quest Expeditions is a nonprofit organization founded in 1989 that specializes in outdoor environmental education and scientific research, focusing on sea kayak travel and whale research.

The program: Trips are from five to seven days and are offered in February, March, and April.

Supervision: All leaders have a comprehensive knowledge of natural history and outdoor education experience. Each trip is accompanied by a field biologist. The ratio of participants to leaders is usually six to one.

Services for persons with disabilities: To be eligible for the program, persons with disabilities must be able to travel by sea kayak or boat.

Requirements: Participants must be at least 16 years of age (unless accompanied by an adult or teacher) and able to paddle a sea kayak or travel by boat in open water.

Living arrangements: Participants stay in tents.

Finances: The cost of the trip is $699, which includes all gear, food, and guides but does not include airfare to and from site. Participants must supply their own sleeping bag, clothes, and personal items.

Deadline: Reservations can be made with a 50-percent deposit; however, the full amount is due not less than 30 days before the trip departs.

Contact: Mark Lewis, Executive Director (address above).

SÉJOURS INTERNATIONAUX LINGUISTIQUES ET CULTURELS

For information on Séjours Internationaux Linguistiques et Culturels and its outdoor activity programs, see its listing in the Homestays section of this book, page 292.

SKI CLUB OF GREAT BRITAIN
118 Eaton Square
London SW1 9AF
England
Telephone: (44) 71–245–1033

The sponsor: Founded in 1903, Ski Club of Great Britain is the world's largest club for recreational skiers.

The program: Ski Club of Great Britain organizes skiing parties to Austria, France, Italy, Switzerland and Canada. Skiing is organized by age group and skill level and always takes place with an instructor. Technique improvement is encouraged in all groups.

Supervision: The ratio of skiers to leaders is 8 or 12 to one. Each skiing party is closely supervised.

Services for persons with disabilities: Special programs for skiers with disabilities are available.

Requirements: Participants must be at least 11 years old.

Living arrangements: Participants live in half-board hotels, whenever possible with private facilities.

Finances: Costs are around 625 British pounds (approximately $1,190) and include accommodations (half-board), travel between London and program site, and compulsory insurance. Ski and boot rental is approximately 50 British pounds extra.

Deadline: A nonrefundable deposit of 50 British pounds per person is required for booking. Participants who book within 12 weeks of the departure date must include payment for the total cost of the trip with the booking form.

STICHTING NEDERLANDSE JEUGDHERBERG CENTRALE (NJHC)
Prof Tulpplein 4
1018 GX Amsterdam
The Netherlands
Telephone: (31) 20–5513155

The sponsor: This national youth hostel association operates 41 youth hostels throughout the Netherlands and a travel agency, Future Line Travel, that caters to young people and budget travelers.

The program: NJHC offers several programs for active holidays, including bike tours through the Netherlands with stays at youth hostels and watersport programs, with or without instruction.

Supervision: Participants in all watersports and instruction programs are supervised during their stay. Other holiday packages do not offer special supervision. All NJHC youth hostels do, however, have a trained managing staff.

Services for persons with disabilities: Several NJHC youth hostels offer special accommodations for disabled persons.

Requirements: Staying at Dutch youth hostels requires a valid Hostelling International membership. (See page 63.)

Living arrangements: Students stay at Dutch hostels.

Finances: Contact the organization for current costs.

Deadline: Bookings are accepted from March to October, but full payment must be received four weeks before the trip is scheduled to begin.

Contact: Information Service (address above).

STRACOMER RIDING CENTRE
Bundoran, County Donegal
Ireland
Telephone: (353) 72–41685
Fax: (353) 72–41002

The sponsor: Stracomer is situated on the edge of six miles of beach and 600 acres of sand dunes off the Atlantic Ocean. The Centre is approved by the British Horse Society.

The program: The Centre specializes in riding lessons for the beginning to advanced rider. Courses are taught year-round.

Supervision: There is one instructor for every seven students. Staff members (including instructors) supervise students while at the Centre.

Services for persons with disabilities: Disabled persons are welcome to apply. Staff is qualified to handle most physical disabilities.

Requirements: Participants should be between the ages of 10 and 18.

Living arrangements: Students stay in owner's home at the school or other homes within the area.

Finances: Write to the Centre for current costs.

Contact: Terry Fergus-Browne, Owner-Director (address above).

STUDENT HOSTELING PROGRAM (SHP)
Ashfield Road
Conway, MA 01341
Telephone: (413) 369–4275 or (800) 343–6132

The sponsor: SHP has offered bicycling trips to teenagers for 20 years.

The program: Bicycle trips are available in Austria, Canada, Denmark, Eastern Europe, England, France, Holland, Hungary, Ireland, Italy, Spain, Switzerland, and countries of the former Soviet Union. They range in length from 2 to 10 weeks and vary in difficulty from easy to challenging. An example of one of SHP's European trips is a 25-day tour of England that involves two weeks of travel by train and bus to see some of England's major sights and two weeks of cycling in the English countryside.

Orientation: At at two-day orientation in Conway, participants get to know their group members and their leaders and work out any "bugs" in their bicycles.

Supervision: Each group of 8 to 11 participants has a senior and an assistant leader. Senior leaders must be at least 21 years old and have had "formidable experience with teenagers."

Services for persons with disabilities: SHP accepts any disability that does not impair participants' ability to cycle in a safe manner.

Requirements: Students ages 12 to 18 are eligible. "Our trips demand self-discipline and a reasonable level of maturity. You will be expected to respect the rights and lifestyles of other people you meet during the trip. You'll be expected to do your share of work and day-to-day chores."

Living arrangements: Participants stay in campgrounds, youth and student hostels, inns, bed-and-breakfasts, dorms, pensions, and occasionally a hotel or motel.

Finances: Program costs range from $650 for an 8-day tour of Vermont to $3,500 for a 57-day trip from England to Austria. Fees include transportation, room and board, and all necessary equipment. Participants provide their own 10- to 18-speed bikes, but rentals are possible.

Contact: Ted Lefkowitz, Director (address above).

STUDENTS ABROAD

For information on Students Abroad and its outdoor activities programs, see its listing in the Organized Tours section of this book, page 218.

TAYLOR STATTEN CAMPS
59 Hoyle Avenue
Toronto, Ontario M4S 2X5
Canada
Telephone: (416) 486–6959

The sponsor: Founded in 1921 and run by three generations of Stattens, this summer camp offers children ages 7 to 16 the opportunity to spend the summer participating in a variety of outdoor activities. Located in Algonquin Park in Ontario's northland, and within a mile of each other, are Camp Ahmek for boys and Camp Wapomeo for girls. The purpose of the camps is "to provide a happy, friendly environment in which young people can develop and mature as individuals, while learning to 'pull together' for the good of the group as a whole." The camps are accredited by the American Camping Association and the Ontario Camping Association.

The program: The camps operate in July and August. Campers attend for one or two sessions lasting 27 days each. Special 12- and 15-day sessions are available for campers age seven to nine. Each camper goes on a canoe trip lasting from 4 to 10 days, traveling into the regions of Temagami, Quettico, Biscotasing, Kipawa, or Killarney. In addition to full camp activities, extended canoe trips are available for campers 10 to 16 years old. Activities and instruction in swimming, canoeing, sailing, windsurfing, horseback riding, ecology, drama, music, and arts and crafts are available. The boys' and girls' camps participate in joint programs weekly.

Supervision: All supervision, instruction, counseling, and evening activities are provided by staff members. There is one staff member for every two campers.

Requirements: The minimum age is 7 (completion of first grade required), and the maximum is 16.

Living arrangements: Campers stay in cabins shared by six or seven children of the same age range; the cabins do not have electricity. Shower and toilet facilities are centralized.

Finances: The 1992 fee of 1,995 Canadian dollars (approximately $1,675) covers all activities, room and board, and laundry service for a one-month session. The full two-month session costs 3,310 Canadian dollars (approximately $2,780). These costs do not include 10-percent tax. Participants from outside of Canada are advised to arrange their own medical insurance. Travel expenses are not included. Buses pick up campers from Montreal, Ottawa, Toronto, and the Toronto airport. Financial aid is available.

Deadline: There is no formal deadline, but various sessions may fill by mid-January.

T.M. INTERNATIONAL SCHOOL OF HORSEMANSHIP
Sunrising Riding Centre
Henwood Nr. Liskeard
Cornwall PL14 5BP
England
Telephone: (44) 579–62895

The sponsor: T.M. International is a residential riding school that provides riding holidays and training for those wishing to take British Horse Society exams.

The program: The Riding Centre provides instruction at all levels. Programs last from a week to nine months (September to June).

Supervision: There is one group leader for every six students.

Services for persons with disabilities: Ground-floor accommodations are available for people with minor physical disabilities.

Requirements: Students must be at least 16 years old.

Living arrangements: Dormitory-style accommodations.

Finances: Courses cost 70 British pounds (about $130) per week, including room, full board, riding lessons, and lectures on horse care and stable management. Prices for holidays start at about $350 per week.

Deadline: There is no formal deadline; however, it is advisable to apply as early as possible.

Contact: Captain E. W. R. Moore, Principal (address above).

VILLAGE CAMPS
CH-1296 Coppet
Switzerland
Telephone: (41) 22–776–2059
Fax: (41) 22–776–2060

The sponsor: Village Camps was founded in 1972 with the purpose of "education through recreation." The program aims to bring children of different nationalities and languages together so they may better appreciate each other's background and culture. In addition, the camps endeavor to provide an educational experience.

The program: Village camps offers two-week educational and sports programs for youth ages 8 to 17. Included are English, French, and German language institutes in England, Switzerland, and Austria; a computer and leadership training course in Switzerland; golf and tennis in England; and canoeing, caving, and outdoor adventure in the south of France. In addition to these specialty camps, participants can choose from a variety of multi-activity programs in Austria, England, and Switzerland.

The program in Switzerland is the only camp outside of North America to be accredited by the American Camping Association.

Supervision: Adult group leaders are responsible for daily supervision of students. The ratio of students to counselors is five to one.

Requirements: Students should be between 8 and 19 years old, depending on the program.

Living arrangements: Students live in shared rooms in a group hotel.

Finances: Fees range from 1,450 to 2,100 Swiss francs (approximately $1,090 to $1,575). Individual scholarships are sometimes available.

Contact: Roger Ratner, Director (address above).

WESTCOAST CONNECTION TRAVEL CAMP

For information on Westcoast Connection and its outdoor activities programs, see its listing in the Organized Tours section of this book, page 220.

WEST OF IRELAND CAMP
Brampton Lodge
Newcastle
Staffordshire ST5 0QW
England
Telephone: (44) 782–616415

The sponsor: The Camp, which is based in the United Kingdom but located in the west of Ireland, has been in operation since 1919.

The program: Set in ''the breathtaking beauty and tranquility'' of the west Irish county of Sligo, this camp offers sailing, windsurfing, canoeing, horseback riding, hill walking, fishing, and archery. ''The background of these holidays is a sane and balanced Christian influence.''

Supervision: Many of the leaders are former campers; all are volunteers who pay their own way. There is one leader for every two campers.

Requirements: Campers must be from 8 to 16 years old.

Living arrangements: Campers live in chalet tents and eat together in a dining hall.

Finances: Each two-week camping period costs approximately 310 Irish pounds (approximately $560).

Deadline: Applications should be made as early as possible.

Contact: Mr. J. Caddick-Adams (address above).

WILDERNESS INQUIRY
1313 Fifth Street SE, Box 84
Minneapolis, MN 55414
Telephone: (612) 379–3858

The sponsor: Wilderness Inquiry is a nonprofit organization that integrates people with disabilities and able-bodied people on wilderness trips.

The program: Wilderness Inquiry offers kayaking and canoeing adventures in Canada. Trips last from three days to two and a half weeks, depending on the location.

Orientation: Trip leaders call participants prior to departure to answer questions about the trip.

Supervision: There is a staff leader for every five participants.

Services for persons with disabilities: Equipment is available for participants with physical disabilities.

Requirements: Participants under the age of 18 should be accompanied by an adult.

Living arrangements: Accommodations are in outdoor campgrounds.

Finances: Costs range from $195 to $1,195. Scholarships are available.

Deadline: No set deadline, but it is recommended that people sign up as early as possible.

WORLDTEENS
RR2 Box 81
Lincolnville, ME 04849
Telephone: (207) 338–5165

The sponsor: Worldteens, a nonprofit organization, operates *Worldpeace Exchanges*, a teen exchange dedicated to the memory of Samantha Smith, a girl who traveled to the Soviet Union to promote world peace. The Worldteens International Camp also brings students from the former Soviet Union to Poland Spring, Maine.

The program: During the month of July and early August, American teens live in youth camps in Russia and the Ukraine for four weeks, followed by a homestay with a host family for one week.

Supervision: Group leaders supervise the participants. There is one group leader for every four or five teens.

Services for persons with disabilities: Each case is handled individually.

Requirements: Participants should be between the ages of 13 and 16.

Living arrangements: Participants stay in youth camps for four weeks and with a host family for one week.

Finances: The fee is $2,695 which includes airfare.

Deadline: No set deadline; apply as early as possible.

Contact: Karen and Jay Stager, Directors (address above).

YOUTH FOR UNDERSTANDING (YFU) INTERNATIONAL EXCHANGE

For information on YFU and its outdoor activities programs, see its listing in the Study Abroad section of this book, page 132.

HOMESTAYS

While many of the programs in other sections of this book involve homestays, those in this section offer a homestay as the central feature of the program. Participants spend a week or more living with a host family, taking part in its daily activities. Usually teenagers on a homestay experience have the opportunity to improve foreign language skills in day-to-day conversation and to do some traveling, either on their own or with their host family. They also learn firsthand what it's like to live in another country and establish a personal relationship that crosses international borders.

Most language institutes offer their students the opportunity to live with host families as paying guests. Rather than list each of these programs here, we suggest you look through the Language Institutes section of this book if you're interested in that type of arrangement.

ACCUEIL FRANCE FAMILLE
5, rue François Coppée
75015 Paris
France
Telephone: (33) 1–45542239

The sponsor: This nonprofit organization specializes in homestays with French families.

The program: Participants live with families throughout France for a minimum of one week. According to the sponsor, "These families are willing to let you share their way of life and you should be prepared to adapt accordingly."

Requirements: The minimum age is 16 (18 for Paris homestays). A basic knowledge of French is advisable.

Living arrangements: Participants live in private rooms in comfortable homes. They are matched with appropriate families by filling out a questionnaire. The staff "will do everything in our power to send you to your chosen region of France, but we are principally concerned in placing you with a family whose tastes and interests correspond to your own."

Finances: A week-long homestay with full board costs 2,050 French francs (approximately $410).

AFS INTERCULTURAL PROGRAMS

For information on AFS and its homestay programs, see its listing in the Study Abroad section of this book, page 91.

AMERICAN ASSOCIATION OF TEACHERS OF GERMAN (AATG)

For information on AATG and its homestay program, see its listing in the Study Abroad section of his book, page 94.

AMERICAN COUNCIL FOR INTERNATIONAL STUDIES (ACIS)

For information on ACIS and its homestay programs, see its listing in the Organized Tours section of this book, page 198.

AMERICAN FARM SCHOOL

For information on the American Farm School and its homestay program, see its listing in the Worker/Volunteer section of this book, page 222.

AMERICAN HERITAGE ASSOCIATION

For information on American Heritage Association and its homestay program, see its listing in the Study Abroad section of this book, page 96.

AMERICAN INTERCULTURAL STUDENT EXCHANGE (AISE)

For information on AISE and its homestay program, see its listing in the Study Abroad section of this book, page 97.

ANGLO-CONTINENTAL HOLIDAYS

For information on Anglo-Continental Holidays and its homestay programs, see its listing in the Organized Tours section of this book, page 200.

ANIMATIONS LOISIRS JEUNES
58 bis, rue Sala
69002 Lyons
France
Telephone: (33) 72409642

The sponsor: This nonprofit exchange organization, approved by the Ministère de la Jeunesse et des Sports, (the French ministry of youth and sports) offers homestays for young people visiting France. It has been in operation since 1971.

The program: Participants live with French families for up to four weeks.

Supervision: Participants are supervised by the host family.

Requirements: The maximum age is 18.

Living arrangements: Participants may choose between half and full board.

Finances: One week with full board costs 1,219 French francs (approximately $240). Half-board costs 1,115 French francs (approximately $220). Airfare is not included.

Contact: Ms. Laurence Fine, Director of International Exchanges (address above).

AQUITAINE SERVICE LINGUISTIQUE (ASL)
6, rue Louis Pasteur
33127 Martignas
France
Telephone: (33) 56214096
Fax: (33) 56780401

The sponsor: This nonprofit organization has been organizing homestays for visitors to France since 1978. ASL also places French students in England, Ireland, Germany, Spain, Italy, and the United States.

The program: Participants live with French families on a weekly basis year round. Host families are located in the regions of Bordeaux and Charente. Homestays in Charente (the region surrounding Cognac) include the option of scheduled French instruction in the home.

Supervision: Participants are supervised by their host families. Representatives of ASL are available for assistance.

Services for persons with disabilities: ASL does not restrict participation by persons with disabilities as long as families can be found to accommodate them.

Requirements: The minimum age is seven.

Living arrangements: Host families are expected to treat participants as members of the household. "Students will take their meals with their families and will be taken on outings and will be given every opportunity of meeting French people of their own age."

Finances: Family accommodation with full board costs 1,490 French francs (approximately $300) per week. Ten hours of French lessons per week cost 700 French francs (approximately $140).

ARES
Druzsteunicka 20
736 01 Havířov
Czechoslovakia
Telephone: (42) 69231412
Fax: (42) 699425312

The sponsor: ARES is a commercial Czechoslovakian homestay organization founded in 1991.

The program: Homestays, usually in apartments with university students, last from two days to eight weeks during the summer months. Participants should be aware that their hosts are eager to practice English. ARES offers another program in which foreign visitors are offered employment as language instructors in children's summer camps.

Requirements: The minimum age is 17; maximum is 35.

Living arrangements: Most participants live with university students, typically in three-room apartments. Homestays with families are also possible. Breakfast and dinner can be arranged.

Finances: ARES charges a $10 fee for arranging the homestay. Participants pay their hosts approximately $4 per day. Breakfast and dinner cost an extra $3 per day. The salary for English instructors is approximately $200 per month, plus free room and board.

Deadline: May 31.

Contact: Martin Gres (address above).

ASPECT FOUNDATION

For information on ASPECT and its homestay programs, see its listing in the Study Abroad section of this book, page 99.

ASSE INTERNATIONAL STUDENT EXCHANGE PROGRAMS

For information on ASSE and its homestay programs, see its listing in the Study Abroad section of this book, page 100.

BANGLADESH WORKCAMPS ASSOCIATION (BWCA)

For information on BWCA and its homestay programs, see its listing in the Work/Volunteer section of this book, page 224.

CHILDREN'S INTERNATIONAL SUMMER VILLAGES (CISV)

For information on CISV and its homestay programs, see its listing in the Outdoor Activities section of this book, page 252.

CITIZEN EXCHANGE COUNCIL (CEC)

For information on CEC and its homestay program, see its listing in the Organized Tours section of this book, page 204.

ECI
62, avenue DeLattre de Tassigny
13100 Aix-en-Provence
France
Telephone: (33) 42–210768
Fax: (33) 42–214293

The sponsor: ECI, a nonprofit organization whose main purpose is to send French students to the United States, also arranges homestays for U.S. students in France.

The program: Students live with families in Aix-en-Provence, a city of around 130,000 inhabitants in the south of France. ECI can also arrange programs for student groups with language courses and excursions.

Supervision: Students are supervised by their host families.

Requirements: The minimum age is 15. Students must have at least two years of French language study.

Living arrangements: "Our families are carefully selected and will provide room, board, and activities."

Finances: One week at half-board costs 1,140 French francs per day (approximately $230); full board costs 1,350 French francs (approximately $270).

Deadline: Two weeks before intended stay.

Contact: Valerie Deltour, Director of Incoming Programs (address above.)

EF FOUNDATION

For information on EF Foundation and its homestay programs, see its listing in the Study Abroad section of this book, page 104.

EUROVACANCES

For information on Eurovacances and its homestay programs, see its listing in the Study Abroad section of this book, page 106.

FORMATION INTERNATIONALE VOYAGES ETUDES (FIVE)
9, rue Barla
06300 Nice
France
Telephone: (33) 93–267255
Fax: (33) 93–268774

The sponsor: Founded in 1980, FIVE is a nonprofit organization that offers homestay programs, language courses, excursions, and residence accommodations in Paris and the French Riviera.

The program: FIVE offers two programs for teenagers:

- *French Riviera Homestay:* Participants spend two or three weeks during the summer in Cannes, Nice, or Antibes, taking French language courses and living with a French family.
- *Paris/French Riviera Excursion:* Participants spend three days touring Paris and ten days on the French Riviera in June or July. (The excursions can be arranged at any time of the year for groups.)

Orientation: Students meet with FIVE staff in the United States two weeks before departure for the homestay program. There is no orientation for the French Riviera excursion.

Supervision: There is one group leader for every eight students.

Requirements: Participants should be between the ages of 13 and 20.

Living arrangements: Students live with a French family in the *French Riviera Homestay* program and stay in a hotel or a homestay in the *Paris/French Riviera Excursion.*

Finances: The homestay program is 4,300 French francs ($860) for two weeks and 6,500 French francs ($1,300) for three weeks. Write FIVE for the current price of the Paris/French Riviera excursion.

FULBRIGHT-GESELLSCHAFT

For information on Fulbright-Gesellschaft and its homestay programs, see its listing in the Study Abroad section of this book, page 108.

FUTURE FARMERS OF AMERICA (FFA)

For information on FFA and its homestay programs, see its listing in the Study Abroad section of this book, page 109.

GERMAN-AMERICAN PARTNERSHIP PROGRAM (GAPP)

For information on GAPP and its homestay programs, see its listing in the Study Abroad section of this book, page 110.

IBEROAMERICAN CULTURAL EXCHANGE PROGRAM (ICEP)

For information on ICEP and its homestay programs, see its listing in the Study Abroad section of this book, page 111.

INTERCAMBIO INTERNACIONAL DE ESTUDIANTES
16 Broadway, Suite 107
Fargo, ND 58102
Telephone: (800) 437–4170

The sponsor: Founded in 1959 in Mexico City, Intercambio sponsors exchanges between the U.S. and countries in Central America.

The program: U.S. students spend July and August in Costa Rica, El Salvador, Guatemala, Panama, or Mexico. Each participant lives with a local family and "becomes a true family member."

Supervision: Local delegates and the head of the host family supervise the participant's day-to-day activities.

Services for persons with disabilities: Intercambio, which has accommodated disabilities in the past, handles each case individually.

Requirements: Students ages 11 to 16 are eligible; applicants should have a working knowledge of Spanish.

Living Arrangements: Students live with families in urban or rural areas.

Finances: Fees range from $1,300 to $1,700, depending upon the destination. Members of families who host Intercambio students receive a $200 to $300 deduction. The fee includes round-trip airfare, health and accident insurance, and supervision.

Deadline: Three months before departure.

INTERFON
Koroglu Cd. Kahramankadin Sok. 18/3
Gaziosmanpasa, Ankara 06700
Turkey
Telephone: (90) 4–446–1097

The sponsor: Interfon is a commercial organization established in 1982 with the aim of introducing Turkish culture to young visitors.

The program: From June through September, Interfon runs its *Holiday in Turkey* program, in which visitors live with host families in Ankara, Antalya, Bursa, Istanbul, Izmir, Konya, and summer resort towns.

Orientation: Participants are met at the airport by an Interfon representative, who introduces them to the host family.

Supervision: Interfon representatives are in Ankara, Istanbul, and Izmir. Participants are supervised by their hosts.

Requirements: The minimum age is 12.

Living arrangements: Participants may live in houses or apartments, depending on the family.

Finances: Participants pay a registration fee of $150, which includes full board and accommodation. The fee is valid for stays of one to three months. Host families are volunteers; participants are expected to teach their native language to their hosts by speaking with them.

Deadline: Write two months in advance, enclosing letter of introduction, medical report, and three photographs.

INTERNATIONAL ASSOCIATION OF LIONS CLUBS
Youth Programs Department
300 22nd Street
Oak Brook, IL 60521-8842
Telephone: (708) 571–5466

The sponsor: Lions Clubs International is the world's largest service club organization, with 40,000 clubs in 174 countries.

The program: The Lions Youth Exchange Program offers exchanges throughout the year that last from two to six weeks. The exchanges are conducted by local Lions clubs. In most cases, youths stay in the home of a club member in another country. Lions Clubs in many countries also have International Youth Camps, which last from four to six weeks.

Supervision: Youths are supervised by the host Lions Club or host district youth exchange chairman.

Services for persons with disabilities: Students with disabilities have been accommodated in the past, often as guests of families in which someone has a similar disability.

Requirements: Students must be between the ages of 15 and 21. Participants are interviewed and chosen by their local Lions Club. More than 3,000 young people participate each year.

Living arrangements: Exchanges live with host families, and it is hoped that the sending community will, in turn, host a foreign visitor.

Finances: Costs for transportation and insurance vary. These costs may be paid by the participant, his or her host family, a Lions Club, or some combination of these sources. Room and board in the host country is paid by the host family. The host club may pay for special events. About $75 per week is suggested as pocket money.

Deadline: Varies, but applications should be initiated six months before departure date.

Contact: Your local Lions Club for addresses of District Youth Exchange Chairmen, or write to the address above.

INTERNATIONAL CATHOLIC CORRESPONDENCE AND EXCHANGE SERVICE
Veilchenweg 2
D-6634 Wallerfangen
Germany
Telephone: (49) 6831–60638

The sponsor: Since 1950, this nonprofit organization has arranged homestays for young people primarily in Germany, but also in Austria and France. It is also active in establishing written correspondences between people throughout the world.

The program: Participants are placed in the homes of local families as paying guests. Participants are expected to become "integrated members" of their foreign families.

Orientation: Students correspond with their hosts before arrival.

Supervision: Participants are supervised by their hosts.

Requirements: Students must be between 13 and 18 years of age and have studied at least two years of German.

Living arrangements: "Host families can by no means provide the lavish services one would expect in a hotel or pension-house. We want to provide a sensible balance, presenting the 'average family.'"

Finances: Costs range from 400 deutsche marks to 1,000 deutsche marks (approximately $270 to $670) for stays of two to four weeks.

Deadline: Four weeks ahead of time.

INTERNATIONAL CHRISTIAN YOUTH EXCHANGE (ICYE)

For information on ICYE and its homestay programs, see its listing in the Study Abroad section of this book, page 113.

LABO INTERNATIONAL EXCHANGE FOUNDATION
Suite 1850
1201 Third Avenue
Seattle, WA 98101
Telephone: (206) 554–7255

The sponsor: The Labo International Exchange Foundation is a non-profit foundation based in Tokyo, Japan, that has hosted educational exchange programs between Japan and the United States, Australia, China, and other countries since 1972.

The program: Labo offers a five-week summer homestay program in conjunction with 4-H organizations in 38 states. During the homestay, U.S. students participate in weekly Labo club activities and attend a four-day camp in the countryside. They also have time for sight-seeing in Tokyo prior to their return to the United States. Labo also offers a three-week intensive Japanese-language program immediately prior to the homestay exchange. In addition to language lessons, students go on field trips and attend courses on Japanese history, society, and culture.

Supervision: All Japan programs are supervised by Labo staff members and club leaders, and by U.S. chaperons.

Services for persons with disabilities: Labo does not discriminate on the basis of disabilities.

Requirements: Students should be between the ages of 12 and 20.

Living arrangements: On both the homestay and language programs, students live with a Japanese family. For the homestay program, the host family has a child the same sex and age as the U.S. participant.

Finances: The fee for the homestay program is $650 plus airfare; the fee for the language program is $700 plus airfare.

Deadline: March 15.

LEX AMERICA
68 Leonard Street
Belmont, MA 02178
(617) 489–5800

The sponsor: Lex, the Institute for Language Experience, Experiment and Exchange, is a nonprofit organization that offers international homestay programs in Japan and Korea.

The program: The Lex Exchange is offered during July and August in four- and six-week programs. ''The emphasis is on mutuality: not only do participants learn to see the world as the host family does, but the members of the host family also learn what it is like to be an American. Participants are not tourists; the role is much more like that of an ambassador. They discover many new things about themselves and come home changed, with a clearer sense of what it means to be a member of the family of humankind.'' Participants visit historic sites and participate in local festivals.

Orientation: An initial one-day orientation provides an opportunity for participants to meet their respective Japanese or Korean family and also to prepare to enter another culture. Upon arrival in their host country, participants receive the second half of their orientation.

Supervision: Host families are fully screened and all have some English ability. Families host because they are interested in sharing their life with a new family member. Group leaders are responsible for participants during travel, with a ratio of fifteen participants to one leader.

Services for persons with disabilities: Lex America does not discriminate.

Requirements: Students must be 12 or older to be eligible.

Living arrangements: Homestays. Participants absorb the customs and characteristics of their host culture by taking part in activities of daily life as a member of the family.

Finances: The program fee ranges from $2,500 to $3,000 dollars and includes round-trip airfare, supplemental travel insurance, and all costs abroad except for personal expenses and any local transportation costs.

Deadline: May 1.

Contact: Steffi R. Samman, Program Manager (address above).

NACEL CULTURAL EXCHANGES
3460 Washington Drive, #109
St. Paul, MN 55122
Telephone: (800) 622–3553

The sponsor: Nacel has coordinated exchanges between the United States and France since 1969. Exchanges were added with Germany and Spain in 1981, with Ireland in 1986, and with Côte d'Ivoire in 1988. Nacel Cultural Exchanges is dedicated to promoting international understanding and language education. It specializes in summer homestay programs, which offer affordable opportunities for international friendships, bringing together students and families from all walks of life.

The program: Nacel offers both a study program and a homestay program. In the homestay, students from the United States learn firsthand about another way of life, make new friends, and improve their language skills by living for four weeks with a family in France, Germany, Spain, or for three weeks with a family in Côte d'Ivoire.

Study options allow middle-school students to participate in language classes and cultural enrichment activities for three weeks in Paris or Madrid. High-school students can take an enrichment course in Irish literature and history while living with a family for four weeks in Dublin.

Orientation: Predeparture orientations are arranged regionally by Nacel coordinators.

Supervision: The host family assumes responsibility for the students. A chaperon (an American language teacher who accompanies the students on their trip) is on call for help or advice for the duration of the stay. Local Nacel coordinators ensure a support network.

Services for persons with disabilities: Nacel is pleased to accept participants with disabilities in homestay programs, provided coordinators abroad are able to find appropriate host families.

Requirements: The minimum age is 13, maximum is 18; participants must have at least two years of language study and three recommendations. For the Study Seminar in Ireland, participants must have completed 11th or 12th grade and have three recommendations.

Living arrangements: Homestay participants live in homes during the entire stay. Middle-school study-program participants stay in boarding schools with teacher-chaperons.

Finances: A fee of $1,295 for the homestay program, $2,295 for the middle-school program, and $1,835 for the Irish study seminar includes round-trip airfare from New York, ground transportation, an escort, American chaperons during the stay, and insurance. Coordinated group departures are offered from 60 cities throughout the United States.

Deadline: Programs usually fill up by April.

Contact: Liane Mattson, National Coordinator (address above).

NATIONAL ASSOCIATION OF SECONDARY SCHOOL PRINCIPALS (NASSP)
1904 Association Drive
Reston, VA 22091
Telephone: (703) 860–0200, ext. 280

The sponsor: NASSP is a nonprofit organization that "serves all administrators and other educators who are committed to the goal of providing youth with the best possible education." NASSP was founded in 1916 and is a member of CIEE.

The program: NASSP's *School Partnerships, International (SPI)* program is a short-term exchange between paired schools, designed to foster long-term partnerships between secondary schools in the United States and other countries. SPI pairs U.S. schools with schools in Austria, Canada, Costa Rica, France, Germany, Italy, Japan, Mexico, Spain, the United Kingdom, and countries of the former Soviet Union. U.S. students and teachers live in the homes of their counterparts and participate in school and community activities. In turn, they host groups from the partner schools coming from abroad.

Orientation: All programs offer an optional, several-day cultural orientation in the host country. There is also an all-day workshop for teachers and principals participating in the program.

Supervision: Students are supervised by their home teachers, who accompany them on the trip.

Services for persons with disabilities: SPI programs are open to all youth.

Requirements: Requirements are generally established by individual schools.

Living arrangements: Students and teachers live with host families.

Finances: Fees range from $700 to $1,900, including transportation.

Contact: School Partnerships, International (address above).

NATIONAL 4-H COUNCIL

For information on the National 4-H Council and its homestay programs, see its listing in the Study Abroad section of this book, page 118.

ÖSTERREICHISCHE VEREINIGUNG FÜR AUSTAUSCH UND STUDIENREISEN (ÖVAST)
Dr.-Gschmeidler-Strasse 10/4
A-3500 Krems
Austria
Telephone: (43) 2732–85793

The sponsor: ÖVAST is an organization founded in 1964 that offers student-exchange programs, study tours, and homestays throughout Austria and England.

The program: The *Exchange and Study Program* allows participants to experience Austria as part of a homestay-study tour, living and eating with their Austrian hosts as well as visiting the sites of Austria. ÖVAST oversees this program for about 500 students.

Orientation: A one-day orientation takes place in Vienna before the program begins.

Supervision: Group leaders are chosen for their foreign language ability and prior experience. There is one leader for every 10 to 15 students.

Services for persons with disabilities: ÖVAST does not accept persons with disabilities.

Requirements: Requirements for each program vary. Contact ÖVAST for details.

Living arrangements: Homestays. Participants stay with middle-class Austrian families. Families are selected by local organizers, mostly teachers.

Finances: The fee is 300 Austrian schillings (approximately $30) per day, which includes room, board, and a group leader. Insurance is available for an additional charge; contact ÖVAST for details. Travel arrangements to and from Austria as well as rail travel within the country also can be arranged through ÖVAST.

Deadline: Options are available throughout the year. Deadline is two months before departure date.

Contact: Dr. Hans Kapitan, Director (address above).

PEOPLE TO PEOPLE INTERNATIONAL
501 East Armour Boulevard
Kansas City, MO 64109
Telephone: (816) 531–4701

The sponsor: People to People began in 1956 when President Dwight D. Eisenhower invited a group of business leaders to a White House conference to establish a citizen organization dedicated to the pursuit of world peace. Thirty years later there are People to People chapters and international committees in 156 cities of the world.

The program: People to People's *High School Student Ambassador Program* sends approximately 4,500 students to any of 30 countries each summer. While abroad, the students attend briefings by overseas government officials and make field visits to manufacturing facilities, farms, universities, and so on. The heart of the program is the homestay aspect: Student Ambassadors live with families for five-day periods in several different countries. The entire trip lasts 21 to 29 days.

Orientation: Student Ambassadors attend six two-hour orientation meetings locally. When school ends in June, they assemble in Washington, DC, for a two-day orientation which includes intensive briefings on U.S. government, business, and history.

Supervision: Student Ambassadors travel in groups of 30 to 35 with three or more leaders in each group. All leaders are certified teachers.

Requirements: Applicants must be 13 to 18 years old and enrolled in junior high or high school at the time of application. They must supply four letters of recommendation and pass a screening review conducted by a local committee of professional, business, and education leaders. "Maturity, well-rounded interests, and the ability to adapt are as important to a student's selection as academic standing."

Living arrangements: When students are not living with host families, they stay in hotels.

Finances: Fees range from $2,950 to $4,000, which includes airfare, food, lodging, and all travel and educational visits while overseas. Accident insurance is provided; health insurance is required, but is not included in the fee.

Deadline: April 1.

Contact: Paul Watson, Associate Director, People to People High School Student Ambassador Program, Dwight D. Eisenhower Building, S-110 Ferrall, Spokane, WA 99202.

ROTARY INTERNATIONAL

For information on Rotary International and its homestay programs, see its listing in the Study Abroad section of this book, page 123.

SCHOOL PARTNERS ABROAD

For information on School Partners Abroad and its homestay program, see its listing in the Study Abroad section of this book, page 125.

SÉJOURS INTERNATIONAUX LINGUISTIQUES ET CULTURELS
32, Rempart de l'Est
16022 Angoulême Cedex
France
Telephone: (33) 45958356

The sponsor: Founded in 1965, Séjours Internationaux is a nonprofit organization that operates homestays in France and 18 other countries in order to foster language skills and cultural understanding.

The program: Participants stay with host families, and have the option to take private or group French lessons with experienced language teachers. Also available is a homestay complemented by coaching in a specific sporting activity such as tennis, golf, horseback riding, squash, and various water sports. Stays last from one week to a full semester.

Supervision: Host families provide parental supervision and guidance in a cultural immersion that includes family responsibilities and experiences.

Requirements: Participants must be between the ages of 15 and 18 and have had at least two years of French.

Living arrangements: Homestays. Participants usually share a room with host family children of about the same age.

Finances: Vacation homestays cost 1,545 French francs (approximately $300) per week. Two-week homestays with language lessons start at 3,860 French francs (approximately $770).

Contact: J. M. Roques, General Delegate (address above).

VISTAS IN EDUCATION
1400 West Lake Street
Minneapolis, MN 55408
Telephone: (612) 823–7217

The sponsor: Founded in 1976, Vistas in Education specializes in organized trips to France for French teachers and their students.

The program: The programs vary in length from 10 days to three weeks and take place in the spring and early summer. The main focus of each program is a six-day family homestay, followed by a tour and several days in Paris. Each group is accompanied by a bilingual guide certified by the French government. Participants usually enroll through their French teacher; however, individual students are welcome to participate and are assigned to a group, preferably from their area.

Supervision: Classroom teachers accompany their students. Usually, one teacher is responsible for every 10 students. A Vistas in Education office in Paris offers continuous support to teachers as needed.

Services for persons with disabilities: Due to the lack of access in many of the facilities in France, the organization is not able to accommodate most physically disabled participants.

Requirements: Participants must be in high school and studying French at the time of enrollment.

Living arrangements: Students spend one week with a family; during the tour they stay in two-star tourist-class hotels. Breakfast and most dinners are included.

Finances: Program prices range from $995 for a 10-day spring program from New York, to $2,045 for a three-week summer program from the West Coast. Costs include round-trip airfare from most major U.S. cities, land transportation in France, hotel accommodations, most meals, homestay arrangements, travel insurance, entrance fees, and guides.

Deadline: For group enrollment, October 1 for spring programs; November 15 for June programs. Individuals should contact Vistas in Education for availability after these dates.

Contact: Jane Weinstein, Program Director (address above).

WORLD EXPERIENCE (WE)

For information on WE and its homestay programs, see its listing in the Study Abroad section of this book, page 129.

WORLD LEARNING INC.
Box 676, Kipling Road
Brattleboro, VT 05302
Telephone: (802) 257–7751, or (800) 345–2929 outside Vermont

The sponsor: For more than 60 years, World Learning Inc., formerly The Experiment in International Living, has provided more than 100,000 young people with "the opportunity to build bridges of cross-cultural understanding and to develop lasting friendships through a broad range of international programs designed to illustrate the simple but powerful idea advanced by the founder of World Learning—that people learn to live together by living together. Programs artfully combine travel, study, and a variety of activities with the cornerstone feature, an extended homestay with a host family." The organization is a member of CIEE.

The program: World Learning Inc. sponsors a number of comprehensive summer programs. During the summer, participants can choose from a variety of program formats in fifteen different countries as diverse as France, Australia, Kenya, Thailand, and Ecuador.

- *The Homestay* lasts from two to four weeks and includes regional sight-seeing.
- *Language Study* is offered in selected countries. College credit is granted in some cases.
- *Multicountry Tours* are offered in various combinations such as Spain, Morocco, and Portugal, or France, Italy, and Switzerland.
- *Youth Service Programs* provide students an opportunity to take part in projects overseas such as working with refugees, or building a children's playground.

Orientation: Programs include predeparture orientations focusing on cross-cultural adaptation, introduction to the host country, role-playing, and discussions, so that group members can get to know one another.

Supervision: There is one leader for every group of 8 to 15 young people, and in every host country a representative is available to help. Leaders are responsible for daily supervision—their duties include "absolutely everything!"

Services for persons with disabilities: Persons with disabilities are considered on a case-by-case basis.

Requirements: The summer program age range is 15 to 20. The language requirement varies with the country.

Living Arrangements: Participants live with families. This is the part of the program for which World Learning Inc. is most famous—it's the heart of the experience. "The homestay is perhaps the richest, warmest, and most satisfying part of the program." Homestay placements are arranged by national offices in the host country; host families undergo extensive interviews and must provide excellent references.

Finances: The cost of the summer program ranges from $1,600 to $5,200 and includes transportation and all costs in the host country, with the exception of personal spending money. Insurance is included.

Deadline: April 15.

WORLDPEACE EXCHANGES

For information on Worldpeace Exchanges and its homestay program, see the listing for Worldteens in the Outdoor Activities section of this book, page 274.

YOUTH EXCHANGE SERVICE (YES)

For information on YES and its homestay programs, see its listing in the Study Abroad section of this book, page 131.

YOUTH FOR UNDERSTANDING (YFU) INTERNATIONAL EXCHANGE

For information on YFU and its homestay programs, see its listing in the Study Abroad section of this book, page 132.

APPENDIX: MEMBERS OF THE COUNCIL ON INTERNATIONAL EDUCATION EXCHANGE

Members

Adelphi University
Adventist Colleges Abroad
AFS International/Intercultural
    Programs
Albertson College of Idaho
Alma College
American Council on the Teaching
    of Foreign Languages
American Graduate School of
    International Management
American Heritage Association
American University
American University in Cairo
American Youth Hostels
Antioch University
Arkansas College
Associated Colleges of the
    Midwest
Association for International
    Practical Training

Association of Student Councils
    (Canada)
Attila Jozsef University
Augsburg College
Austin Community College
Babson College
Bates College
Beaver College
Beloit College
Boston College
Boston University
Bradford College
Bradley University
Brandeis University
Brethren Colleges Abroad
Brigham Young University
Brown University
Bucknell University
Butler University
California State University
California State University, Long
    Beach

California State University,
Sacramento
Carleton College
Carroll College
Central Michigan University
Central University of Iowa
Central Washington University
Chapman University
College of Charleston
Colorado College
Colorado State University
Cornell University
Curtin University of Technology
Dartmouth College
Davidson College
DePauw University
Drake University
Earlham College
Eastern Michigan University
Eckerd College
École Centrale de Paris (École
Centrale des Arts et
Manufactures)
Elmira College
Empire State College—SUNY
The Experiment in International
Living
Flagler College
Florida Atlantic University
Georgetown University
Gonzaga University
Goshen College
Great Lakes Colleges Association
Grinnell College
Guilford College
Gustavus Adolphus College
Hampshire College
Hartwick College
Harvard College
Hebrew University of Jerusalem
Heidelberg College
Hiram College
Hollins College
Hope College
Illinois State University
Indiana University
Institute of International Education
International Christian University
International Christian Youth
Exchange
International Student Exchange
Program
Iowa State University

James Madison University
Kalamazoo College
Kent State University
Lake Erie College
Lancaster University
LaSalle University
Lehigh University
Lewis and Clark College
The Lisle Fellowship
Longwood College
Louisiana State University
Loyola Marymount University
Macalester College
Marquette University
Mary Baldwin College
Marymount College, Tarrytown
Memphis State University
Miami University
Michigan State University
Middlebury College
Millersville University
Monterey Institute of International
Studies
Moorhead State University
Murdoch University
National Association of Secondary
School Principals
New York University
North Carolina State University
Northeastern University
Northern Arizona University
Northern Illinois University
Northern Michigan University
Northfield Mount Hermon School
Oberlin College
Ohio University
Ohio State University
Old Dominion University
Open Door Student Exchange
Pace University
Pennsylvania State University
Pepperdine University
Pitzer College
Pomona College
Portland State University
Purdue University
Ramapo College of New Jersey
Reed College
Rochester Institute of Technology
Rollins College
Rosary College
Rutgers, the State University of
New Jersey

St. John Fisher College
St. Lawrence University
St. Olaf College
St. Peter's College
Scandinavian Seminar
School Year Abroad
Scripps College
Skidmore College
Southern Illinois University at
  Carbondale
Southern Methodist University
Southwest Texas State University
Spelman College
Springfield College
Stanford University
State University of New York
Stephens College
Stetson University
Syracuse University
Texas A&M University
Texas Tech University
Trinity College
Tufts University
Tulane University
Universidad Autónoma de
  Guadalajara
Universidad de Belgrano
Université de Bordeaux III
Universidad del Salvador
University College London
University of Alabama
University of Alabama at
  Birmingham
University of Arkansas at Little
  Rock
University of British Columbia
University of California
University of Colorado at Boulder
University of Connecticut
University of Copenhagen (DIS
  Program)
University of Denver
University of Essex
University of Evansville
University of Hartford
University of Illinois
University of Iowa
University of Kansas
University of La Verne
University of Louisville
University of Maine
University of Maryland
University of Massachusetts

University of Michigan
University of Minnesota
University of New Hampshire
University of New Orleans
University of North Carolina at
  Chapel Hill
University of North Texas
University of Notre Dame
University of Oklahoma
University of Oregon
University of the Pacific
University of Pennsylvania
University of Pittsburgh
University of Rhode Island
University of St. Thomas
University of South Carolina
University of Southern California
University of Sussex
University of Tennessee at
  Knoxville
University of Texas at Austin
University of Toledo
University of Utah
University of Vermont
University of Virginia
University of Washington
University of Wisconsin at Green
  Bay
University of Wisconsin at
  Madison
University of Wisconsin at
  Milwaukee
University of Wisconsin at
  Platteville
University of Wisconsin at River
  Falls
University of Wollongong
University of Wyoming
University System of Georgia
Valparaiso University
Volunteers in Asia
Wake Forest University
Washington State University
Wayne State University
Wesleyan University
Western Michigan University
Western Washington University
Westminster College
Whitman College
Whitworth College
Wichita State University
Wilmington College
Wittenberg University

Wofford College
Worcester Polytechnic Institute
World College West
YMCA of the USA
Youth for Understanding
  International Exchange

Associates

American Center for Students and
  Artists
Association of College
  Unions—International

Canadian Bureau for International
  Education
European Association for
  International Education
Fontainebleau Fine Arts and Music
  Schools Association
NAFSA: Association of
  International Educators
National Association for Equal
  Opportunity in Higher
  Education
United Negro College Fund

INDEX

LOCATION

PROGRAM TYPE

GENERAL INDEX
including organizations